Southeastern

of

The Religious Society of Friends

FAITH

AND

PRACTICE

4th Edition   2013

The Southeastern Yearly Meeting *Faith and Practice* is published by
SOUTHEASTERN YEARLY MEETING PUBLICATIONS, under the auspices of
Southeastern Yearly Meeting (SEYM) of The Religious Society of Friends, a
nonprofit corporation founded in 1963.
Address: www.seym.org, publications@seym.org

Content submitted by Faith and Practice Committee (F&PC); seasoned by
SEYM affiliated Monthly Meetings and Worship Groups.
Content editing by F&PC; approved at Yearly Business Meeting Annual Sessions.
2011-2013 Editors: Phoebe Andersen, Carol Bechtel, and Harold Branam, F&PC.
Content layout and design by Phoebe Andersen, clerk, F&PC.
Copy editing: Eleanor Caldwell

© 2013 by SEYM, *February Sky*, artistic rendering by Lyn Cope of original
photograph by Roger Little, 2013.
Cover design by Lyn Cope and Phoebe Andersen.

Title and text are set in WarnockPro™ designed by Robert Slimbach for Adobe
Originals, U.S. Patent Des. 454,152.

Print masters provided by SEYM Publications.
Print on demand by Lightening Source, Ingram Content Group.
Digital eBook formats by Publishgreen.com.

Cataloging-in-Publication Data
Southeastern Yearly Meeting of the Religious Society of Friends, 2013
        Religion
        Quaker, Society of Friends
        <u>Includes Index</u>

Copies available through Quaker Bookstores, e-bookstores, or from SEYM.
Contact: www.seym.org—admin@seym.org—publications@seym.org—faith@
seym.org

ISBN 978-1-939831-00-2 (paperback)
ISBN 978-1-939831-01-9 (eReader: MOBI)
ISBN 978-1-939831-02-6 (eReader: EPUB)

Southeastern Yearly Meeting
of the Religious Society of Friends

FAITH AND PRACTICE
Fourth Edition 2013

We are not searching for a perfect book, but rather a serviceable book for our time. It is for our comfort and discomfort, a book which affirms the unities which we have found. We recognise and welcome diversity within Yearly Meeting. Still we feel the pain that has been caused by past and continuing failures to accept and value the experience of us all.
London Yearly Meeting, 2 August 1994

Southeastern Yearly Meeting of the Religious Society of Friends was established in 1962 and first met April 12, 1963 and comprised those Friends Meetings previously recognized by Friends World Committee for Consultation and loosely organized in 1950 as Southeastern Friends Conference. Southeastern Yearly Meeting is affiliated with Friends General Conference and Friends World Committee for Consultation.

Faith and Practice is an evolving record and guide, reflecting the growing experience of Friends in Southeastern Yearly Meeting as we seek to know and follow the Inner Light. This 2013 fourth edition reflects changes in the way Southeastern Yearly Meeting Friends have conducted their affairs over these years since the last revision, the third edition in 1987, which succeeded a second edition in 1979 of the original document created in 1963.

The Faith and Practice Committee has labored to create a clear and readable revision that Friends can also use as a text to teach basic Quakerism for adult religious education within our meetings. Members and attenders are urged to study, use, and evaluate this book in the Spirit of the Inner Light. The committee solicits your feedback as you study this book.

As you read through the *Faith and Practice* you will notice that each chapter contains several quotations from Friends, both early and contemporary. These quotations were chosen to add the voice of Friends' experience to each chapter's discussion. The Faith and Practice Committee asks Friends to read all of the text including the quotations as the whole of the guidance of the *Faith and Practice*.

Suggested changes which arise from individuals or committees are to be forwarded to the Faith and Practice Committee. After consideration, they are seasoned through the actions of monthly meetings, interim meetings and the Yearly Meeting. When Friends unite in the need to change practice, then the next revision of *Faith and Practice* will occur.

The Faith and Practice Committee is deeply indebted to all of the yearly meetings for the help of their published *Faith & Practice* in creating the text of SEYM's *Faith and Practice*. When we struggled for words to define and explain our faith, we found reading many of these *"books of discipline"* to be inspirational as well as instructive. In particular we are grateful to Baltimore YM Draft 2011; Britain (London) YM 1960, 1995; Canadian YM 1991; New England YM 1985; New York YM 2001; North Pacific YM 1993; Pacific YM 1985; and Philadelphia YM 1997.

For those Friends wishing to understand in full the detailed responsibilities of the yearly meeting clerks, officers, standing committees, and representatives to SEYM-affiliated organizations, in addition to the *Faith and Practice*, please consult the *SEYM Operational Handbook, Procedures, and Job Descriptions* available from SEYM Publications and QuakerBooks.org.

History of the Faith and Practice Committee

The Faith and Practice Committee was re-convened in 1996 and tasked with preparing the fourth edition of Faith and Practice. The committee has been made up of several Friends who have since served one or more terms on the committee: Phoebe Andersen, Carol Bechtel, Harold Branam, Vicki Carlie, Lyn Cope, Jan Dahm, Doris Emerson, Cathy Gaskill, Gay Howard, Gerry O'Sullivan, Connie Ray, and Neil Andersen (adopted member). Additionally, we remember the service of those Friends who have had their service on the committee truncated due to death: Ed Bertsche (clerk of the third revision), Beverly Bird, Heather Moir, Christine O'Brien, and James Weston.

The Southeastern Yearly Meeting Faith and Practice was first adopted in 1963, revised in 1979, 1987, and revised section by section from 1998 through 2011, comprising the fourth edition.

Advices

In 1656 the elders of the Meeting at Balby, near Doncaster, in Yorkshire, England, drafted the earliest known letter of advices on Christian practice issued by any general body of Friends. The most remembered of those advices is the following postscript:

> *Dearly beloved Friends, these things we do not lay upon you as a rule or form to walk by, but that all, with the measure of light which is pure and holy, may be fulfilled in the Spirit, not from the letter, for the letter killeth, but the Spirit giveth life.*
> **Balby Postscript, 1656**

Modern Friends still aspire to use *Faith and Practice* with this attitude in mind. In 1954 Jan Palen Rushmore spoke similarly, but in a different metaphor:

> *The teachings of our Quaker forefathers were intended to be landmarks, not campsites.*
>
> **Jan Palen Rushmore, 1954**

TABLE OF CONTENTS

Friends' Spiritual Practices in Southeastern Yearly Meeting

Friends' Structure in Southeastern Yearly Meeting

Friends' Revision Process

Friends' History

Friends' References

CHAPTER 1

The Light Within and the Meeting for Worship

Friends' Experience of the Meeting for Worship

*Be still and cool in thy own mind and spirit from thy
own thoughts, and then thou wilt feel the principle of
God to turn thy mind to the Lord God, whereby thou
wilt receive his strength and power from whence life
comes, to allay all tempests, against blusterings and
storms. That is it which molds into patience, into
innocency, into soberness, into stillness, into stayed-
ness, into quietness, up to God, with his power.*
George Fox, 1658

*When you come to your meetings . . . what do you
do? Do you then gather together bodily only, and
kindle a fire, compassing yourselves about with the
sparks of your own kindling, and so please yourselves, and walk in the "Light of your own fire, and
in the sparks which you have kindled?" . . . Or rather, do you sit down in the True Silence, resting from
your own Will and Workings, and waiting upon the
Lord, with your minds fixed in that Light wherewith
Christ has enlightened you, until the Lord breathes
life into you, refresheth you, and prepares you, and
your spirits and souls, to make you fit for his service,
that you may offer unto him a pure and spiritual
sacrifice?*
William Penn, 1678

*As iron sharpeneth iron, the seeing of the faces one
of another when both are inwardly gathered into the
life, giveth occasion for the life secretly to rise and
pass from vessel to vessel. And as many candles
lighted and put in one place do greatly augment the*

light and make it more to shine forth, so when many are gathered together into the same life, there more of the glory of God and his powers appears, to the refreshment of each individual.

Robert Barclay, 1671

On one never-to-be-forgotten Sunday morning, I found myself one of a small company of silent worshipers, who were content to sit down together without words, that each one might feel after and draw near to the Divine Presence, unhindered at least, if not helped, by any human utterance. Utterance I knew was free, should the words be given; and before the meeting was over, a sentence or two were uttered in great simplicity by an old and apparently untaught man, rising in his place amongst the rest of us. I did not pay much attention to the words he spoke, and I have no recollection of their import. My whole soul was filled with the unutterable peace of the undisturbed opportunity for communion with God, with the sense that at last I had found a place where I might, without the faintest suspicion of insincerity, join with others in simply seeking His presence. To sit down in silence could at least pledge me to nothing; it might open to me (as it did that morning) the very gate of heaven.

Caroline E. Stephen, 1890

Our worship is a deep exercise of our spirits before the Lord, which doth not consist in exercising the natural part or natural mind, either to hear or speak words, or in praying according to what we, of ourselves, can apprehend or comprehend concerning our needs; but we wait, in silence of the fleshly part, to hear with the new ear what God shall please to speak inwardly in our own hearts, or outwardly through others, who speak with the new tongue which he unlooseth and teacheth to speak; and we pray in the spirit, and with a new understanding, as God pleaseth to quicken, draw forth, and open our hearts towards himself.

Isaac Penington, 1661

How does a Quaker Meeting work? Its foundation is the conviction that God is not a distant remote being but a living presence to be discovered in the deep centre of every human being. . . . The Quaker experience is that, in the silence, as we are open to one another in love, we help each other by sharing our strengths and weaknesses. The Quaker conviction is that as we go deeper into ourselves we shall eventually reach a still, quiet centre. At this point two things happen simultaneously. Each of us is aware of our unique value as an individual human being, and each of us is aware of our utter interdependence on one another.

George Gorman, 1982

I have never lost the enjoyment of sitting in silence at the beginning of meeting, knowing that everything can happen, knowing the joy of utmost surprise; feeling that nothing is preordained, nothing is set, all is open. The Light can come from all sides. The joy of experiencing the Light in a completely different way than one has thought it would come is one of the greatest gifts that Friends' meeting for worship has brought me.

Ursula Franklin, 1979

As I silence myself I become more sensitive to the sounds around me, and I do not block them out. The songs of the birds, the rustle of the wind, children in the playground, the roar of an airplane overhead are all taken into my worship. I regulate my breathing as taught me by my Zen friends, and through this exercise I feel the flow of life within me

*from my toes right through my whole body. I think
of myself like the tree planted by the "rivers of water" in Psalm 1, sucking up God's gift of life and being restored. Sometimes I come to meeting for worship tired and weary, and I hear the words of Jesus,
"Come unto me, all that labour and are weary, and
I will give you rest." And having laid down my burden, I feel refreshed both physically and spiritually.
This leads me on to whole-hearted adoration and
thanksgiving for all God's blessings. My own name,
Tayeko, means "child of many blessings" and God
has surely poured them upon me. My heart over-
flows with a desire to give Him something in return.
I have nothing to give but my own being, and I offer
Him my thoughts, words, and actions of each day,
and whisper, "Please take me as I am."*

Tayeko Yamanouchi, 1980

The Light Within

The Light Within is the fundamental and immediate experience for Friends. It is that which guides each of us in our everyday
lives and brings us together as a community of faith. It is, most
importantly, our direct and unmediated experience of the Divine.

Friends have used many different terms or phrases to designate the source and inner certainty of our faith–a faith which we
have gained by direct experience. The Inward Light, the Way, the
Truth and the Life, the Spirit of Truth, the Divine Principle, the
Christ Within, the Seed, Inward Teacher, Presence, and the Inner
Light are examples of such phrases. George Fox's Journal refers
to "that Inward Light, Spirit, and Grace by which all might know
their salvation" and to "that Divine Spirit which would lead them
into all truth." Fox wrote, "There is one, even Christ Jesus, that can
speak to thy condition" and encouraged Friends "to walk cheerfully
over the world, answering that of God in every one." Many Friends
interpret "that of God" as another designation for the Light Within.

The Light Within is not the same as the conscience or moral faculty. The conscience, a human faculty, is conditioned by education and the cultural environment; it is not, therefore, an infallible guide to moral practice. It should nevertheless be attended to, for it is one of the faculties through which the Light shines. Friends are encouraged to test their leadings by seeking clearness through direct communion in the meeting for worship, through the clearness process (see Chapter 10, Clearness Committees), and through other ways. Such testing enhances and clarifies insight so that the conscience may be purged of misconceptions and become more truly obedient to the Light Within. When conscience has been transformed by experiencing the Light, it gives more reliable guidance even though it may seem to point in an unexpected direction.

Friends' experience is that following the Light Within brings a release of the spirit and a state of peace that are independent of the tangible results of the action taken. Spiritual power arises from living in harmony with the Divine Will. George Fox and others often spoke of the power they experienced in times of need and of the relationship between that power and the Light. For instance, Fox writes that "the power of God sprang through me," and he admonishes us to "hearken to the Light, that ye may feel the power of God in every one of you."

Continuing obedience to the Light increases our gratitude for God's gifts. Among these gifts are an awareness of enduring values, the joy of life, and the ability to resolve problems in accord with divine leading, as individuals or as a meeting. Under the guidance of the Light, the monthly meeting is enabled to use and transform the aspirations and judgments of its members. This waiting on the Light helps the meeting make decisions and face undertakings in a spirit detached from self-interest or prejudice. Fundamental Quaker testimonies such as equality, simplicity, peace, integrity, and community have arisen from a deep sense of individual and corporate responsibility guided by the Light Within.

Recognizing "that of God" is in every person overcomes our separation and our differences from others and leads to a sympathetic awareness of their needs and a sense of responsibility toward them. Friends believe that the more widely and clearly the Light is recognized and followed, the more humanity will come into accord. "Therefore," writes George Fox, "in the Light wait, where unity is."

Worship

> *Life grows from freely adopted self-discipline main-*
> *tained by prayer, persuasion, the guidance of the*
> *Spirit and the motions of love.*
> **T. Canby Jones, 1972**

Worship is our response to what we feel to be of ultimate importance. Worship is always possible, alone or in company, in silence, in music or speech, in stillness or in dance. It is never confined to place or time or form, and it is open to everyone.

When Friends worship, we reach out from the depths of our being to God, the giver of life and of the world around us. Our worship is a search for communion with God and the offering of ourselves—body and soul—for the doing of God's will. The sense of worship can be experienced in the awe we feel in the silence of a meeting for worship or in the awareness of our profound connectedness to nature and its power. In worship we know repentance and forgiveness by acknowledging God as the ultimate source of our being and feel the serenity of accepting God's will for our lives. Individual leadings are often made clearer by reference to the life and teachings of Jesus and by the transforming power of the Inner Light. From worship there comes a fresh understanding of the commandment to

> *. . . love the Lord your God with all your heart, and*
> *with all your soul, and with all your strength, and*
> *with all your mind; and your neighbor as yourself.*
> **Luke 10:27 NRSV**

Careful listening to the Inward Teacher can lead to fresh openings: an in-pouring of love, insight, and interdependence. True listening can also bring the worshiper to new and sometimes troubling perceptions, including clear leadings that may be a source of pain and anxiety; yet it can also bring such wholeness of heart that hard tasks can become a source of joy. Even when we worship while torn with our own pain or that of another, it is in worship that we discover new strength for what faces us in our everyday lives.

Each experience of worship is different. There is no one right way to prepare for spiritual communion, no set practice to follow when worship grows from expectant waiting in the Spirit. Vital worship depends far more on a deeply felt longing for God than upon any particular practice.

Ask, and it will be given you; seek, and you will find; knock, and it will be opened to you.
Matthew 7:7 NRSV

And one of the scribes came near and heard them disputing with one another, and seeing that he answered them well, he asked him, "Which commandment is the first of all?" Jesus answered, "The first is, 'Hear, O Israel: The Lord our God, the Lord is one; and you shall love the Lord your God with all your heart, and with all your soul, and with all your mind, and with all your strength.' The second is this, 'You shall love your neighbor as yourself.' There is no other commandment greater than these."
Mark 12:28-32 NRSV

The Corporate Meeting for Worship: the Spiritual Heart of the Monthly Meeting

The meeting for worship is the heart of the monthly meeting and of the Religious Society of Friends. It draws us together in the enlightening and empowering presence of God, sending us forth with renewed vision and commitment. Its basis is direct communion with God. The meeting for worship is the only Quaker practice which has existed from the beginning of the Religious Society of Friends. Meetings for worship are held at established times, usually once a week; appointed or "called" meetings for worship are arranged by the monthly meeting at the time of marriages, memorial meetings, or other special occasions.

Friends find it useful to come to meeting with hearts and minds prepared for worship by a practice of daily prayer, meditation, and study. Some find help through Bible study in the Quaker manner (such as that described by Joanne and Larry Spears in the pamphlet *Friendly Bible Study*), through thoughtful reflection, listening to the Inward Teacher, and through the experiences of others in daily life and service. We thereby deepen our awareness of the wonder of God and of God's love and acquire the words with which to understand and express that awareness as we worship.

Such preparation helps us to set aside our preoccupation with ourselves and our affairs and, as Friends arrive for meeting, to settle into worship.

> *The first that enters into the place of your meeting*
> *. . . turn in thy mind to the light, and wait upon God*
> *singly, as if none were present but the Lord; and here*
> *thou art strong. Then the next that comes in, let*
> *them in simplicity of heart sit down and turn in to*
> *the same light, and wait in the Spirit; and so all the*
> *rest coming in, in the fear of the Lord, sit down in*
> *pure stillness and silence of all flesh, and wait in the*
> *light. Those who are brought to a pure still waiting*
> *upon God in the Spirit are come nearer to the Lord*
> *than words are; for God is spirit and in the spirit He*
> *is worshipped.*
> **Alexander Parker, 1660**

> *The first thing that I do is to close my eyes and then*
> *to still my body in order to get it as far out of the way*

as I can. Then I still my mind and let it open to God in silent prayer, for the meeting, as we understand it, is the meeting place of the worshiper with God. I thank God inwardly for this occasion, for the week's happenings, for what I have learned at His hand, for my family, for the work there is to do, for Himself. And I often pause to enjoy Him. Under His gaze I search the week, and feel the piercing twinge of remorse that comes at this, and this, and this, and at the absence of this, and this, and this. Under His eyes I see again–for I have often been aware of it at the time–the right way. I ask His forgiveness of my faithlessness and ask for strength to meet this matter when it arises again. There have been times when I had to reweave a part of my life under this auspice.

I hold up persons before God in intercession, loving them under His eyes–seeing them with Him, longing for His healing and redeeming power to course through their lives. I hold up certain social situations, certain projects. At such a time I often see things that I may do in company with or that are related to this person or this situation. I hold up the persons in the meeting and their needs, as I know them, to God.

Douglas V. Steere, 1937

Worship in meeting may thus begin with stilling of the mind and body, letting go of tensions and everyday worries, feeling the encompassing presence of others, and opening oneself to the Spirit. It may include meditation, reflection on a remembered passage from the Bible or other devotional literature, silent prayer, thanksgiving, praise of God, consideration of one's actions, remorse, request for forgiveness, or search for direction. Even in times of personal spiritual emptiness, Friends find it useful to be present in meeting for worship.

Worshiping together strengthens the sense of the corporate body and deepens the act of worship itself. Such communal worship is like a living organism whose individual but interdependent members are essential to one another and to the life of the greater whole. It is like the luminous unity and individual fulfillment that arises when musicians, responding to the music before them, offer up their separate gifts in concert. Friends sometimes use Paul's image and speak of the meeting for worship as a "body whose head is Christ" (taken from "Now you are the body of Christ and individually members of it" [I Cor. 12:27 NRSV] and "And he has put all things under his feet and has made him the head over all things for the church, which is his body, the fullness of him who fills all in all" [Ephesians 1:22-23 NRSV]). The gifts and participation of each member are important in maintaining and enriching the spiritual life of the meeting for worship. Corporate worship is distinct from individual worship. There is a power that can often be experienced in the group that is much greater than that within an individual alone.

There is a renewal of spirit when we turn away from worldly matters to rediscover inward serenity. Friends know from experience the validity of Jesus' promise: "For where two or three are gathered in my name, I am there among them" (Matthew 18:20 NRSV). Often we realize our hopes for a heightened sense of the presence of God through the cumulative power of the worship of the group, communicated in silence as well as in vocal ministry. When we experience such a profound and evident sense of oneness with God and with one another, we speak of a "gathered" or "covered" meeting for worship.

Friends gather for worship in quiet waiting upon God. We come together out of our care for one another and out of our shared hunger to know God, to follow the leading of the Spirit, to feel with clarity our shortcomings and the reality of forgiveness, to give voice to our anguish, faith, praise, joy, and thanksgiving. At the close of the meeting for worship, we shake or hold hands, in acknowledgment of our commitment to one another and to God, and go forth with renewed trust in the power and reality of God's grace and love.

In a truly covered meeting an individual who speaks takes no credit to himself for the part he played in the unfolding of the worship. ... For the feeling of being a pliant instrument of the Divine Will characterizes true speaking "in the Life." Under such a covering an individual emerges into vocal utterance, frequently without fear and trembling, and subsides without self-consciousness into silence when his part is played. For One who is greater than all individuals has become the meeting place of the group, and He becomes the leader and director of worship. With wonder one hears the next speaker, if there be more, take up another aspect of the theme of the meeting. No jealousy, no regrets that he didn't think of saying that, but only gratitude that the angel has come and troubled the waters and that many are finding healing through the one Life. A gathered meeting is no place for the enhancement of private reputations, but for self-effacing pliancy and obedience to the whispers of the Leader.

Thomas Kelly, 1945

Meeting for worship can be more than just an occasion on which one's private religious needs are satisfied. Silent devotion should lead to an awareness that the meeting is less and less a place we choose ourselves, and more and more a place to which, out of love, God has called us. To understand this is to sense the meaning of those lovely phrases about the community of faith being the body of Christ.

John Punshon, 1987

Communion and Communication

One day, being under a strong exercise of spirit, I stood up and said some words in a meeting; but not keeping close to the Divine opening, I said more than was required of me. Being soon sensible of my error, I was afflicted in mind some weeks without any light or comfort, even to that degree that I could not take satisfaction in anything. I remembered God, and was troubled, and in the depths of my distress he had pity on me, and sent the Comforter. I then felt forgiveness for my offense; my mind became calm and quiet, and I was truly thankful to my gracious Redeemer for his mercies. About six weeks after this, feeling the spring of Divine love opened, and a concern to speak, I said a few words in a meeting, in which I found peace. Being thus humbled and disciplined under the cross, my understanding became more strengthened to distinguish the pure spirit which inwardly moves upon the heart, and which taught me to wait in silence sometimes many weeks together, until I felt that rise which prepares the creature to stand like a trumpet, through which the Lord speaks to his flock.

John Woolman, 1740

Direct communion with God is a wholeness that transcends mere communication, and it constitutes the essential life of the meeting for worship. Into its living stillness may come leadings and fresh insights that are purely personal, not meant to be shared. At other times they are meant for the meeting at large to hear. It is incumbent on the Friend receiving the message to make the sometimes difficult discernment whether the message is meant for the meeting as a whole or for the individual.

When a leading is to be shared, the worshiper feels a compelling inward call to vocal ministry. The very name "Quaker" is by tradition derived from the evident quaking of early Friends witnessing under the power of the Spirit. Ministry today may sometimes be accompanied by such outward signs, and many feel the inward quaking. Vocal ministry may take many forms, such as prayer, praise of

God, song, teaching, witnessing, and sharing. These messages may center upon a single, vital theme; often apparently unrelated leadings are later discovered to have an underlying unity. Such ministry and prayer may answer the unrecognized or unvoiced needs of other seekers.

When someone accepts the call of the Spirit to speak, fellow worshipers are likewise called to listen with openness of minds and hearts. Reticent and tender spirits should feel the meeting community's loving encouragement to give voice, even if haltingly, to the message that may be struggling to be born within them. Friends whose thought has been long developing and whose learning and experience are profound serve the meeting best when they, like all others, wait patiently for the prompting of the Inward Teacher. Anyone moved to speak should first allow others time to absorb and respond inwardly to what has already been said.

Friends should not put obstacles, including their own feelings of unworthiness, in the way of the call to speak. Deciding in advance to speak or not, or feeling a duty to speak to provide some balance between silence and the spoken word, interferes with the guidance of the Spirit. Even if not a word is spoken, a meeting for worship can be profoundly nurturing.

All present should be mindful that spiritual opportunities entail responsibilities as well, including attention to the time of assembling and consideration for those already settled. Speaking carried on in a spirit of debate, lecturing, discussion, or news reporting is destructive to the life of the meeting for worship and of the meeting community. Friends' experience has shown that it is not helpful to answer or rebut what has been said previously during meeting for worship. Also, any who habitually settle into silent reading or sit in inattentive idleness cut themselves off from their fellow worshipers and from the Spirit. If hindrances to worship occur within a meeting for worship, members of the worship and ministry committee or others as appropriate should move quickly and in love to provide counsel.

Friends moved to vigorous support of causes need to voice their insights outside of meeting for worship in brief and sensitive ways. Similar sensitivity should be practiced by those who bring material to be posted or shared with the meeting community.

I think it's extremely important that we learn to listen. Listening is a lost art. And when I say learn to listen I mean listen to our spouses, listen to our children, listen to our fellow believers in our communities of faith. But I also want us to learn to listen to God. I know from personal experience that God speaks through the Scriptures. He speaks through preaching. He speaks through friends. But He also speaks directly. We can know that, but we must make time and space and silence in our lives if we are to learn this in real ways and be the beneficiaries of His leading and His guidance directly. We are told in the 46th Psalm, "Be still and know that I am God." In another translation it says, "Stop fighting and know that I am God." Let's take time to listen to God.

Kara Cole Newell, 1982

It is unfortunate that much formal training in ministry does not even recognize that . . . inward preparation exists. In our world of degrees, exams, and training programs, it is easy to forget that ministry is not primarily a task; it is a way of being in the world. It is living in relationship with God and being a witness to God. Ministry is being able to listen to the Word of God and thereby have a word of life to share with others. Fundamentally, we do not do ministry. We are ministers.

Sandra Cronk, 1991

CHAPTER 2

THE RELIGIOUS EXPERIENCES
OF SOME SEYM FRIENDS

Love is like light; it enters wherever there is a crack or door ajar in one's heart. If you don't love yourself, then you maybe find that you love one other person; then maybe you find that you love another person. And, if you don't love another person, then perhaps you love a work of art or an animal or a mathematical formula or a sweater. You begin somewhere and practice loving. And, once you open your heart to loving one thing, then another, you may eventually find yourself enjoying how loving makes you feel. If we love others only as much as we love ourselves, then perhaps we feel God's love for us only as much as we feel our love for ourselves.

Wendy Clarissa Geiger, 2008
Jacksonville Meeting

Surely you know that you are God's temple, where the Spirit of God dwells.

1 Corinthians 3:16
Revised English Bible

Out of my experience comes the sense of a loving and sustaining presence in whom I am grounded and overshadowed. God, with infinite patience, draws from me love, trust and worship as my response, and service as I come to recognize the presence at work in the lives of my sisters and brothers. God cares about the way I respond and does not ask to be defined, and thus limited, as one or three or male. In this awesome mystery are hidden my source and my goal, and God is growing in me now.

Robert Allenson, 1987
Gainesville Meeting

I believe in one Supreme Being who I call God. I believe that God is within me and without, and that every single thing is God. I also believe that God is too complex and incomprehensible to be described. Naturally, I don't go along with the sole divinity of Jesus Christ as I believe that there is that of God in all of us. Nor am I still awaiting a Messiah. We all have the potential for being a Messiah; some of us use it, some of us don't. My belief in the power of prayer is very strong, whether it's the verbal intercessory request or the non-verbal swelling of the heart in gratitude. I believe in miracles and magic and that we have gifts we haven't even used yet. I believe that whatever you believe is true and that if you don't believe it, that's OK, too. And that the greatest sin we can commit is not to enjoy life fully. I subscribe to the following quotations, the first from the Talmud, which Jesus of Nazareth probably read, and the second from Anthony de Mello, a contemporary Roman Catholic priest living in India:

> *On Judgment Day, a man will have to give account for every good thing which his eye saw and he did not enjoy.*
>
> **Palestinian Talmud, Kiddushin**

> *I am fortunate indeed!*
> *I have been granted*
> *the wealth*
> *of another day of life.*
>
> **Anthony de Mello, *Wellsprings***

You might say I'm a practicing Hedonist, but cursed at birth by three wicked witches: "Protestant Work Ethic," "Jewish Guilt," and "Twentieth-Century Anxiety." They curse me daily and stand in the way of my wholehearted delight in the utter beauty of the Florida sky and the enjoyment of love for my fellow man. When I learn how to get rid of the wicked witches who live on my shoulders and shout in my ears, I will have become the person I want to be. However, I believe God loves me anyway, witches and all, because He/She/It has given me multiple blessings, and today I am very, very grateful!

Marie Stilkind, 1986
Miami Meeting

I'm a Lutheran minister's daughter—therefore I'm a Christian Quaker. Due to my husband being a C.O., we were invited to become members. All I can say is—I love my Bible, my various devotionals, including one put out by Quakers, "Fruit of the Vine," and of course our journals. I have that Inner Peace. All in all, it gives me the knowledge of what God expects of me. I'm thankful that I have the strength and joy in my commitments to our Meeting and am thankful for my family of Friends. Being a Quaker is a challenge! I love challenges. Religion and art is my thing.

Hildegard Herbster, 1986
Miami Meeting

At this moment in my spiritual journey I pause to try to make a statement of my faith. I know that I am only a child in this journey and that today's statement is different from the one I would have made a year ago and from one I might make a year from now. From my experience this far in my journey I believe that God is love and that this spirit of love is within me and at the same time envelops me. This spirit is caring and steadfast and, as I become more awake and aware, is increasingly persistent, teaching me that I must pay constant and careful attention to this inner guide. I know that when I am obedient, getting my self out of the way as far as it is possible for me to do so, I feel a deep joy. More and more, God becomes the single reality of my life, and my goal is to become whatever God would have me be.

Without understanding or needing to understand how this can be so, I believe that God is in each person and each particle of creation, and encompasses not only all that we know of the universe but even more than we can possibly imagine. I believe that God wills only good for us and that we are all one in God.

Dorothy Ann Ware, 1986
Clearwater Meeting

I am drawn to the Society of Friends for a number of reasons. For me, the most important is that I feel at home in the silence of Meeting for Worship. It satisfies my heart's longing for peace and I think enables me to live my life in a way that is more integrated, more whole.

My observations and readings lead me to think that I am also in harmony with Friends around the following:

As a group Friends seem to live what they believe and I am trying to do that too.

It appears that Friends are a more open system, allowing for a range of thoughts and beliefs which is a position that I also work to maintain.

I am a seeker of truth and divine guidance and I have faith in continuing revelation as do Friends.

I hold that simplicity, honesty, equality, and peace are important principles to live by.

Conceptualizing God as Inner Light is consistent with what I believe about the nature of spirituality.

Finally, I think that the structure of Friends Meeting for Worship, Business, etc., is one that provides for two natural forces that exist in humankind—a need for closeness with others and an equally important need to be autonomous persons.

Alice Wald, 1986
Charleston Meeting

My faith rests in an uncomprehendable God.

I have experienced God both within and without.

The record of the life and teachings of Jesus, in the Bible, has been one of the guides in my quest to reach God.

Knowing people of God and imitating them is another guide. I know I am becoming more in the Light, the more I work at establishing a constant relationship with God.

Cathy Gaskill, 1987
Winter Park Meeting

I see the Quaker experience as incorporating three spheres: spiritual, political, and social. Of course, these overlap. For instance, our dealings with others may be guided by our Spirituality. And, because of individual interests and personal needs these are balanced differently in each person. For some, the social aspect of meeting is important to the degree that the meeting becomes an extended family. For others, the spiritual component is pivotal because it gives them strength for their political commitments.

Recently I heard a Quaker woman in Texas tell a group of refugees that while Quakers believed in peace there was an increasing movement within the Friends which averred that the violence done to individuals by evil governments, such as the depriving of food, was equal to acts of violent self defense. I was appalled. It does not matter that one violence equals another, what matters is that it is in <u>addition</u> to the other. We are fundamentally a peace church and I have heard this echoed repeatedly in SEYM. Peace and our silent meetings are cornerstones of the uniqueness that is Quaker faith.

We are tolerant, and we are brave because of our tolerance. That is, we have the courage to face our own hidden bigotries. The early Quakers did it when they loved individuals who happened to be black while the masses despised the negro, and we are doing it today when we love individuals who happen to be gay when the masses treat them with contempt.

India Aditi, 1986
Winter Park Meeting

If I am not God,
 what am I?
If Thee is not God,
 what is thee?
If Here is not Infinity,
 where is it?
If Now is not Eternity,
 when is it?

The above expresses my current state of awareness. However, the following intimates my prediction of future states:

> *on that final day*
> *how shall I know I am dead?*
> *I'll stop Becoming.*

Kenneth C. Leibman, 1987
Gainesville Meeting

I have come to believe that all life is holy, for there is nowhere that God is not. We "swim" in God. We "live and move and have our being" in God, who is "nearer to us than we are to ourselves." God is life and the life energy is love permeating the universe.

I believe that our sense of being separate one from another and from God is our misperception, and this false sense of separateness is the source of fear and of every evil (error or ignorance).

I believe we all walk our own path (like the prodigal son) toward self-realization of our spiritual reality and oneness. And though we may be in different places, we are where we should be for growing into that reality. We teach and we learn from one another, and as we give we receive.

I tend to believe in reincarnation because it makes of this earth experience a fair and a just one, and places the responsibility for our actions and our consequences squarely on ourselves, and that feels right.

I feel–in prayer and meditation and silent worship–that God's healing love is channeled: And I find that in the silence I feel a connection with that spirit of God within me, and the more aware I am of that holy presence the more peaceful I am, the more harmony I feel around me.

Finally, I believe that life (consciousness) is ongoing, that all life is tending toward wholeness, and love, and forgiveness will bring it into being.

Mary Dee, 1987
Palm Beach Meeting

As I look back over my life, I find that it has been gradually drawing closer to God. I have always felt the nudge of Spirit to go into a certain path. Sometimes I would follow the nudge and grow closer to God. Other times (most of the time) I have been absolutely certain that I can handle the crisis and ignored the spiritual nudge. As a matter of fact, I got very good at ignoring the nudge. Then, I had a Bibical "Job" experience. At age 46, I lost my job, my reputation, and had to move back home with family. After the shock wore off, I was humbled and heartsick. I finally asked God for a measure of his everlasting and healing Love. I was embraced by the Spirit, lifted up and transformed. I was filled with Love, Light and Trust. I understood that God is always present with us but I had spent most of my existence dwelling on past hurts and slights or worried about the future or, even worse, absorbed in busy-ness. If I could stand still in the present, I would find God present and His Love for me manifest. From this experience, Love has called me closer and closer to God. I am filled to overflowing with God's love for everyone and all of creation. I have tried to let Love be the first motion in my life and have humbly ministered as way opened, and learned to accept that Love and ministry from wherever it comes to me.

I was fortunate a few years ago to participate in an <u>ad hoc</u> committee charged to come to some clarity regarding an item of great concern for the yearly meeting. As the committee convened it was clear we needed to try another approach to come to clarity on this great concern. It was also clear that none of us were called to clerk this committee. We settled into worship to find clarity. After a while, we stayed worshipful and shared our Light with each other. The worship felt right-ordered, so we continued in worship. After a period of time, we felt clear that this worship time was the way forward, letting the Inner Light be our Guide and our clerk.

In worship, we lost track of time and experienced a gathering into God's love for all of us, all of his creation. It became clear over time and several meetings that we were blessed with both new understandings and openings. We were reminded that we could not focus on the "wrongs" of the "other" without looking at our own behavior and our tendency to judgment, moral outrage and "other-izing" (my words for us vs. them). We struggled to find ways to be a loving witness. Participating in this process of extended worship and worship sharing opened us as a group. Our openings were both simple and deep. They were:

•   **Love God and love one another.**
We are each called to Love God with all of our heart, mind, soul and strength, and we are called to love everyone, especially those with whom our measure of the Light may differ.

•   **Avoid judgment; seek forgiveness.**
We are called to be mindful of judging others and rather seek their forgiveness instead. We are called as well to be forgiving of those who judge us.

•   **Listen and seek healing.**
We are called to be about the process of listening to and helping Friends heal who are hurt by discrimination and division, as well as called to promote spiritual healing of all Friends through deep listening, forgiveness, and love.

These openings that we received from the Spirit on the surface offered no particular guidance on the resolution of the yearly meeting's great concern. However, continued prayer and discernment by the committee brought clarity that following these openings were where God had called us to do our work.

The <u>ad hoc</u> committee had done its work and reported back to the yearly meeting. However, the openings we received have stayed with me. Through continued prayer and discernment, I am called to the greater action of love, forgiveness and healing, as well as the challenge to avoid judgment. This is a difficult and rewarding calling. It is extremely hard to avoid judgment; however, it is easy to listen and forgive, even easier still to love as I am loved by God.

Phoebe Biers Andersen, 2012
Tallahassee Meeting

CHAPTER 3

Concerns, Leadings, and Testimonies

For Friends the most important consideration is not the right action in itself but a right inward state out of which right action will arise. Given the right inward state, right action is inevitable. Inward state and outward action are component parts of a single whole.

Howard Brinton, 1943

Friends are sometimes called "practical mystics" or "prophetic Christians" because Quaker worship has been a wellspring for service in the community and world that arises out of the ongoing revelation of the Light experienced in worship. An old story relates the whispered question asked by someone attending meeting for worship for the first time and puzzled by the absence of overt activity: "When does the service begin?" The response: "When the meeting for worship ends."

Concerns and Leadings

A concern is God-initiated, often surprising, always holy, for the life of God is breaking through into the world. Its execution is in peace and power and astounding faith and joy, for in unhurried serenity the Eternal is at work in the midst of time, triumphantly bringing all things unto Himself.

Thomas Kelly, 1941

Leading and being led: the words are simple enough. But for Quakers they have their most profound resonance as defining religious experience. Friends speak variously of being drawn to an action, feeling under the weight of a concern, being called or led to act in specific ways. We speak of being open to the leadings of the Light, of being taught by the Spirit or the Inward Christ. Extraordinary claims lie embedded in those phrases. They say that it is not only possible but essential to our nature for human beings to hear and obey the voice of God; that we can be directed, daily, in what we do, the jobs we hold, the very words we say; and that our obedience may draw us to become leaders in all spheres of human life—in the professions, arts, and sciences, but also in discovering the ethical, political, social, and economic consequences of following the will of God.

Paul Lacey, 1985

A Quaker social concern seems characteristically to arise in a sensitive individual or very small group. ... The concern arises as a revelation to an individual that there is a painful discrepancy between existing social conditions and what God wills for society and that this discrepancy is not being adequately dealt with. The next step is the determination of the individual to do something about it—not because he is particularly well fitted to tackle the problem, but simply because no one else seems to be doing it.

Dorothy H. Hutchinson, 1961

A concern is an interest deeply rooted in the Spirit, which may move an individual and the meeting to action. A leading is an inner conviction that impels one to follow a certain course of action under a sense of divine guidance. Modern Friends sometimes use the words interchangeably. Our testimonies were initially leadings inspired by the Spirit in an individual, tested by the individual Friend and later by the meeting, and accepted as a concern of the meeting. Continued discernment over time by ever wider bodies of Friends eventually led all to come to unity with the concern, and thus the concern was transformed into a testimony.

The impetus for service is often a concern, which, as Friends use the word, is a quickening sense of the need to do something or to demonstrate sympathetic interest in an individual or group, as a result of what is felt to be a direct intimation of God's will. A concern as an impetus to action arises out of Friends' belief that the realm of God can be realized here and now, not just in another place or time. A concern may emerge as an unexpected insight from prayerful study of a problem or situation, such as a concern to support national policies which promote international peace. It may also grow from an anxious interest in the welfare of a person or group, which may result in inquiries or practical support.

When it initially arises, a concern may not yet be linked to a proposed course of action but may simply be a troubled sense that something needs attention. A leading is a sense of being drawn or called by God in a particular direction or toward a particular course of action. Friends speak of "feeling led" or "being called." The leading may be short-term and specific in its fulfillment, or it may involve transformation of one's life and even the life of the meeting.

Friends have long believed it important that leadings be tested before action is taken. The process of testing is a form of spiritual discipline for Friends. A Friend's concern and consequent leading may be an individual matter–something which one person is called to attend to without requiring assistance. In many cases, however, a Friend may receive guidance, aid, and encouragement from other members of the meeting. Therefore, it has long been the practice of Friends to inform and consult with their meeting when they feel a leading resulting from a major concern laid upon them.

The Meeting's Response

> "Concern" is a word which has tended to become debased by excessively common usage among Friends, so that too often it is used to cover merely a strong desire. The true "concern" [emerges as] a gift from God, a leading of his Spirit which may not

be denied. Its sanction is not that on investigation it proves to be the intelligent thing to do–though it usually is; it is that the individual . . . knows, as a matter of inward experience, that there is something that the Lord would have done, however obscure the way, however uncertain the means to human observation. Often proposals for action are made which have every appearance of good sense, but as the meeting waits before God it becomes clear that the proposition falls short of "concern."

Roger Wilson, 1949

The meeting's responsibility is to give serious consideration to requests from those seeking unity for a proposed course of action–and the meeting may not always approve. Its worship and ministry committee or other designated committee may appoint a clearness committee (see Chapter 10, Clearness Committees) to help such persons gain clarity on whether to act upon a concern. Such a committee may also provide longer-term support, including ongoing testing and reevaluation. Sometimes just testing a leading in a clearness committee is all the action that is needed for a particular concern. In other instances, the concern needs to be brought to the meeting for business for seasoning by the whole meeting. In cases where meeting approval is given to a proposed course of action which may result in allowing the Friend to be released to follow a leading, the meeting often takes responsibility for providing financial assistance and family support and continues to give oversight until the leading is fulfilled or laid down.

When a meeting fails to unite with a member's concern, the member is asked to reconsider the concern very carefully, perhaps setting it aside and waiting for further Light. Sometimes the individual and meeting agree that the concern should be dropped, and the member may feel released from responsibility for action since the concern has been laid on the meeting. Occasionally, the meeting may be able to encourage the member to go forward even when the meeting is unable to participate in furthering the witness.

Where the concern cannot be furthered without meeting

unity, and a member does not feel right about dropping it, the process of discernment continues. Often this process involves the formation of a small group, which includes Friends who come to the matter at hand from different perspectives. The concern, perhaps with a modified proposal for action, may be brought to the meeting many times before unity is reached either in support or nonsupport of the concern.

Submitting the concern to the discernment of the meeting is of value. The meeting may be enlightened by the insights of those who bring concerns, and these Friends may be helped, through the sympathetic consideration of the meeting, to clarify their leadings. The meeting's care for its members causes it to take interest in all concerns felt by its members, even when it cannot unite with them or may feel obliged to admonish members against "running ahead of their Guide" (see Chapter 17, Glossary of Terms).

Depending on the nature and scope of the concern, the monthly meeting may wish to lay it before the Fall or Winter Interim Business Meeting and the Southeastern Yearly Meeting through a Minute accompanied by personal presentation where possible. A meeting may also request that a concern, brought by a member and deemed significant by the meeting, be considered at a threshing session during the annual sessions of the yearly meeting.

Individuals also may bring concerns to yearly meeting committees. After testing such a concern, a committee may or may not include it in its reports to the yearly meeting, either through interim business meeting or at the annual sessions of yearly meeting.

When a concern is thus presented, the yearly meeting may reach a decision or may provide for further consideration of the matter. Deep sensitivity to divine leading and to the insights of others is required on the part of both individuals and meetings when controversial concerns are considered. Concerns involving intensely personal witness or public policy demand a special degree of forbearance, and unity may not always be reached.

Testimonies

Ever since I first came among Friends, I was attracted to the testimonies as an ideal. I wanted to belong to a church, which made the rejection of warfare a collective commitment and not just a personal option. I admired simplicity, a devotion to equality, and a respect for others, which reflected what I already knew of Christ. In a deceitful world I warmed to those who did not swear oaths and strove to tell the truth in all circumstances. But this was a beginning in the spiritual life. The seed that was sown in my mind and my politics struck root in my soul and my faith.

The choice of the word "testimony" is instructive. The testimonies are ways of behaving but are not ethical rules. They are matters of practice but imply doctrines. They refer to human society but are about God. Though often talked about, they lack an authoritative formulation. . . .

A "testimony" is a declaration of truth or fact. . . . It is not an ejaculation, a way of letting off steam, or baring one's soul. It has a purpose, and that is to get other people to change, to turn to God. Such an enterprise, be it in words or by conduct and example, is in essence prophetic and evangelical.

John Punshon, 1987

Since the 1650s, Friends have acted upon shared concerns through practices which historically have been distinctive and definitive. While the specifics of Friends' practice have varied as times have changed, Friends today continue to have concerns and underlying beliefs similar to those of past generations. Primarily, we testify that God is active in the world today, and there is that of God in everyone.

The term "testimonies" is used to refer to this common set of deeply held, historically rooted convictions and modes of living in the world. They are based on "openings," or revelations experienced by Quakers beginning with George Fox, who preached that "Jesus Christ has come to teach his people himself." He also taught that "There is one, Christ Jesus, that can speak to thy condition."

Testimonies bear witness to the Truth as Friends in community perceive it, Truth known through relationship with God. The testimonies are expressions of lives turned toward the Light, outward expressions reflective of the inward experience of God's leading, differently described by various Friends and in changing eras. Often in the past the testimonies were defined specifically, such as the testimony against taking oaths; recently it has become customary to speak of them more generally, as in the testimony of integrity or simplicity. Through the testimonies, with that measure of the Light that is granted, Friends strive for unity and integrity of inner and outer life, both living with ourselves and each other and living in the world. Trusting strongly in the Holy Spirit to guide sincere seekers, Quakers today refrain from placing on each other particular outward requirements.

> *Let all nations hear the sound by word or writing. Spare no place, spare no tongue nor pen, but be obedient to the Lord God; go through the world and be valiant for the truth upon earth; tread and trample all that is contrary under. ... Be patterns, be examples in all countries, places, islands, nations, wherever you come, that your carriage and life may preach among all sorts of people, and to them. Then you will come to walk cheerfully over the world, answering that of God in everyone; whereby in them you may be a blessing, and make the witness of God in them to bless you.*
>
> **George Fox, 1656**

> *We are a people that follow after those things that make for peace, love, and unity; it is our desire that*

others' feet may walk in the same, and do deny and bear our testimony against all strife and wars and contentions. . . . Our weapons are not carnal, but spiritual. . . . And so we desire, and also expect to have liberty of our consciences and just rights and outward liberties, as other people of the nation, which we have promise of, from the word of a king. . . . Treason, treachery and false dealing we do utterly deny; false dealing, surmising or plotting against any creature on the face of the earth; and speak the Truth in plainness and singleness of heart; and all our desire is your good and peace and love and unity.

Margaret Fell, 1660

The Cross of Christ . . . truly overcomes the world, and leads a life of purity in the face of its allurements; they that bear it are not thus chained up, for fear they should bite; nor locked up, lest they should be stole away; no, they receive power from Christ their Captain, to resist the evil, and do that which is good in the sight of God: to despise the world, and love its reproach above its praise; and not only not to offend others, but love those that offend them.... True godliness doesn't turn men out of the world, but enables them to live better in it, and excites their endeavors to mend it; not hide their candle under a bushel, but set it upon a table in a candlestick.

William Penn, 1682

Every degree of luxury of what kind so ever, and every demand for money inconsistent with divine order, hath some connection with unnecessary labor. . . . To labor too hard or cause others to do so, that we may live conformable to customs which Christ our Redeemer contradicted by his example in the days of his flesh, and which are contrary to divine order, is to manure a soil for propagating an evil seed in the earth.

John Woolman, c. 1763

Love was the first motion, and then a concern arose to spend some time with the Indians, that I might feel and understand their life and the spirit they live in, if haply I might receive some instruction from them, or they be in any degree helped forward by my following the leadings of Truth amongst them. . . . Afterward, feeling my mind covered with the spirit of prayer, I told the interpreters that I found it in my heart to pray to God, and I believed, if I prayed right, he would hear me, and expressed my willingness for them to omit interpreting, so our meeting ended with a degree of Divine love. Before our people went out I observed Papunehang (the man who had been zealous in laboring for a reformation in that town, being then very tender) spoke to one of the interpreters, and I was afterward told that he said in substance as follows: "I love to feel where words come from."

John Woolman, 1763

These testimonies are presented as a reference to actions Friends may be called to take. It is just as likely, however, that we will be challenged in different ways to live according to such key Quaker testimonies as equality, peace, simplicity, and integrity. Our testimonies are our guides as we seek to apply George Fox's advice in a world that is beyond his imagining, yet which offers myriad opportunities to be "valiant for the Truth." For Friends, faith and practice are inseparable.

Testimony of Integrity

The call for honesty lies at the heart of Quakerism. It is a testimony rooted in the Quaker respect for truthfulness. . . . Respect for this kind of integrity

calls for a correspondence between what one pro-
fesses and how one translates that into action in
real life.

Wilmer Cooper, 1990

Integrity was in a sense the first of the Quaker testimonies. Ever since Friends embraced Jesus' challenge to "Be ye perfect," the basis of our personal living has been laid deeper than mere respectability, deeper than the observance of some moral minimum based on the old law of "Thou shalt not." Friends are called to live with integrity Jesus' teachings and example in obedience to the Holy Spirit. This way of living causes a transformation in the fabric of our lives. A simplicity of purpose arises to live in the present in the Truth and order one's life so as to help bring about the realization of God's kingdom of heaven here on earth.

Integrity, essential to all relationships between one and another and between one and God, has always been a basic goal of Friends. Friends have been concerned to interact with integrity, to make our words and actions fit the Truth as we understand it. We endeavor to speak and act honestly and forthrightly, speaking plainly from our own experience of the Light in our lives. Friends strive to make their statements as accurate as possible, without exaggeration or omission. Thoughtful listening is as important as speaking and is a necessary part of communication. If we listen attentively to the expression of the Spirit, in ourselves and in others, words and action can become a means of knowing God. It sometimes takes courage to live according to our faith that God's power operates in us. As we attempt to conform our lives to the leadings of the Spirit, to integrate our beliefs and our actions, and to become more honest and authentic, we receive the strength and courage to follow our religious principles.

Friends regard the custom of swearing oaths as not only contrary to the teachings of Jesus but as implying the existence of a double standard of truth. Early Quakers were persecuted for refusing to take judicial or loyalty oaths. On all occasions when special statements are required, it is recommended that Friends take the opportunity to make simple affirmations, thus emphasizing that their statements are only a part of their usual integrity of speech.

"However, I say to you do not swear at all. . . . Let your word be 'Yes, Yes' or 'No, No.'"
Matthew 5:34-37 (NRSV)

People swear to the end they may speak the truth, Christ would have them speak the truth to the end they might not swear.
William Penn (1644-1718)

Another by-product of truth-telling was the establishment of the one-price system of exchange. Prior to the introduction of this method by Friends, the price of goods and services was always haggled over and bartered until agreement was reached between buyer and seller. Often merchants had one price for the nobility and a different, sometimes higher, price for the commoner. With the one-price system of trade, people knew they wouldn't be taken advantage of by a Quaker merchant.

At the first convincement, when Friends could not put off their hats to people, or say You to a single person, but Thou and Thee; when they could not bow, or use flattering words in salutations, or adopt the fashions and customs of the world, many Friends, that were tradesmen of several sorts, lost their customers at the first; for the people were shy of them, and would not trade with them; so that for a time some Friends could hardly get money enough to buy bread. But afterwards, when people came to have experience of Friends' honesty and truthfulness, and found that their Yea was yea, and their Nay was nay; that they kept to a word in their dealings, and that they would not cozen and cheat them; but that if they sent a child to their shops for anything, they were as well used as if they had come themselves; the lives and conversations of Friends did preach, and reached to the witness of God in the people.
George Fox, 1653

Living The Testimony of Integrity

[Excerpted from *The Testimony of Integrity in the Religious Society of Friends* by Wilmer A. Cooper.]

The testimony of integrity can be articulated and practiced by Friends in four distinct ways.

• *The first is truth-telling, or simply not telling lies.* *This is the most obvious place to begin to live out the testimony of integrity. Friends have always been known for truthfulness and honesty in their relationships and dealings with others. This standard of truthfulness was grounded in Jesus' and James' Biblical injunction not to take an oath or to swear that one will tell the truth (Matthew 5:33-37; James 5:12). Friends were very conscientious about this, not only because taking oaths and swearing was forbidden by the Scriptures but because it implied a double standard of truth, thus suggesting that when not under oath it is all right to lie. Friends' concern was that followers of Christ should be known for telling the truth all the time and not just when called before a judge and sworn to tell the truth.*

... Many Quakers suffered persecution and imprisonment because they refused to exercise a double standard before judges in courts of law. Early Friends were thrown into jail more often for refusing to take the oath than for any other reason. Anybody who didn't like the Quakers could make a charge against them, have them arrested and brought before a judge, whereupon they were automatically thrown into jail, guilty or not, because they refused to swear that now they would tell the truth. ... The testimony of integrity calls for truth-telling under all circumstances and at all times.

• Second, integrity calls for authenticity, for genuineness, and for veracity in one's personhood. It calls us to be truly who we are and not be two-faced by trying to be something or somebody we are not. ...

The opposite of integrity of course is hypocrisy, which means phoniness, sham, and deception. Jesus has some scathing words for hypocrites in Matthew 23. He declares seven woes against the religious authorities of his time, the Scribes and Pharisees, who were hypocrites and pretenders of virtue and piety. We are all tempted to become pretenders in this way. The tendency to misrepresent our true selves is a common shortcoming we all have, but we do not always realize that we are violating our integrity every time we respond this way.

• Third integrity calls for obedience or, if you prefer, faithfulness to conscience illumined by the Light Within. For Quakers this is the seat of religious authority and, therefore, the touchstone of our faith. Here Quaker truth and integrity take on an existential quality. It is truth which may well have objective validity, as I believe it does, but if it is not truth which is internalized in each of us, and for which we take ownership, then it is not truth which is valid and binding for us. But once it lays hold of us, it is truth that will not let us go until we have acted upon it. This kind of truth is new and fresh and therefore vital. It is not grounded in dogma, creeds, abstract philosophical ideas, or theological affirmations. It is not to be found in religious textbooks or Quaker books of discipline, but it is grounded in a living faith and experience of the present moment. It is the basis for the Quaker testimonies – the testimonies which are a living witness to the inward leading of the Spirit of God in our lives.

• *Fourth, the root meaning of the word "integrity" calls for wholeness.* The word comes from the Latin "integritas," which refers to a state or quality of being complete, that is, a condition of wholeness. The word "integrity" and the mathematical term "integer" all have a common meaning. When we look at this common meaning of "integritas," or "integrity," it points to a unity, which, when applied to persons, we call community. Integrity creates a sense of togetherness and belonging when applied to persons in community. Integrity forms the basis for a covenant relationship in which persons exercise a sense of responsibility and accountability toward one another. Individualism, which is preoccupied with doing one's own thing, often with little concern for how it affects other people, dominates much of our behavior in Western society, and in our American culture in particular, and it affects the Religious Society of Friends as well. Thus, we need to recover the testimony of integrity, to balance this other attitude (individualism) when applied to wholeness in the corporate life of persons where there is a sense of responsibility and accountability toward one another. . . .

Integrity in its root meaning and search for wholeness leads to an even deeper sense of community than we have described so far. This level of wholeness goes beyond the community of persons to a spiritual community with "the ground of our being," to use the words of Paul Tillich. Here we need to associate integrity with the religious concept and experience of salvation. Now that may seem strange, because the word "salvation" is not fashionable anymore, except among radio and television evangelists and a few Fundamentalist church folk. But according to Paul Tillich the root meaning of "salvation" can be derived from the Latin salvus (or *salus), which means "health" or "wholeness." Surely all of us hope for health and wholeness in our lives, both physical and spiritual. If the wholeness aspect of integrity leads to a sense of community of persons, likewise it can lead us to an experience of spiritual wholeness in our relationship with God. This comes very close to what Saint Augustine meant when he prayed: "Thou hast created us for Thyself [Oh God], and our hearts are restless until they find their rest in Thee."*

Wilmer A. Cooper, 1990

Testimony of Equality

The testimony of human equality before God is one of the earliest Quaker social testimonies and is a cornerstone of Friends' belief. Quaker equality does not imply equality of ability or economic resources but is based on the concept that there is that of God in every person and therefore that each person is due equal respect. This has led to a conscious effort to eliminate negative words and behavior that arise from distinctions in class, race, gender, sexual orientation, social status, age, or physical attributes.

It was opened to early Friends that God does not distinguish between priesthood and laity. Within the meeting, there are no positions of privilege. We are all responsible for the spiritual life of the meeting and the practical aspects of continuing and strengthening the community of Friends. All may be called to ministry and service according to their gifts.

As the Quaker movement became more organized through the establishment of regular local and regional gatherings for the care of Friends (monthly, quarterly, and yearly meetings), questions arose regarding church authority. Unity emerged through listening closely to the Spirit, particularly in the leadings of more experienced Friends.

And thus the Lord Jesus hath manifested himself and his Power, without respect of Persons; and so

*let all mouths be stopt that would limit him, whose
Power and Spirit is infinite, that is pouring it upon
all flesh.*

Margaret Fell, 1666

In the highly stratified English society of the seventeenth century, Friends' adherence to this testimony outside the meeting often made them seem rude or ill mannered. Quakers refused to use titles of honor or salutations implying superiority. It was common among English society at that time to address superiors in the royal plural "you" and familiars or inferiors in the singular "thee" or "thou."

*This way of speaking proceeds from a high and
proud mind . . . because that men commonly use the
singular to beggars and to their servants; yea and
in their prayers to God–so hath the pride of men
placed God and beggars in the same category.*

Robert Barclay, Apology, 1678

In keeping with this testimony Friends also refused to practice "hat honor," the taking off of one's hat in the presence of superiors or magistrates as a mark of respect. Even before Friends became pacifists, they were dismissed from the army for refusing to treat officers as superiors.

Friends pioneered in recognizing the gifts and rights of women. Women were members and leaders of their early meetings, listened to, and respected.

*And may not the spirit of Christ speak in the female
as well as in the male? Is he there to be limited?
Who is it that dare limit the holy one of Israel? For
the light is the same in the male and the female,
which cometh from Christ, he by whom the world
was made, and so Christ is one in all and not divided; and who is it that dare stop Christ's mouth?*

George Fox, 1656

In 1671 George Fox urged the monthly meetings to set up parallel men's and women's meetings for business. A significant aspect of early Friends' organization was separate regular meetings of women, which arose to free women from customary social restraints on women's self-expression.

Women shared in the work of Quaker ministry as well as taking the lead in caring for the poor and for imprisoned Friends. The first person that George Fox convinced was Elizabeth Hooten, an English General Baptist minister, who shortly afterward became one of the first Quaker ministers. She preached in the public places, wrote pamphlets, and penned letters to King Charles II professing the innocence of Quakers. This Quaker grandmother traveled in the ministry to the New World and died in Jamaica on her second missionary trip traveling with George Fox.

As much as George Fox is credited with the vision that gave rise to the movement, Margaret Fell must be recognized as the nurturing spirit that helped sustain Friends through years of persecution and for establishment of the practical groundwork of our religious community. She had the gift of organization and concern for Friends in need. She wrote letters to struggling Friends encouraging them in their witness, pamphlets in support of women's public preaching, and letters to King Charles II petitioning for the release of George Fox and other imprisoned Friends. She provided a safe haven at Swarthmoor Hall for Friends to recuperate after prison or persecution. She visited Friends in prison and was herself imprisoned for her public witness.

> *And now also some ancient women-friends did meet together, to consider what appertained to them as their most immediate care and concern to inspect the circumstances and conditions of such who were imprisoned on truth's account, and to provide things needful to supply their wants. And what did or might more immediately concern men-friends, the women would acquaint them therewith. These women did also inquire into, and inspect the wants*

*and necessities of the poor, who were convinced of
the truth. And they sat not still until the cry of the
poor came to their houses.*

William Crouch, 1712

*How healing to come into the Religious Society of
Friends, whose founder saw clearly that the Light of
God is not limited to the male half of the human
race. Membership and participation have helped
me grow toward wholeness, as I have followed my
calling into a ministry that embraces all of life.
Though I believe deeply in women's liberation, I cannot put men down, or I join in consciousness-raising
activities that foster hatred of everything masculine.
I have loved the men in my life too deeply for that
kind of betrayal.*

*As women gain rights and become whole human
beings, men too can grow into wholeness, no longer
having to carry the whole burden of responsibility
for running the affairs of humankind, but in humility accepting the vast resources, as yet not very much
drawn on, and the wisdom of women in solving the
colossal problems of the world.*

Elizabeth Watson, 1975

Friends believe that everyone is a "child of God" and should
relate to one another in those terms. Everyone is regarded as of
infinite worth and must be treated as a person who can be drawn by
love to live a full and worthwhile life, which manifests respect and
consideration for others. When Friends are at their best, that love
leads to unity in their meetings. It can also be effective in relations
among all people.

*There is no longer Jew nor Greek, there is no longer
slave nor free, there is no longer male nor female, for
all of you are one in Christ Jesus.*

Galatians 3:28 NRSV

Friends came more slowly to recognize the evil of slavery and of discrimination in general, and some have been guilty of the prejudices of the broader society. In recent years, however, most have taken increasingly clear stands against all forms of discrimination. As we continue to seek the Light, habits and attitudes of a less sensitive past must increasingly give way to new understandings that affirm the value of all human beings.

Living the Testimony of Equality

Social Justice

Friends have worked in a variety of ways to further social justice. Historically, Friends have worked for the abolition of slavery, improvement of conditions in prisons and mental health hospitals, and women's right to vote, among other concerns. Today some Friends work with groups who have been victimized by prejudice or exploitation. Friends should recognize that prejudices are very prevalent even within the Religious Society of Friends and that the problem of prejudice is complicated by advantages that have come to some at the expense of others. Exploitation impairs the human quality of the exploiter as well as of the exploited.

Enunciation of the principle of equality of human beings in the sight of God is important and necessary, but it is not sufficient. Realization of equality involves such matters as independence and control of one's own life. Friends seek to bring to light structures, institutions, language, and thought processes which subtly support discrimination and exploitation. Therefore, Friends are led to aid the efforts of the exploited to attain self-determination and social, political, and economic justice and to change attitudes and practices taken for granted.

Racial Equality

What began as an understanding that all men were equal, and was first manifested in Quaker practices that denied class and social distinctions, was expanded over time to recognition of gender equality and later to racial equality as well. John Woolman's long witness–from approximately 1745 to his death in 1772–against slavery put many Friends at the front of an ongoing effort against racial bigotry. Today, we are brought to a new consciousness of the continuing need for that self-examination and witness by various Quaker committees on racism.

It is a simple truth to say that if we would cast out racism we must "love one another as Jesus has loved us," yet most need more detailed instruction. The goal of good human relations is a community in which each individual and each group can feel sure of opportunities for self-development, full realization of potential, and rewarding relations with others.

> *If one begins with presumptions of moral and mental greatness founded upon body color, the conduct and conclusions flowing there from will be erroneous. If one begins with prayer and intellectual honesty, profound consideration of the Queries together with a sharing of truthful–if embarrassing–answers will prime our spiritual pumps so we may start to reverse the descent from grace and begin to move towards spiritual wholeness.*
> **Almanina Barbour and Walter Sullivan, 1984**

Testimony of Peace

All human beings are children of God; thus Friends are called to love and respect all persons and to seek to overcome evil with good. Friends' peace testimony arises from the power of Christ working in our hearts. Our words and lives should testify to this power and should stand as a positive witness in a world still torn by strife and violence. In explaining his unwillingness to serve in the army, George Fox said of the Commonwealth in 1651:

*I told them . . . that I lived in the virtue of that life
and power that takes away the occasion of all wars.*

George Fox, 1651

To early Friends, pacifism flowed so inevitably and directly
from other more fundamental principles that little was said about
it until Quakers were accused of plotting to overthrow the English
government. In 1660, a few Friends were arrested in the belief that
they were involved with a group called the "Fifth Monarchy." This
group tried to seize London by force in preparation for the second
coming of Christ. In response George Fox and other Quaker ministers stated the position of the Religious Society of Friends clearly in
the following declaration to Charles II (1660):

> *We utterly deny all outward wars and strife, and
> fightings with outward weapons, for any end, or
> under any pretense whatsoever; this is our testimo-
> ny to the whole world. . . . The Spirit of Christ, by
> which we are guided, is not changeable, so as once
> to command us from a thing as evil, and again to
> move us unto it; and we certainly know, and testify
> to the world, that the Spirit of Christ, which leads
> us into all truth, will never move us to fight and war
> against any man with outward weapons, neither
> for the Kingdom of Christ nor for the Kingdoms of
> this world. . . . Therefore, we cannot learn war any
> more.*

Friends Declaration to King Charles II, 1660

The Religious Society of Friends is a historic peace church.
Since Friends' first allegiance is to a loving God, we are called to
obey God rather than human law when this allegiance is challenged
by the demands of the state. We support those who oppose war by
performing work as conscientious objectors and those who resist
any cooperation with the military. We hold in love, but disagree
with, those of our members who feel that they must enter the armed
forces. We recognize that the entire military system is inconsistent with Jesus' example of love. We work toward the day when

armaments and conscription will no longer be tolerated and we can live in the peaceable kingdom.

Our historic peace testimony is nothing if not also a living testimony as we work to give concrete expression to our ideals. We would alleviate the suffering caused by war. We would refrain from participating in all forms of violence and repression against people. We would make strenuous efforts to secure international agreements for the control of armaments and to remove the domination of militarism in our society. We would seek to be involved in building interpersonal skills and local, national, and transnational institutions to deal with conflict nonviolently. We seek to model to others the path of love and non-violence in the face of the horrors of warfare so that all can come to understand that war is not the way.

> *O that we who declare against wars, and acknowledge our trust to be in God only, may walk in the light and therein examine our foundation and motives in holding great estates. May we look upon our treasures, the furniture of our houses, and our garments, and try whether the seeds of war have nourishment in these our possessions?*
> **John Woolman, 1763**

The most basic task of our peacemaking is to fill the spiritual void in our world by replacing the fear which cripples human efforts with faith in the power of God's love. We look beyond the evil we oppose to the establishment of the "blessed community." Lifelong, sacrificial efforts in peacemaking require us to acknowledge our inability in a complex society to disengage ourselves completely from it. Each Friend has the responsibility to seek and to live the full personal implications of the peace testimony. This is a spiritual and very practical challenge. Following God's promptings, the Inward Christ roots out that which is selfish and impels us to share each other's suffering in that which brings unity and peaceful relationships. Our hope lies in the power of God's peace moving through our meetings, small devotional groups, and wider associations.

Living the Testimony of Peace

The Individual and the Peace Testimony

In our individual lives, the peace testimony leads us to accept differences as an opportunity for loving engagement with those with whom we disagree. That love can often be expressed in creative, nonviolent resolution of the disagreement. When we encounter people of sincere religious conviction whose views are profoundly different from our own, that love can also be manifested by acknowledging the sincerity of the other while faithfully expressing our own convictions.

The peace testimony also leads us as individuals to consider seriously our employment, our investments, our purchases, our payment of taxes, and our manner of living as they relate to violence. We try to become sensitive to the covert as well as the overt violence inherent in some of our long-established social practices and institutions. Friends wish to avoid, for example, benefiting not only from the manufacture of arms or the excessive use of natural resources but also from company practices that do violence to employees, consumers, or the natural world.

Friends and Military Activity

We support those who do not cooperate with conscription and those who oppose war by performing work as conscientious objectors. While counseling against military service, we hold in love our members who feel they must undertake it. Some Friends have decided to serve in the military as noncombatants.

Friends work as we are able to alleviate the suffering caused by war. We acknowledge the contribution that military forces have made in some situations to the relief of suffering, but we are troubled by the use of agents of destruction for such purposes and by the failure of nations to support the creation of nonviolent groups to undertake humanitarian missions.

Alternatives to War

The almost unimaginable devastation that results from modern war makes ever more urgent its total elimination. We work for greater understanding at all levels, from the kindergarten to the United Nations, of proven techniques for the nonviolent resolution of conflict. We would promote and assist programs of conversion to peaceful uses of facilities built for war. Friends are led to support the Peace Tax Fund, the World Court, and the United Nations as alternatives to war.

World Order

Friends in America since William Penn have sought to promote institutions of peace. In this era we promote a vision of global living that recognizes the essential unity of a human family sharing a fragile planet. We prefer governing institutions that work face-to-face within small communities. But we acknowledge the need for governing institutions at all levels, both as supportive, coordinating bodies and as courts of appeal from the arbitrary actions of lesser jurisdictions. We are deeply distressed by a world dominated by heavily armed nation-states. We apply our gifts—of spirit, of intellect, of time and energy—to work for a new international order, within which our communities will be able to redirect their resources from dependence on the manufacture of arms to human needs and the preservation of the earth.

Testimony of Simplicity

Simplicity, also called simple living, has long been a testimony of Friends. A life of simplicity is one that is centered in God and focused on core values and faith. It need not be cloistered and may even be a busy life, but its activities and expressions should be correlated and directed toward the simple, direct purpose of keeping one's communication with God open and unencumbered. Simplicity is cutting away all that is extraneous. Simplicity is being without sham and is based in the right ordering of one's priorities in placing devotion to God at the center of life. When sought intentionally, simplicity, like the other testimonies, is not something one should be driven to achieve. It is in essence a free gift of God's grace.

It's a dangerous thing to lead young Friends much into the observation of outward things, which may be easily done, for they can soon get into an outward garb, to be all alike outwardly, but this will not make them true Christians: it's the Spirit that gives life. I would be loath to have a hand in these things....
Margaret Fell Fox, 1698

My mind through the power of Truth was in a good degree weaned from the desire of outward greatness, and I was learning to be content with real conveniences that were not costly; so that a way of life free from much Entanglements appeared best for me, tho' the income was small. I had several offers of business that appeared profitable, but saw not my way clear to accept of them, as believing the business proposed would be attended with more outward care & cumber than was required of me to engage in. I saw that a humble man, with the Blessing of the Lord, might live on a little, and that where the heart was set on greatness, success in business did not satisfy the craving; but that commonly with an increase of wealth, the desire for wealth increased. There was a care on my mind so to pass my time, as to things outward, that nothing might hinder me from the most steady attention to the voice of the True Shepherd.
John Woolman, c. 1744

I wish I might emphasize how a life becomes simplified when dominated by faithfulness to a few concerns. Too many of us have too many irons in the fire. We get distracted by the intellectual claim to our interest in a thousand and one good things, and before we know it we are pulled and hauled breathlessly along by an over-burdened program of good committees and good undertakings. I am persuaded that this fevered life of church workers is not wholesome. Undertakings get plastered on from the outside because we can't turn down a friend. Acceptance of service on a weighty committee should really depend upon an answering imperative within us, not merely upon a rational calculation of the factors involved. The concern-oriented life is ordered and organized from within. And we learn to say No as well as Yes by attending to the guidance of inner responsibility. Quaker simplicity needs to be expressed not merely in dress and architecture and the height of tombstones but also in the structure of a relatively simplified and coordinated life-program of social responsibilities. And I am persuaded that concerns introduce that simplification, and along with it that intensification which we need in opposition to the hurried, superficial tendencies of our age.

Thomas R. Kelly, 1941

For some there is a danger that care for the future may lead to undue anxiety and become a habit of saving for its own sake, resulting in the withholding of what should be expended for the needs of the family or devoted to the service of the Society. The temptation to trust in riches comes in many forms, and can only be withstood through faith in our Father and his providing care.

London Yearly Meeting, 1945

Simplicity consists not in the use of particular forms but in avoiding self-indulgence, in maintaining humility of spirit, and in keeping the material surroundings of our lives directly serviceable to necessary ends. This does not mean that life need be poor and bare or destitute of joy and beauty. All forms of art may aid in the attainment of the spiritual life, and often the most simple lines, themes, or moments, when characterized by grace and directness, are the most beautiful.

Living a simple life can take forms as diverse as the people we are and requires listening to the Inward Light for guidance in making choices. Considerations involve all aspects of our lives, including what material possessions we acquire, how much and what kind of activities and relationships we engage in and how we nurture our spiritual lives. Do we choose what is simple and useful? Do we take joy in our commitments?

Living the Testimony of Simplicity

Walking Gently on the Earth

> *Poverty [Simplicity] does not mean scorn for goods and property. It means the strict limitation of goods that are for personal use. It means the opposite of the reckless abuse and misuse of property that leaves our country spotted with the graveyards of broken and abandoned machinery. It means a horror of war, first because it ruins human life and health and the beauty of the earth, but second because it destroys goods that could be used to relieve misery and hardship and to give joy. It means a distaste even for the small carelessnesses that we see prevalent, so that beautiful and useful things are allowed to become dirty and battered through lack of respect for them. We have in America in this day the strange spectacle of many comely and well-equipped small homes kept in a state of neglect and disorder that would shock peasants anywhere.*
>
> **Mildred Binns Young, 1956**

We recognize that the well-being of the earth is fundamentally a spiritual concern. From the beginning, it was through the wonders of nature that people saw God. How we treat the earth and its creatures is a basic part of our relationship with God. Our planet as a whole, not just the small parts of it in our immediate custody, requires our responsible attention.

As Friends become more aware of the interconnectedness of all life on this planet and the devastation caused by neglect of any part of it, we have become more willing to extend our sense of community to encompass all living things. We must now consider how to combine the belief that we humans are called to act as stewards of the natural world with the growing view of human actions as the major threat to the ecosystem.

Friends are indeed called to walk gently on the earth. Wasteful and extravagant consumption is a major cause of destruction of the environment. The right sharing of the world's remaining resources requires that developed nations reduce their present levels of consumption so that people in underdeveloped nations can have more and the earth's life-sustaining systems can be restored. The world cannot tolerate indefinitely the present rate of consumption by technologically developed nations.

Friends are called to become models and patterns of simple living and concern for the earth. Some may find it difficult to change their accustomed lifestyle; others recognize the need and have begun to adopt ways of life which put the least strain on the world's resources of energy, clean air, water, and soil.

Rapid population growth leads to famine, war, and destruction of natural resources. In simplifying our own lives we may find it difficult to limit the number of children we have. Voluntary restraint in procreation along with simplicity in living hold the promise of restoring ecological balance.

Recreation

Recreation can promote spiritual well-being; it may bring a needed balance into life and contribute to the wholeness of personality. Simplicity directs the individual to choose those forms of recreation that rest and build up the body, that refresh and enrich mind and spirit. Consideration needs to be given to the proper expenditure of time, money, and strength and the moral and physical welfare of others as well as oneself. Healthful recreation includes games, sports, and other physical exercise; gardening and the study and enjoyment of nature; travel; books; the fellowship of friends and family; and the arts and handicrafts, which bring creative self-expression and appreciation of beauty. Recreations in which one is a participant rather than merely a spectator are particularly beneficial. Also, Friends find that simplicity involves refraining from excess in general, including avoiding the addictive use of alcohol, drugs, tobacco, gambling, and even a compulsive engagment in work, causes, or hobbies. Such excess can lead to a life harmful to health, loving relationships, and spiritual experience.

In 1755 London Yearly Meeting issued this query on alcohol:

Are Friends careful to avoid the excessive use of spirituous liquors, the unnecessary frequenting of taverns and places of diversions and to keep to true moderation and temperance on account of births, marriages, burials and other occasions?

Implicit in the above reference to "places of diversions" is the Friends' testimony against gambling:

Gambling by risking money haphazardly disregards our belief that possessions are a trust. The persistent appeal to covetousness . . . is fundamentally opposed to the unselfishness which was taught by Jesus Christ and by the New Testament as a whole. The attempt, which is inseparable from gambling, to make profit out of the inevitable loss and possible suffering of others is the antithesis of that love for one's neighbor on which our Lord insisted. Moreover, we must consider the moral and spiritual plight of those who by indulgence in gambling become possessed of large

*financial resources for which they have rendered no
service to the community.*

London Yearly Meeting, 1959

Concerns Arising From Multiple Testimonies

Unity in the Community

One of the queries in longest continuous use asks, *"Are love
and unity maintained among you?"* (1682). Early Friends did not
consider themselves a sect, an institutionalized permanent minor-
ity, but rather part of a great movement that would soon sweep the
world. Unity and mutual care within the Quaker community in
the face of persecution demonstrated as a witness to the world the
working of Christ among his people. Without formal church membership, doctrine, or creed, early Quakers relied on the movings of
the Spirit, seeking God's will in the "sense of the meeting" and the
leadings of "weighty Friends." The process of individuals submitting themselves to the corporate revelation of God's truth forms the
basis of Friends' approach to Christian unity.

> *The way is one; Christ the truth of God; and he that
> is in the faith, and in the obedience to that light
> which shines from his Spirit into the heart of every
> believer, hath a taste of the one heart and of the one
> way, and knoweth that no variety of practices, which
> is of God, can make a breach in the true unity.*

Isaac Penington, 1659

> *True unity may be found under great apparent dif-
> ferences. This unity is spiritual, it expresses itself in
> many ways, and we need divine insight that we may
> recognize its working. We need forbearance, sympa-
> thy, and love, in order that, while remaining loyal to
> the truth as it has come to us, we may move forward
> with others to a larger and richer experience and
> expression of the will of God.*

London Yearly Meeting, 1916

Stewardship of Economic Resources

All that we have, in our selves and our possessions, are gifts from God, entrusted to us for our responsible use. Jesus reminds us:

> *Do not store up for yourselves treasures on earth.*
> *... For where your treasure is, there your heart will*
> *be also. ... You cannot serve God and mammon*
> *[wealth].*
>
> **Matt. 6: 19-24 NRSV**

Stewardship is an outgrowth of our major testimonies. To be good stewards in God's world calls on us to examine and consider the ways in which our testimonies for integrity, peace, equality, and simplicity interact to guide our relationships with all life.

In a world of economic interactions far more complex than George Fox or John Woolman could have imagined, Friends need to examine their decisions about obtaining, holding, and using money and other assets to see whether they find in them the seeds not only of war but also of self-indulgence, injustice, and ecological disaster. Good stewardship of our resources consists both of avoidance of those evils and of actions that advance peace, simple living, justice, and a healthy ecosystem. Good stewardship also requires attention to the economic needs of Quaker and other organizations that advance Friends' testimonies.

Right Sharing

Friends worldwide have accepted the idea that the testimony of equality implies a commitment in the economic realm to the right sharing of the world's resources. Friends in comfortable circumstances need to find practical expression of the testimony of simplicity in their earning and spending. They consider what economic equality and simplicity mean for their own lives and what level of income is consonant with their conclusions. They should consider likewise what portion of that income could be shared beyond the immediate family. That decision entails balancing the social value of self-sufficiency against the social value of greater help for those more needy. It also requires judgments about what expenditures are essential and what are discretionary and about the values that will underlie discretionary expenditures.

Civic Duties

As a part of our witness to what society may become, Friends may be called to participate in public life as voters, public officials, or participants in community groups or professional societies. As private citizens in the public arena, Friends bear witness by respect for others, flexibility, reconciliation, and forgiveness in difficulties, as well as faithful persistence in pursuit of their leadings. In public office, Friends have an opportunity to bear witness to the power which integrity, courage, respect for others, and careful attention to different points of view can exert in creating a just community. Where there is a conflict between loyalty to God and a seeming necessity for action as a public official, a prayerful search for divine guidance may lead to a suitable resolution of the conflict or to a decision to resign. Our primary allegiance is to God.

Criminal Justice

Many early Friends were victims of an arbitrary and unreasonable legal system. Knowledge of that experience has opened many later Friends to that of God in convicted persons. Friends continue to undertake work in prisons by ministering to the spiritual and material needs of inmates. Believing that the penal system often reflects structural and systemic injustice in our society, Friends seek alternatives. Friends have acted out of the conviction that redemption and restorative justice, not retribution, are the right tasks of the criminal justice system. We strongly oppose capital punishment, finding it contrary to the teachings of Jesus and the principle of "that of God in every person."

Seeking to heal the wounds of criminal actions, Friends are called to many different kinds of service in the criminal justice system. Prison visiting, victim support services, conflict resolution training for staff of correctional institutions and offenders, and work to abolish the use of the death penalty are typical of these services. Such service is undertaken in order to restore the victim, the offender, and the community to the greatest extent possible. The healing love, and the trust in divine leading that such disciplined service requires, can greatly assist the rebuilding of broken lives.

Civil Disobedience

From their earliest days Friends have counseled obedience to the state except when the law or ruling involved has appeared to be contrary to God's leading. The state has no claim to moral infallibility. Primary allegiance is to God.

If the state's commands appear to be contrary to divine leading, Friends take prayerful counsel before responding. This usually also involves testing one's proposed action by the judgment of the meeting. When the decision is to refuse obedience to the law or order of the state, in accordance with the dictates of one's conscience as revealed in the Light, Friends act openly and make clear the grounds of their action.

If the decision involves incurring legal penalties, Friends generally have suffered willingly for the sake of their convictions. Friends not personally involved in such actions can strengthen the meeting community by supporting their fellow members with spiritual encouragement and, when necessary, with material aid.

Membership in Secret Societies

Friends' testimony against membership in secret societies has some of its source in the opposition in England to the Quaker Act of 1662 and the Conventicle Acts of 1664 and 1670. These acts forbade attendance at Friends' meetings (Quaker Act) and later at any other nonconformist religious services (Conventicle Acts). While Quakers continued to meet openly and publicly, others of the "separated peoples" (separated from the Church of England) began to meet in secret for fear of the resulting persecution. Quakers have noted the inherent ethical and moral problems of groups who meet in secret. The <u>1953 edition of the discipline of Iowa Yearly Meeting (Conservative)</u> states:

> *The Society of Friends bears testimony against membership in any secret organizations. While some of these are less objectionable than others, wherever the obligation to secrecy exists, Friends should not join. We believe no one has any moral right to pledge obedience by oath or affirmation to the dictates of another and thus surrender independence of judgment. Secret societies are capable of producing much evil and incapable of producing any good, which might not be effected by safe and open means.*

And more specifically from <u>New England Yearly Meeting, 1930</u>:

> *We especially admonish our younger members against college societies whose proceedings are hedged with secrecy. ... The exclusiveness of secret societies gives to the fellowship which they promote a flavor of selfishness.*

Sexuality

Quakers, like others, in recent years have experienced a growing understanding and appreciation of human sexuality and its important role in our lives. In the words of the British Friends who wrote <u>Towards a Quaker View of Sex.</u>

> *Sexuality, looked at dispassionately, is neither good nor evil—it is a fact of nature and a force of immeasurable power. But looking at it as Christians we have felt impelled to state without reservation that it is a glorious gift of God. Throughout the whole of living nature it makes possible an endless and*

fascinating variety of creatures, a lavishness, a
beauty of form and colour surpassing all that could
be imagined as necessary to survival.

In contrast to this recognition of vibrancy and beauty, there are lingering misunderstandings and ignorance about sexuality, especially in relation to our sexual needs and urges. This can be harmful to people of all ages. Fuller knowledge and understanding are sorely needed. Sex education is therefore important for everyone. Readily available information and open discussion of human sexuality are to be encouraged for both children and adults.

People experience their sexuality from the beginning of life and need to learn what this means to them. Parents and the meeting can encourage children in their learning about this meaning by constructively supporting the child's natural interest in his or her own sexuality and in that of others. Parents teach their children primarily by the example of their lives together. Ideally they demonstrate mutual love, affection, consideration, and trust in a lasting relationship that includes sexual gratification and joy.

We are challenged to discipline our sexual behavior in the light of our growing awareness of overall sexuality. This concept includes keeping sexual behavior in the context of the total interpersonal relationship rather than treating sexual activity as an end. Casual, exploitative, or promiscuous sexual behavior can produce emotional and physical suffering. In dealing with sexual matters, care and concern for others is no less important than care and concern for one's self.

The mystery of sex continues to be greater than our
capacity to comprehend it, no matter how much we
learn about it. We engage in it, in often too fran-
tic efforts to enjoy it but, more subtly, also to try
to fathom its ever recurring power over us. Surely
this power and its mystery relate to the mystery of
God's relationship to us. The mistake we have made

throughout the ages has been to load onto sex the
incubus of success or failure of marriage, to look
upon sex as a resolution, an ending. In reality it
offers us, if we could only see it, a fresh beginning
every time in that relationship of which it is a part.

Mary S. Calderone, 1973

Sexual Preference

We are concerned with the quality of relationships, not with their outward appearances. This insight has brought increasing light to our views of those who are in nontraditional relationships, both gay and straight, and we are looking anew and without judgment at, for example, committed relationships outside of marriage and the choice to be a single parent.

Now more aware of the socially-inflicted suffering
of people who love others of the same sex, we affirm
the power and joy of non-exploitive, loving relation-
ships. As a Society and as individuals, we oppose
arbitrary social, economic, or legal abridgement of
the right to share this love.

Pacific Yearly Meeting, 1972

In a world which hears vitriolic statements against homosexuals made by elected officials and religious persons, we who proclaim a concern for equality and our love for all are called to act. In our Religious Society, the call may not find unity in expression, yet it exists. We work to create and sustain a loving, affirming, safe community within the Society of Friends where all committed relationships can be honored, nurtured, and celebrated in the manner of Friends. We are called to love "that of God" in the world's peoples and strive to bring about this same loving, affirming, and safe community worldwide.

Home and Children

Parents are the child's first teachers. It is in the home that Friends' principles first become practices. The home is founded upon love and depends constantly upon loving sympathy, understanding, and cooperation. Love binds the family together and yet allows freedom for each member to develop into the person he or she is meant to be. Loving guidance that is constructive, and not authoritarian or possessive, will help children discover their potential and their interests. Love reaches further than words and is understood long before words have meaning. The love of parents for God, for each other, and for their children brings stability and security. This outpouring of the Spirit contributes to the religious atmosphere of the home.

Hospitality in the home is a vital force in spiritual nurture. The contacts of parents with their children's companions and the children's association with adult guests are important influences. Parental attitudes toward neighbors and acquaintances are often reflected in the children. Family conversation may determine whether or not children will look for the good in the people they meet, and whether they will be sensitive to that of God in everyone.

The organization of the business of living so that there is time for companionship, for sharing the beauty and the wonder of small, everyday happenings, is an important responsibility of parents. A home that is not cluttered with too many possessions, where there is orderliness without a sense of constraint, and where there is time for the family to enjoy one another will help to develop well-integrated lives.

The home provides an opportunity for devotional reading and prayer. Many parents feel the need for regular times of daily worship. Children may not consciously feel this same need, but in everyday happenings, they are often keenly aware of the closeness of the Holy Spirit. Family worship is especially appropriate in hours of joy, sorrow, or special difficulty.

I have seen much advantage to children, and indeed to whole families, from the practice of a solemn pause at meals. It learns children stillness, decency, and reverence; and where it is done in a feeling manner, with minds rightly turned to feel after God, and experience his blessing, and is not practiced in a slight formal manner, it tends to season and solemnize the minds of young and old. I am morally certain, that I have many a day gone through the cares and concerns of life, with much more composure, stability, satisfaction and propriety, for the strength and assistance I have found in drawing near to God in solemn silence in my family; and I wish the practice of reverently adoring him in this way, may increase more and more.

Job Scott, (1751-1793)

Friends' Experience of Living the Testimonies

The promise of the Holy Spirit was to a group. We need one another to strengthen each other's will to goodness. The concern of an individual should be laid before the worshipping group, so that corporate guidance may be given by an expression of unity or disunity. The life and teachings of Jesus, seen not so much in detail as in totality, provide another check, which should be employed in seeking guidance.

Friends World Conference, 1952

Our testimonies arise from our way of worship. Our way of worship evokes from deep within us at once an affirmation and a celebration, an affirmation of the reality of that Light which illumines the spiritual longing of humanity, and a celebration of the continual resurrection within us of the springs of hope and love; a sense that each of us is, if we will, a channel for a power that is both within and beyond us.

Lorna M. Marsden, 1986

A Quaker testimony is a belief that stems from our fundamental understanding of religious truth. It is a corporately held belief about how we should individually act. In practicing them, we witness to our understanding of the very nature of God's spirit of love and truth.

Jonathan Dale, 1996

CHAPTER 4

BLESSED COMMUNITY: QUAKER FAITH, TESTIMONY, AND PRACTICE

Community as Quaker Faith and Testimony

> *. . . for when I came into the silent assemblies of God's people, I felt a secret power among them, which touched my heart, and as I gave way unto it, I found the evil weakening in me and the good raised up, and so I became thus knit and united unto them, hungering more and more after the increase of this power and life, whereby I might feel myself perfectly redeemed.*
>
> **Robert Barclay, 1678**

> *For the first generation of Friends the testimonies were a prophetic challenge to what they perceived as a vain, unrighteous order around them. To be a prophetic challenge meant to follow the examples of the Hebrew prophets, who, following a direct leading from God, called society to righteousness and articulated what must change for the people to be able to live in justice, mercy, and love.*
>
> **Sandra Cronk, 1991**

The Quaker meeting is a faith community, grounded in the shared experience of God's guidance and grace felt in our meetings for worship, our meetings for worship with a concern for business, and our fellowship. We are a diverse group of individuals who have been drawn together by the Spirit. At some point in each of our spiritual journeys, a longing to find a faith and community that could speak to our condition brought us to Quaker meeting. Many Friends describe the experience of their first visit to meeting as "coming home." It is only with God's Spirit that such a diverse group of individuals can realize and embody the kind of unity, belonging, and community that answers to that of God within us.

The Quaker meeting is meant to be a blessed community –a living testimony to a social order that embodies God's peace, justice, love, compassion, and joy, and is an example and invitation to a better way of life. Like our other testimonies, community can be a prophetic call to the rest of society.

From their earliest beginnings, Quakers have witnessed to their experience of the wholeness that God intends for us in this lifetime on earth. The Spirit calls us to live in a loving relationship with God, with each other, and with all of creation. George Fox showed us a way that was to be found not only through individual pursuit but especially in a worshiping community. Early Quakers identified their experience of God's presence among them with the Biblical message about living as a "people of God"–a community living under God's guidance embodying peace, justice, joy, wisdom, and all the fruits of the Spirit.

We hold the calming peace of the Presence in our being, yet Friends today may feel overwhelmed with the many needs and injustices we see in our society and the world. Some may point to the loss of community as a reason that these problems are multiplying–and to the need for reclaiming and building community in order to solve the world's problems.

Living in blessed community requires a shift in our thinking as the Light shows us our interdependence and increases our empathy with all creation. We come to understand that building compassionate and healthy relationships with others and with all creation is what God asks us to do. Our spiritual growth depends on it.

Because of this emphasis on interconnectedness and compassion, living in blessed community can be a vital part of our witness for peace, social justice, and care for the earth.

Our inability to get along with each other threatens all life on this planet. . . . I think our meetings become Blessed Communities by becoming places where we can engage in learning how to get along with each other, where we consciously learn by doing. Our meetings are the place we can experiment and experience, the place where we can make mistakes and then learn from our mistakes.

Marty Walton, 1994

If there is to be a religious solution to the social problem there must also be renewed in a disintegrating society the sense of community, of mutuality, of responsible brotherhood for all . . .

American Friends Service Committee, 1955

The Individual in Community

You are the light of the world. A city on a hill cannot be hid. No one after lighting a lamp puts it under the bushel basket, but on the lampstand, and it gives light to all in the house. In the same way, let your light shine before others, so that they may see your good works, and give glory to your Father in heaven.

Matt. 5: 14-16 NRSV

Each of us has unique and creative contributions to make as we allow the Light to shine through us. A meeting community needs the God-given leadings and spiritual gifts of each of its members. Individuals, in turn, need the meeting community to be a safe place to explore whether their leadings are from the Light and to exercise their gifts and abilities. This individuality and diversity of gifts can develop and be celebrated because the unity of the group resides in the Spirit through real connections and commitments to God and to each other, not in outward conformity.

The spiritual understanding of individuality stands in sharp contrast to the "rugged individualism" which is rampant in our culture. For generations, people have abandoned traditional forms of community—small towns and extended families—for various reasons, among them the pursuit of personal economic mobility, "progress," and wealth. Individualism has become a value system in which the rights of the individual are often believed to be in conflict and competition with the needs of the community and the environment.

> *Our meetings are living entities, not theories. . . .*
> *We can't nurture our spirits in isolation from all*
> *the other ways we relate to each other—our spiritual*
> *lives can't be separated out. Whether we want it to*
> *be this way or not, we inevitably find that our whole*
> *being is engaged in spiritual growth.*
>
> **Marty Walton, 1994**

> *. . . Here in the United States we put great value in*
> *our individual freedom, in our right to choose, and*
> *we hold very tightly to that right. But it grieves me*
> *that so little is trumpeted about our responsibility*
> *to choose wisely. . . .*
>
> *People have come to believe it is our right to act*
> *however we wish, without looking at the conse-*
> *quences to either the human or wider community in*
> *which we are embedded. This is a big current battle*
> *zone: individual rights versus responsibility and the*
> *taking into account of long-term consequences. . . .*
> *If Quakers have nothing else to offer the wider world*
> *it might be this: our practice of using corporate dis-*
> *cernment to determine what is best for the body as*
> *a whole, balancing the needs of the individual with*
> *the good of the community.*
>
> **Lisa Lofland Gould, 2002**

> *Our Gracious Creator cares and provides for all*
> *His Creatures. His tender mercies are over all His*
> *works; and, so far as His love influences our minds,*
> *so far we become interested in His workmanship*
> *and feel a desire to take hold of every opportunity*
> *to lessen distresses of the afflicted and increase the*

happiness of the Creation. Here we have a prospect
of one common interest from which our own is in-
separable, that to turn all the treasure we possess
into the channel of Universal Love becomes the
business of our lives.

John Woolman, 1772

Community is the context in which people come to
understand their relatedness.

Parker Palmer, 1977

Quaker Social Order (Gospel Order)

. . . [A]nd keep the gospel order . . . so that in all
your men's and women's meetings, see that virtue
flow, and see that all your words be gracious, and
see that love flows, which bears all things, that kind-
ness, tenderness and gentleness may be among you,
and that the fruits of the good spirit may abound.
. . . For you have the light to see all evil, and the
power to withstand it, and to see that nothing be
lacking.

George Fox, 1671

Another aspect of our Quaker testimony of community also
requires a shift in our thinking as we learn to live in a new social
order. Friends' experience is that the creative power of the Spirit
empowers us to recognize our interdependence and to live in a
cooperative relationship with others. Gospel order is a traditional
Quaker term for the social order the Spirit desires for us.

Living in gospel order, also known as good order or right
order, requires giving up our reliance on those social structures that
are based in power over others. Friends' experience is that a social
order based on hierarchies and privilege inevitably leads to injustice
and war. In gospel order we learn to rely on God's power and guidance in building a non-hierarchical social order which values equality and peacemaking.

Our Quaker organizational structures of monthly meetings and yearly meetings, committees, and affiliations with other Friends organizations embody a non-hierarchical order. All of our Quaker practices help to keep us organized according to our discernment of how the Spirit is leading us forward.

> . . . *living in Gospel Order means living in the power of God, in the organizing and harmonizing power of God. Dozens of times in his* Journal *Fox wrote "The Power of God was over all." He and early Friends saw this as a power which can bring forth the words and organizational arrangements which are appropriate in a given situation.*
>
> **William Taber, 1994**

> *Organization is a good servant but a bad master; the living fellowship within the Church must remain free to mould organization into the fresh forms de-manded by its own growth and the changing needs of the time.*
>
> **William Charles Braithwaite, 1905**

> *One might say that gospel order is the vessel, which contains (and therefore shapes) the Quaker edition of the Christian gospel, giving the Quaker mes-sage its particular flavor. Gospel order is not God or any aspect of the Trinity, but it is an organizing principle by which Friends come to a clearer under-standing of our relationship to God in all of the di-vine manifestations and the responsibilities of that relationship. An attention to gospel order enables the meeting faith community to perceive and ac-cept the spiritual gifts, which God offers, as well as to develop and exercise those gifts as God desires. Finally, gospel order is both a distinctive aspect of Quaker witness and testimony and the means by which Friends come to understand how they are to witness to the world.*

Gospel order is pervasive; it is the order and har-mony that characterizes every part of creation when that part is functioning according to the divine will –the shining of stars as well as the making of bread. It has been the experience of Friends that no part of their lives as individuals or as a faith community is separate from their vision of gospel order.

Lloyd Lee Wilson, 1993

The Practice of Community

Responsibilities of Friends

And Friends, meet together, and know one another in that which is eternal . . .

George Fox, 1657

The way that Jesus lived among men shows us the way that God lives among men and the way in which we are to live with one another. It was a way of fellowship. And fellowship, as Jesus understood it, was not mastery, but a living comradeship which respected the freedom of others and safeguarded in-stead of crushing out the growth of their personali-ties.

William Charles Braithwaite, 1921

God guides us to a place of empathy, care, and joy in each other's company. Fellowship in the Spirit has a distinctive liveli-ness, openness, mutuality, and ease.

The more we grow in the Spirit, the more we care about the spiritual growth of others and learn to do the work of love. Friends listen, are patient, respect each other's viewpoints, accept differ-ences, and work through difficulties. Here, love is more than a feel-ing. It is action arising out of our faithfulness to the Light. To be faithful means to make a conscious effort to pay attention to the choices we make and how our behavior affects others.

William Penn said of George Fox that he was "civil beyond all forms of breeding." Courtesy, considered not as a formal code of good manners, but as a supple and sensitive pattern of response to other people's needs, moods, and desires, has marked the lives of many Friends. Even in his last illness, John Woolman was "exceedingly afraid from the first of giving needless trouble to any . . ."

London Yearly Meeting, 1959

Community is a place where the connections felt in the heart make themselves known in bonds between people, and where the tuggings and pullings of those bonds keep opening up our hearts.

Parker Palmer, 1977

Responsibilities of the Meeting

The meeting has responsibilities for cultivating our relationships and building community. Time needs to be set aside for open fellowship, group discussion, and education, and fun. Community-building activities such as shared meals, workdays, committee work, retreats, workshops, and community service projects are recommended. The meeting is responsible for seeing that the work of the group is shared and that members are not unduly or unnecessarily burdened. Friends of all ages need to be included in activities as appropriate.

The group is responsible for recognizing and encouraging spiritual gifts among its members. The meeting community is the place where an individual can find help in testing leadings, clearness for personal decisions and difficulties, and support for leadings and witnesses of conscience.

A meeting that cultivates a strong sense of its Quaker identity, practice, and testimonies, as well as a sense of mission and service to the wider community, will find that its unity and fellowship are strengthened as well.

Group discernment is vital for ensuring that activities, responsibilities, and commitments the group takes on are leadings from God. Our meetings can become overcommitted when we try to live up to imposed expectations of what the meeting "should" be doing. This is destructive of community. If we consciously allow space in our time and emotional energy for the Spirit to lead us, we will not be overburdened with work.

> *Let love be genuine; hate what is evil, hold fast to what is good; love one another with mutual affection; outdo one another in showing honour. Do not lag in zeal, be ardent in spirit, serve the Lord. Rejoice in hope, be patient in suffering, persevere in prayer. Contribute to the needs of the saints; extend hospitality to strangers.*
>
> *Bless those who persecute you; bless and do not curse them. Rejoice with those who rejoice, weep with those who weep. Live in harmony with one another; do not be haughty, but associate with the lowly; do not claim to be wiser than you are. Do not repay anyone evil for evil, but take thought for what is noble in the sight of all. If it is possible, so far as it depends on you, live peaceably with all.*
>
> **Romans 12: 9-18 NRSV**

> *Keep up your meetings for worship, and your men and women's meetings for the affairs of truth, both Monthly and Quarterly. And after you are settled, you may join together and build a meeting-house. And do not strive about outward things; but dwell in the love of God, for that will unite you together, and make you kind and gentle one towards another; and to seek one another's good and welfare, and to be helpful one to another; and see that nothing be lacking among you, then all will be well. And let temperance and patience and kindness and brotherly love be exercised among you, so that you may abound in virtue, and the true humility; living in*

peace, showing forth the nature of Christianity, that you all may live as a family.

George Fox, 1676

Our life is love, and peace, and tenderness; and bearing one with another, and forgiving one another, and not laying accusations one against another; but praying one for another, and helping one another up with a tender hand.

Isaac Penington, 1667

Over-busyness is one of the diseases that has infected Quakerism, not only here, but throughout the Society of Friends. . . . Too many of us too often find ourselves caught in a merry-go-round of activities and responsibilities, and we do not take adequate time to get centered or sufficient time to nurture ourselves. . . . The world of the spirit is real, and our journey into wholeness has to include time for us to be consciously aware of the life of our spirits.

Marty Walton, 1994

. . . One common dilemma in Friends meetings today is the inability to hear when God is asking us <u>not</u> to take on more committee work, more projects, attendance at more gatherings.

Sandra Cronk, 1991

Pastoral Care

The spiritual welfare of a meeting is greatly helped if its social life is vigorous, and its members take a warm personal interest in one another's welfare. The pastoral work of the Society is specially committed to the overseers [also known as the Care and Counsel Committee], but our members generally should not allow themselves to feel that they are relieved from responsibility. In the greater events

of life, such as marriage, birth of a child, illness or death, it is our duty and privilege to share in one another's joys and sorrows; and sympathy thus shown is a potent means of binding us in closer fellowship.
London Yearly Meeting, 1925

"Pastoral Care" is a traditional term for the many ways the faith community extends aid and concern for the spiritual, mental, emotional, and physical well-being of all its members. All of us from time to time need someone to confide in, a listening ear to help us in working through personal life changes, dealing with loss, coping with circumstances, and making wise decisions.

While much of this care for each other flows spontaneously as all Friends listen and help one another, the meeting may appoint a Care and Counsel Committee (see Chapter 11, The Monthly Meeting) to provide leadership and to carry the more formal aspects of this work on behalf of the meeting. The work of this committee is best served if it functions with dedication, tact, and discretion–the ability to listen, to "speak the truth in love," to maintain confidentiality, and to listen with empathy without giving advice unless asked and without making judgments. Gifts of insight, experience, and emotional maturity are most helpful.

The Care and Counsel Committee seeks to maintain humility in carrying out its work, particularly in acknowledging its limitations in abilities and resources and in recognizing when an individual or the community could best be helped by finding expert assistance from other Friends or from outside the meeting. The Care and Counsel Committee needs to be able to recognize when an individual's difficulties require professional counseling. It needs to feel empowered to make that recommendation, even if it may not be well-received; the sincere desire to help someone takes precedence. It is not compassionate to enable someone's mental illness or to allow destructive behavior.

The work of facilitating the resolution of conflicts within the meeting community is usually given first to the Care and Counsel Committee.

Conflict Resolution and Peacemaking

> *Then Peter came and said to him, "Lord, if another member of the church sins against me, how often should I forgive? As many as seven times?" Jesus said to him, "Not seven times, but, I tell you, seventy times seven."*
>
> **Matthew 18:21-22 NRSV**

> *Our meetings can be where we practice making life heaven on earth. . . . [I]f we engage wholeheartedly, we'll find areas of disagreement, differences of approaches, even differences in values. How we handle those differences is critical. To make our meetings Blessed Communities, we have to be willing to face issues, we have to be willing to tell our truth, and we have to be willing to hang in there in the difficult times. There are few things as destructive to a meeting community as keeping your truth hidden, or leaving when things don't go your way. And the extent to which people in the meeting make it safe for each other to tell their truth and safe to disagree will determine the all-over health of the meeting, and its possibility of being, for the people who are part of it, a living example of heaven on earth. Heaven on earth doesn't mean "no problems." It means the full reality, the loving creative spirit at work in all our lives together, and in the spaces between our lives.*
>
> **Marty Walton, 1994**

> *It has been the experience of this Yearly Meeting in the past to know that Friends have met in division and uncertainty, and that then guidance has come, and light has been given to us, and we have become finders of God's purpose. This gives us ground for confidence. We shall not be held back by the magnitude of the questions which are to come before us, nor by a sense of our own unworthiness.*
>
> **London Yearly Meeting, 1936**

The peaceful resolution of disagreements and conflicts that arise in our meetings is vital if we are to carry our testimonies of peace, community, and integrity to the wider world. Friends' experience is that disagreement is inevitable in any community where people are honestly engaged in dealing with important issues. Sometimes conflict erupts in our Meetings despite our best efforts to prevent it. Friends' experience is that we need not despair when conflicts arise, but rather face our difficulties with courage and faith that the Light will guide us.

The foundation for peacemaking needs to be laid long before conflict arises. Peacemaking is grounded in how we relate to God and each other in meeting for worship, meeting for worship with a concern for business, fellowship, and service. Understanding of our Faith and Practice, knowledge gained from Friends' writings, and regular practice of our spiritual disciplines are important if Friends are to be equipped with the spiritual maturity and guidance to be peacemakers. The development of skills in resolving differences peacefully is acquired over time as we walk in the Light, learning how to handle differences and disagreements with love and forbearance in everyday conversation, committee meetings, and meetings for business. Friends need to feel that their meeting is a place where it is safe to disagree and that when they express themselves they will be listened to because they are valued.

It is often hard to discern when a disagreement between Friends "crosses the line" and becomes a battle of wills. Yet it is important that we learn to recognize the symptoms of conflict and begin our peacemaking quickly. We can more readily identify when discord begins if we understand where it comes from. George Fox often used this paraphrase of James 4:1

> *What causes war and fightings among you? Those conflicts and disputes among you, where do they come from? Do they not come from your cravings that are at war within you?*
> **George Fox paraphase of James 4:1**

to illustrate how conflict comes from our desire to have things our way, to get what we want without due regard for others. We invite conflict into our lives when we value our own judgments and desires more than seeking God's guidance and the shared Light of the group.

The peaceful resolution of conflict requires a covering of prayer and true humility. True humility is not about "being a doormat" or stifling one's light but means accepting ourselves for who we are, acknowledging our limits and our need for others and for God. It depends upon our understanding that self-respect and respect for others go hand in hand.

A process for conflict resolution may proceed in different ways according to who brings forward the concern and who is involved or affected. Friends' practice, in general, is to try to maintain confidentiality and care for the reputation of others as much as is possible while also considering the need to prevent further hurtful behavior.

When individuals carry a concern for the difficulties between them, they are advised first to try to work out their differences together, with or without the help of others as they may mutually agree. If this fails, they may take their concerns to the Care and Counsel Committee, which can work with them in confidentiality, separately and/or together, to continue to engage with both parties while taking care to avoid even the appearance of taking sides.

> *So when you are offering your gift at the altar, if you remember that your brother or sister has something against you, leave your gift there before the altar and go; first be reconciled to your brother or sister, then come and offer your gift.*
>
> **Matt 5:23-24 NRSV**

The Care and Counsel Committee is entrusted and empowered by the monthly meeting to initiate a response to conflict when it is recognized. The committee works with those involved, in confidentiality, to solve the problem using resources such as a clearness committee for each participant in the conflict, or outside professional help. If they are not successful, they may bring the matter to the monthly meeting for worship with a concern for business for discernment and direction.

If a conflict is brought to meeting or already involves the group as a whole, the monthly meeting must pay attention to the matter promptly. They may ask the Care and Counsel Committee or Friends from another meeting or the yearly meeting to provide the impartial leadership and facilitation required for the next steps in a group process. Some form of structured and facilitated listening for the group is recommended, such as threshing sessions or worship sharing, along with continued private dialogue with individuals as necessary. It is recommended that Friends also pay close attention to the group's need for closure and healing.

Each difficult situation a meeting faces is unique. There is no set process for Friends to follow in dealing with conflict. We turn to the Spirit and to the gathered group for insights and leadings to guide us. Nevertheless, we can identify some important ingredients of peaceful resolution, at any or various points in the process:

- Friends may need to be reminded lovingly of their commitment to peaceful reconciliation and to acknowledge together that their difficulties are shared. In community, it is a fact that we are all in this together, and blaming one another for a problem only works to prevent us from solving it.

- Friends are advised neither to deny their feelings nor to become ruled by them. While it is normal to have strong feelings at times, Friends are advised to learn to recognize them and to avoid any sense of acting out of crisis or anger. Strong emotions can become hurtful, irrational, and overpowering. Where a group of Friends have come together to listen to each other and God, anger can prevent centering down and the exercise of love and patience. When this happens, Friends are urged to enter into worship in the silence for a time, to allow the group to re-center.

- Friends are asked to set aside agendas, the desire to control outcomes, and any attempts to convert others to their point of view. We are asked and expected not to engage in gossip, make or take sides on an issue, or use other attempts to manipulate others. These behaviors not only show profound disrespect for others but are also a departure from the Quaker path of seeking God's guidance and unity in the Light.

- Friends are encouraged to strive to dispel confusion and misconception by practicing reality-testing and information-sharing. Recognize how different issues are interwoven and seek clearness in identifying them.

- Friends are urged to practice compassionate listening, compassionate speaking, and nonjudgmental language.

- Friends are asked to consider what true forgiveness is and what it is not and to attend to closure and healing.

The Inner Light does not lead men to do that which is right in their own eyes, but that which is right in God's eyes. As the Light is One, so its teaching is ultimately (though not superficially) harmonious. In actual experience, it is not found that souls truly looking to the Inner Light as their authority will break away from each other in anarchy.

Ellen S. Bosanquet, 1927

And be it known unto all, we cast out none from among us; for if they go from the Light and the Spirit, in which our unity is, they cast out themselves. And it has been our way to admonish them, that they may come to that spirit and light of God which they are gone from, and so come into the unity again.

George Fox, 1669

Advices on Community

Maintaining Gospel Order and Good Order

> *. . . Remember that the Lord never lays work upon His people that He does not give them strength or ability to perform . . .*
>
> **Joseph John Armistead, 1913**

> *Life in Christ is not the imposition of a system of "oughts" and "shoulds." George Fox wrote: "Take heed of getting into a form without power; . . . for that will bring deadness, and coldness, and weariness and faintings."*
>
> **Sandra Cronk, 1991**

Our Religious Society endures as a community of Friends who take thought for outward society by first taking care of one another. Friends are advised to strive to maintain love and unity, to avoid tale-bearing and detraction, and to settle differences promptly and in a manner free from resentment and all forms of inward or outward violence. Live affectionately as friends, entering with sympathy into the joys and sorrows of one another's daily lives. Visit one another. Be alert to give help and ready to receive it. Bear the burdens of one another's failings; share the buoyancy of one another's strengths.

Remember that to everyone is given a share of responsibility for the meeting for worship, whether through silence or through the spoken word. Be diligent and prompt in attendance at all meetings and in inward preparation for them. Be ready to speak under the leadings of the Light. Receive the ministry of others in a tender spirit and avoid hurtful criticism. In meetings for business and in all duties connected with them, seek again the leadings of the Light, keeping from obstinacy and from harshness of tone or manner; be teachable, and admit the possibility of being in error. In all the affairs of the meeting community, proceed in the peaceable spirit of "Pure Wisdom," with forbearance and warm affection for each other.

Use your capabilities and your possessions not as ends in themselves but as God's gifts entrusted to you. Share them with others; use them with humility, courtesy, and affection. Guard against contentiousness and love of power; be alert to the personalities and the needs of others. Show loving consideration for all creatures, and cherish the beauty and wonder of God's creation.

Maintaining Unity

> *[It is] our concern that Friends should work with one another in a humble and loving spirit, each giving to others credit for purity of motive, notwithstanding differences of opinion, and being ready to accept the decision of the meeting even when it may not accord with his own judgment. The mutual forbearance and understanding which are produced by a constant dwelling under the power and control of Christ do much to prevent jealousies, misunderstandings, or any breach of love.*
>
> **London Yearly Meeting, 1931**

Focus on "speaking the Truth in love" (Eph. 4:15 NRSV), using nonjudgmental language which invites others into dialogue. For early Friends, "Truth" meant "how the Spirit is working among us," which is much bigger than one's personal ideas. Let the Light show you what your true concerns and motives are. Where the Light reveals a problem, it may show us care for others as well.

To be faithful, follow the process of discerning God's will. Keep an open mind; otherwise, consciously or unconsciously, you will try to impose your own will on a situation. Give up trying to convert others to your viewpoint—instead, share your measure of the Light, respect the views of others and seek the reality that is unfolding. Leave outcomes to God.

Do not gossip or listen to gossip. Do not blame or listen to blaming. Learn to carry a concern for another's behavior as a concern for that Friend's spiritual well-being, and know that that concern supports the unity of the meeting.

If we hope to be forgiven, we must also forgive one another. He who yields to a suspicious and unforgiving spirit is led on to imagine things against his brother that are exaggerated, or even false. . . . It may be that thou hast just ground for offence. Is thy brother's trespass against thee any warrant for thy own disobedience? . . . Wait not until thy brother be reconciled unto thee, or until he shall make the first overture. Be thyself the first to seek reconciliation. . .

London Yearly Meeting, 1870

Maintain that charity which suffereth long, and is kind; put the best construction upon the conduct and opinions one of another which circumstances will warrant. . . . Let each be tender of the reputation of his brother; and be earnest to possess the ornament of a meek and quiet spirit. Watch over one another for good, but not for evil; and whilst not blind to the faults or false views of others, be especially careful not to make them a topic of common conversation. . . .

London Yearly Meeting, 1834

Queries on Community

- How do we recognize and respond to leadings of the Spirit? Do we test our leadings, seeking the help of others in discerning God's guidance and the way forward? Do we wait patiently for "way to open"?

- Do we consider carefully which activities and responsibilities we commit ourselves to, taking into account our gifts and limitations and our sense of leading? Do we leave space for rest and renewal? Do we leave space to respond to needs that may arise and to listen for new leadings of the Spirit? Are we careful not to burden the meeting or each other with preconceived or personal expectations of what they "should" be doing?

- How do we foster participation in the whole life of the meeting? Do members regularly attend meetings for worship and meetings for worship with a concern for business? Do all participate in some way in fellowship and in service?

- How do we care for one another within our meetings? Do we keep good communication with each person? Do we offer aid and support for those who are dealing with difficulties? How is our meeting a place where individuals find healing and encouragement?

- How do we recognize, encourage, and support the development of gifts and leadings among our members?

- Do we deal with disagreements with love and forbearance, seeking God's guidance for peaceful resolution? Do members feel safe to voice their disagreement and concerns, confident that their input is valued?

- Do we have a sense of unity in joining with each other on the Quaker path? Do we foster an understanding of our Quaker identity—faith, testimonies and practice–such that all may find spiritual nourishment and growth?

- How do we reach out to the wider community? Do we serve, participate in, and celebrate the life of our yearly meeting and other Friends organizations? Do we respond to the needs of others in our local communities and the world? Do we build relationships with other organizations in our local communities?

CHAPTER 5

QUERIES AND ADVICES

Friends have assessed the state of this religious society through the use of queries since the time of George Fox. Rooted in the history of Friends, the queries reflect the Quaker way of life, reminding Friends of the ideals we seek to attain. From the Christian tradition, Friends have taken as a standard the life and teaching of Jesus, not only as recorded in the New Testament, but even more importantly as revealed inwardly, as we seek God's truth and its expression through our lives today. Friends approach queries as a guide to self-examination; using them not as an outward set of rules, but as a framework within which we assess our convictions and examine, clarify, and consider prayerfully the direction of our lives and the life of the community.

Philadelphia Yearly Meeting, 1998

The advices have served Friends for many generations in their search for a life centered in the Spirit. Arising from the experience and aspirations of successive generations of Friends, the advices are illustrations of how they seek to carry their faith into all aspects of life.

New England Yearly Meeting, 1985

First Section:

What is the state of our meetings for worship and business?

1.   MEETING FOR WORSHIP

QUERIES:

- Are our meetings for worship held in expectant waiting for divine guidance, with a living silence in which we feel drawn together in the Light by the presence of God?

- Do we respond to the Spirit's prompting to minister, whether in silence, through the spoken word, or through action after the meeting for worship?

- Are we sensitive to one another's needs in meeting for worship?

- Are the spiritual gifts within the meeting fostered and encouraged?

- Are our meetings accessible and welcoming to everyone?

- Are our meetings a source of strength and guidance for daily living?

- Is the vocal ministry in our meetings exercised under the leading of the Spirit?

ADVICES:

- Be prompt and diligent in attendance at meetings.

- Come to meeting with expectant hearts and minds prepared for communion with God.

- Be faithful, be patient, and persevere in our service as messengers of truth.

- To everyone is given a share of the responsibility for the meeting for worship, whether through silence or through the spoken word.

- Quiet our hearts and minds for worship prior to entering the meeting room, so the whole group can be knit together in spiritual fellowship.

- Do not assume that vocal ministry is never to be our part. Be ready to speak under the leading of the Light. Learn to recognize when a message felt within is from God and if it is a message intended for the group to hear.

- Pray that our ministry may arise from deep experience of the Divine.

- Let our spoken ministry be audible and free from unnecessary words.

- Avoid speaking in a manner that brings a sense of discussion or debate.

- Allow for a period of silence after a message has been spoken, so the group can reflect on what has been said and continue to be grounded in silent worship. Overly long or too-frequent messages can hinder the worship of others present.

- Receive the ministry of others in a tender spirit.

- Treat every newcomer as one sent by God.

2. MEETING FOR WORSHIP WITH A CONCERN FOR BUSINESS

QUERIES:
- Are meetings for business held in the spirit of meetings for worship?

- In decision-making, do we promote a spirit of love,

understanding, and patience as we seek unity on an appropriate course of action?

- Do we keep our remarks simple and speak only as the Spirit leads?

- Are we able to unite in good grace with the sense of the meeting when our personal desires tend in another direction?

- Do we maintain respect for others, however strongly our opinions may differ?

- Are meetings for business seen as positive opportunities for testing and practicing our spiritual life?

ADVICES:

- As members, attend the business meetings and extend our support to the meeting's affairs so that the burden will not rest upon a few.

- In meetings for business and in all duties connected with them, seek the leadings of the Light.

- Avoid undue persistence. As we release our attachment to our ideas, the Light may reveal solutions none of us has considered.

- Be willing to admit the possibility of being in error.

- Remember that the foundation of a lasting decision lies in the search for unity—that is, a corporate seeking of the Light in an atmosphere of love, trust, and mutual forbearance.

- Attenders are warmly invited to attend and participate in meeting for worship with a concern for business.

- Have a sense of when to continue to labor on or to lay aside an issue.

3.   Harmony Within the Meeting Community

QUERIES:

- Are love and unity maintained among us?

- When differences arise, do we settle them in a spirit of love and humility?

- Are we careful not to hold an idea too firmly, knowing that another may bring us closer to the truth?

- Are we patient and considerate towards those we find difficult to understand or like?

- Do we demonstrate a forgiving spirit?

- Do we have concern and respect for the reputation of others?

- When people are hurt, do we take care to hold them up with a tender heart?

- Do we respect that of God in each person, though it may be expressed in unfamiliar ways or may be difficult for us to discern?

ADVICES:

- Maintain love and unity by avoiding talebearing and detraction.

- Settle differences promptly, in a manner free from resentment.

- When we have a difference with another person, speak to them in private "in the love and wisdom that is gentle and pure."

- Be aware that verbal violence can be as destructive as physical violence.

- Be careful that our language does not incorporate violence, consciously or unconsciously.

- Listen patiently, and seek the truth another person's expressions may contain for us.

- Be willing to seek and willing to receive counsel and help from one another.

- In our daily lives, seek to know one another in the things that are eternal and to enter with ready empathy and sensitive discretion into the joys, sorrows, and needs of each other.

- Be mindful that everyone is included in the life and activities of the meeting.

Second Section:
How do Friends care for one another?

4. MUTUAL CARE

QUERIES:
- How do we foster a spirit of community among the meeting's members and attenders?

- How does the meeting keep in contact with all of the meeting's members and attenders?

- How does the meeting assist couples and families to communicate, grow together, and rear children in a loving environment?

- Does the meeting community nurture the meeting's children?

- How does the meeting care for those who live alone, the sick, the aging, the widowed, the separated or divorced, and others with families affected by disruption?

- Do we assist Friends in need as their circumstances require?

- How do we labor with and care for those whose conduct or manner of living gives grounds for concern?

- How are visitors to our meeting made to feel welcome?

ADVICES:
- Be truthful and sincere, and thus encourage these qualities in others.

- Through example and education, help each other to recognize and follow the voice of God both in our spiritual lives and in joyful and willing service.

- Watch with tenderness over the opening minds of children. Seek to awaken in them the love and understanding of the life and teachings of Jesus and a sense of security in the love of God.

- Remember that there is a unique potential in each human being as a beloved child of God and that the Holy Spirit may lead children to give wise counsel to listening adults.

- Young people, too, have responsibility to care for the meeting and to participate in meetings both for worship and for business. Faith is needed as a vital part of our living.

5. EDUCATION

QUERIES:
- Do we share our deepest beliefs and values with each other and with our children, while leaving them free to develop as the Spirit may lead them?

- Does the meeting give the children loving care and promote their spiritual life through religious education and other activities?

- Do we encourage our children's participation in the meeting's work and cultivate their desire for service to others?

- How do we educate our members and attenders about the Bible (especially the teachings of Jesus), other spiritual literature, and the history, principles, and practices of Friends?

ADVICES:
- Seek for ourselves and for our children the full development of God's gifts, which is true education.

- Realize that education should continue throughout life and that all should share its opportunities and privileges.

- Make time for regular personal prayer and worship and for reading the Bible, Friends literature, *Faith and Practice*, the queries and advices, and other sources of spiritual value.

- Seek truth together in our families and among Friends in shared worship and discussion.

- Teach by being teachable. Be open to new ideas and approaches.

- Reach out to that of God in everyone, and endeavor to live out the testimonies of Friends in all the expected and unexpected circumstances of daily life.

6. HOME, FAMILY, AND RELATIONSHIPS

QUERIES:
- Do we make our home a place where love, peace, happiness, friendship, and refreshment of spirit are found and where the presence of God is experienced?

- Do all members of our family receive our affection and understanding?

- Do we take care that responsibilities outside the home do not encroach upon the time and loving attention our family needs?

- Do we acknowledge and support all relationships and families, whether conventional or not, that are based on love and commitment?

- Does our family set aside First Day and other times for worship, service, rest, and refreshment of spirit?

ADVICES:
- Live in love, and learn from one another.

- Try to live simply.

- In our family life, encourage reliance upon God's guidance and help for each day's needs.

- Remember the value of beauty in all its forms.

- God's gifts are for all to enjoy; learn to use them wisely.

Third Section:
To what extent is our personal life in accord with Quaker principles?

7. SELF-DISCIPLINE AND RESPONSIBILITY

QUERIES:
- Do we attend meeting for worship regularly and punctually?

- Do we participate in meeting for worship with a concern for business and support it financially and with personal service according to our resources and abilities?

- Are we conscientious in fulfilling all obligations of state and society that are not contrary to our religious convictions?

- Are we punctual in keeping promises, just in payment of debts, and honorable in all our dealings?

- Do we choose recreations that strengthen our physical, mental, and spiritual life, avoiding those that may hinder others, our Earth, and ourselves?

- Do we act responsibly concerning substances and behaviors that can become addictive?

ADVICES:
- Take heed, dear Friends, to the promptings of love and truth in our hearts, which are the leadings of God.

- Bring the whole of our life under the healing and ordering of the Holy Spirit, remembering that there is no time but this present.

- When tempted to do wrong or to despair, call upon God with an open heart, confessing our weaknesses and our needs.

- Be mindful at all times of our connection with the Divine and others—avoid substances, behaviors, and activities which diminish this connection.

- Be aware of the ill effects of mind-altering or habit-forming drugs, intoxicants, gambling, and other detrimental practices.

- Choose recreations that increase our vitality, self-awareness, and peace of mind and strengthen our will to create what is good.

- Make thoughtful use of our time.

- Guard ourselves and our children in our choice of print, electronic media, and other entertainments. Avoid those that promote violence and disrespect for human beings.

- Friends, strive to be courteous and responsible while driving.

8.   PERSONAL INTEGRITY AND RIGHT ACTION

QUERIES:
- Do we keep to simplicity and moderation in speech, manner of living, and vocation?

- Do we make time in our day for silence, solitude, spiritual reflection, and the growth of our inner life?

- Do we remind ourselves each day of our connections with people, other creatures, and all that sustains life?

- Are we ready to live in the Spirit that heals estrangements that may arise from resentment, nagging fears, and alienation from others?

- Do we listen to others, even beyond words, being sensitive to their personal needs and difficulties?

- Are we free from the use of judicial oaths, thus affirming that our statement is only part of our usual integrity of speech?

- Do we regard our possessions as given to us in trust, and do we part with them freely for the needs of others?

- Are we careful to keep our jobs and social activities from absorbing time and energy that need to be given to spiritual growth and service to others?

- Do we stay tender and open to the leadings of the Spirit?

ADVICES:
- Use our capabilities and possessions as God's gifts entrusted to us to share with others in humility, courtesy, and affection.

- Accept and encourage the creativity in others.

- When we have a choice of employment, choose that which gives the fullest opportunity for the use of our talents in the service of others.

- Be willing to seek and be faithful to God's will.

- Remember that we are all one in God.

9. WITNESS

QUERIES:
- Do our lives reflect Quaker testimonies?

- Are we open and responsive to continuing revelation, and do we incorporate it into our spiritual life?

- Is our Quaker witness characterized by humility and a willingness to learn from others?

- Do we recognize that the Spirit works in the world through us?

- Does our witness lead us to the condition in which we "walk cheerfully over the earth answering that of God in everyone"?

- Do we as a meeting try to share in the religious life of our wider community, availing ourselves of opportunities for worship and service with other local religious groups?

ADVICES:
- Strive to keep true to the testimonies of integrity and simplicity.

- Try to keep before us the essential truths, and test our life by them.

- Endeavor to make our lives consistent with the high principles we profess. This involves the often-difficult discernment not only between good and evil but also between the better and the best.

- Live adventurously. Let not failure discourage us.

- Witness so that others can perceive the presence of God within us.

- Be as good as people think you are.
  E. St. John (Jack) Catchpool

Fourth Section:
How do Friends meet our responsibilities to the community and the world?

10.   SOCIAL AND ECONOMIC JUSTICE

QUERIES:
- Do we seek to transform the world with our loving spirit?

- Do we take an active interest in the social and economic conditions of our community?

- Have we objectively considered the causes of discrimination, and are we ready to abandon old prejudices and think anew?

- Do we as individuals and as a meeting do all in our power to end governmental, social, economic, and educational injustices in our community and to create equal opportunity for all?

- How do we as individuals and as a meeting promote the welfare of those in need and work to secure a just distribution of the world's resources?

- What are we doing as individuals and as a meeting to understand and remove the causes of war and violence and to develop the conditions and institutions of peace?

ADVICES:

- Seek to understand the causes of social ills, and work toward their removal.

- Be not content to accept things as they are, but keep an alert, sensitive, and questioning mind.

- Understand and maintain Friends' witness for truth, simplicity, and nonviolence, holding up your personal life to these testimonies.

- Encourage inclusiveness, and discourage discrimination.

- Friends' belief in that of God in everyone should lead to reverence for all life and to personal integrity.

- Encourage all efforts to overcome prejudices and antagonisms.

- Cherish diversity.

- Aid and comfort those afflicted or in prison that they may rebuild their lives.

- Work for the abolition of the death penalty.

- Let the way that we live contribute to the realization of a peaceable kingdom on earth.

11. CARE OF THE NATURAL WORLD

QUERIES:

- Do we live in harmony with nature? Do we live in keeping with the spirit of the unity, sacredness, and integrity of all creation?

- Do we seek to minimize our consumption of the earth's resources?

- Do we encourage equitable and sustainable use of those resources?
- Do we walk gently over the earth, seeing that of God in all of nature?

- Do we seek to educate ourselves, our children, our meeting, and our community about how our lives can be more in harmony with the earth?

- Does the meeting strive to bring all its practices in harmony with the natural world?

ADVICES:
- Maintain in ourselves and encourage in others a sense of responsibility for the environment, both for the present and for future generations.

- Avoid amusements that stimulate destructive emotions, are detrimental to the health or tranquility of others, or are damaging to the natural environment.

- Show a loving consideration for all creatures, cherishing the beauty and wonder of all God's creation.

- Share our sense of reverence and stewardship for the earth.

12. PEACE TESTIMONY AND NONVIOLENCE

QUERIES:
- Do we work for peace in the world? Do we nurture peace within ourselves?

- Do we "live in the virtue of that life and power which takes away the occasion of all wars"?

- Do we seek consistently to carry out this testimony for peace in all our relationships, including family, community, and work life?

- Do we as individuals and as members of a meeting seek to take part in the ministry of reconciliation between individuals, groups, and nations?

- Do we faithfully maintain our peace testimony?

- Do we reject military training, preparation for war, and participation in war as inconsistent with the spirit of Christ's teachings?

- Do we as a meeting take a stand and do all we can to remove the causes of war and violence?

ADVICES:
- War is contrary to the life and teaching of Jesus. Seek through God's power and grace to overcome in our hearts the emotions that lie at the root of conflict.

- Strive for nonviolent approaches to conflicts in all aspects of our lives.

- Every human being is a beloved child of God and has that divine spark which claims our reverence. War is a denial of this truth.

- Friends' peace testimony is the positive exercise of good will calling us to lend our influence to all that strengthens the growth of international friendships and understanding.

- Cultivate an active spirit of love and peace.

The first step to peace is to stand still in the Light. . .
George Fox, 1653

MEETING FOR WORSHIP
WITH A CONCERN FOR BUSINESS

Mind The Oneness . . .

George Fox

In each of us the Spirit is manifested in one particular way, for some useful purpose. . . . But all these gifts are the work of one and the same Spirit, distributing them separately to each individual at will. For Christ is like a single body with its many limbs and organs, which, many as they are, together make up one body.

I Corinthians 12: 7, 11-12 New English Bible

Our belief that people can continually discover more about the will of God makes us eschew dogma. We search for ways to meet human need in shared worship and open ourselves to disagreement as a path to God's higher truths. The spirit leads our community to creative action occasionally in ways that transcend reason, as we listen to God's voice in our prayers and in the messages we have for each other.

New York Yearly Meeting, 1995

Friends are not to meet (in meetings for business) like a company of people about town or parish business; . . . but to wait upon the Lord.

George Fox, 1674

Throughout, the grace of humor can often help to relax the tensions of a Meeting (for Business) so that new Light comes to it.

North Pacific Yearly Meeting, 1993

The presuppositions of the corporate meeting for worship have, from the very beginning, profoundly affected the method of decision making in the meeting for business. In both, there is faith in the Guide. There is faith in a continuous revelation that is always open to produce fresh disclosures. And there is respect and affection for each other that cuts through all diversity and that helps to kindle a faith that, with patience and openness, the group can expect to come to clearness and to resolve the problems that come before it.

Philadelphia Yearly Meeting, 1997

Decision Making

From Faith Into Business

Friends' decision making is rooted in the spiritual oneness of a faith community. We reject majority rule and consensus for the higher goal of reaching decisions in unity, through distinctive attitudes and practices developed by Friends over the centuries. Our process is democratic in the sense that everyone is encouraged to participate. However, it also goes beyond democracy in that it does not rely solely on human will or ability.

The quality of interaction among the Friends present at a meeting for business is as important as the matters on the agenda. The goal of meeting for business lies in its contribution to the growth of the blessed community.

When used with care, this decision-making process is deeply satisfying and produces practical decisions that are in harmony with the Spirit. When the process is used carelessly, its lack of formal rules of order can lead to abuse by neglect or design.

The act of choosing is spiritual when it involves our fundamental values and deepest loyalties. Friends must therefore be rigorous in discerning the ultimate source of their leadings, always looking beyond the self and never letting their own wills become a substitute for God's will.

The Religious Basis of Our Decision Making

Meetings for business are meetings for worship. Both are conducted in the same openness to the leading of the Spirit. For our religious community to thrive, it is essential that we nurture our love for one another, maintain our spiritual unity, and live in harmony with the Spirit. Ideally, these beliefs underlie every attitude and practice in our meetings, including our meetings for business.

As we wrestle with outward issues, the Inner Light gives us new perspectives and creative responses. On all matters, even the mundane, its presence promises a fresh revelation of truth and a clearer understanding of God's will.

One of the practices basic to the Religious Society of Friends is that we test our leadings before acting. We bring our concern into the Light of truth when we speak it to our meeting. When we believe we are called to act out of a concern, we share our vision with the meeting. The meeting worships together asking for divine assistance in discerning whether the leading is of the Spirit.

It is our experience that new openings to truth may come at any time and from any source. Each Friend should therefore listen to all efforts to express that truth. As we listen, we test these expressions against accumulated experience, the life and teachings of Jesus, and moral and spiritual guides in Scripture and elsewhere.

Therefore, we are careful not to rely on the letter of the text but to read the Scriptures "in the Spirit in which they were given forth," as George Fox enjoined us.

The Goal of Friends' Decision Making

Unity

The purpose of meeting for business is to discern God's will for the corporate body of the meeting. The goal of Friends' decision-making is a Spirit-led unity—a crystallization of the search for clarity on the topic under consideration. Even in the face of strong difference of opinion, that goal is achievable when there is spiritual unity.

Our search is for unity, not unanimity. We consider ourselves to be in unity when our search for truth is shared, when our listening for God is faithful, when our wills are caught up in the presence of Christ, and when our love for one another is constant and manifest. A united meeting is not necessarily all of one mind, but it is all of one heart.

We believe that this unity, transcending apparent differences, springs from God's empowering love, and that a meeting, trusting in the leadership of that love and gathered in its spirit, will enjoy unity in its search for truth.

A meeting is a living spiritual entity, a corporate body, which sometimes encompasses strong differences of opinion. It is like an individual who may have many conflicting inclinations but who still has a final sense of how to act. The sense of the meeting is not designed and fitted together but is conceived, born, and nurtured; the meeting's care for the quality of its decision-making process is essential to the rightness of its decisions.

Sense of the Meeting

The term "sense of the meeting" has two meanings. One of the meanings is the same as unity, the point at which the meeting is agreed on a decision. This point is not the same as unanimity. The second meaning of the term "sense of the meeting" is a description of where the meeting now stands in its discernment of a question. For example, the meeting may be in agreement on one part of an issue and in disagreement on another part of the issue, or the meeting may be polarized or in confusion. A statement in the minutes of the sense of the meeting at this point will serve Friends as a reminder of the foregoing experience when they take up the issue again.

Sense of the meeting is not synonymous with consensus. Consensus is a widely used and valuable secular process characterized by a search for general agreement largely through rational discussion and compromise. Sense of the meeting is the result of our religious process, which is characterized by listening for and trusting in God. Both sense of the meeting and consensus result in a course of action agreed to by the participants, but the sense of the meeting relies consciously on the Spirit. Lively discussions may often play a role in Friends' decision making; these are useful only to the extent that they are the expressions of spiritual leadings. Friends' practice avoids secular devices such as debate, persuasion, coercion, and procedures equivalent to voting.

When the meeting has come to unity, those present will know that they have faithfully followed their Guide and will feel a continued affection for each other.

The meeting may find that a matter under consideration evokes considerable emotion in members of the meeting. In such a situation, the clerk sets aside time, either in the present meeting for business or later, for Friends to share their emotions in a worship-sharing format. After the emotions have been shared and understood, the meeting can go on to make a decision on the concern.

Threshing Sessions

In dealing with issues which are difficult, complex, or entailing information with which some Friends may be unfamiliar, it is often helpful to hold one or more preliminary threshing meetings in which no decision is made but through which the chaff can be separated from the grain of truth. Such meetings can clear the way for later action on the issue. Full notice of a threshing session should be given and special efforts made to see that Friends of all shades of opinion can and will be present. To the extent that Friends of a given view are absent, the usefulness of such a meeting will be impaired. If factual material needs to be presented, persons knowledgeable in the area should be asked to present such material and be available to answer questions.

The clerk or moderator of a threshing session should make it clear at the start that the meeting not only expects but welcomes expressions of the widest differences. Friends are urged not to hold back whatever troubles them about the issues at hand. Hesitancy to share a strong conviction, because it may offend someone, reflects a lack of trust. The clerk's job, then, is to draw out the reticent, limit the time taken by too-ready talkers, and see that all have an opportunity to speak. It is useful to ask someone to take notes of the meeting for later reference. At times the threshing meeting may forward a recommendation to the meeting for business. No decisions are made at a threshing session.

Expectations of Participants

Among Friends, the decisions made by a group are enriched when all members commit themselves to regular attendance at meetings for worship as well as at decision-making sessions. By maintaining a spirit of worship throughout the meeting, participants nurture their openness to the leadings of the Spirit and its gifts of trust, humility, compassion, and courage. Anyone can call for silence when the spirit of worship has been disrupted. In the silence, connection to God and each other can be renewed.

Participants are expected to put aside personal desires and allow themselves to be led by the Spirit beyond the self. Although an individual Friend has the designated role of clerk, all share the responsibility for the maintenance of the Spirit-led gathering, for steadfast search for truth, and for the wise use of time. Sometimes, what the truth requires is uncomfortable or painful. All are expected to be attentive and to offer, concisely, such insight as each may have. The meeting is listening to God and listening to each other to hear

God speaking. As we seek God's will, we get closer to each other. In this way, we will all reach a point of unity. None should remain silent in the belief that the conclusion is foregone or that an insight apparently counter to that of the body of the meeting will be divisive or dismissed. Friends are encouraged to actively consider bringing issues which may be difficult or controversial into meeting for business for spiritual discernment. It is better for the meeting to allow full opportunity for differences to be aired and faced.

Friends demonstrate their faith in the meeting's access to divine guidance and its ability to find unity by their attendance and participation in meeting for business even when they feel they cannot agree with what they perceive to be the weight of the meeting. Their absence diminishes the meeting's ability to discern the truth.

Both speaking and listening should be marked by respect for others, with speakers saying only what they know to be worth others' hearing and with listeners seeking the Light as it is revealed through others. An openness of spirit is crucial, especially when differing views are being expressed. Usually an individual speaks only once on any one issue because, in a gathered meeting for business, we trust that our expression of light has been heard and is being considered and tested as part of the truth. Repeated speaking is often a way of forcing one's will on others. One should speak with clarity and brevity. If one's viewpoint has been expressed by another, one can say, "That Friend speaks my mind" or "I approve." In some meetings there is opportunity for each individual to speak more often. All meetings need to use care to see that the meeting for business is Spirit-led and that each person is heard and respected.

Meeting for Worship with a Concern for Business

A meeting may organize the meeting for business in any way it wants. What follows is a brief description of the traditional form of the meeting for business: worship (within which there is a reading of the queries and advices of the month), a reading of the agenda, reading of the minutes of the last meeting for business (perhaps approved at the previous meeting for business), the treasurer's report, reports from committees (which if written may be attached to the minutes), other items of business, reading of the minutes of the present meeting for business (for approval), and a final period of worship.

Seasoning

It is an integral part of Quaker process to consider a given concern repeatedly, giving time for Friends to consider the matter alone (perhaps in prayer), to sleep on it, and to talk about it with different people. This process is called seasoning. In the traditional meeting for business process, an issue is first discerned in a committee. Then it is discerned in meeting for business at least in one meeting, and perhaps successive meetings. If a meeting does not have committees and acts as a committee of the whole, it can consciously decide not to make a decision on an item at the first meeting for business at which the concern is raised. Instead the item can be fully considered at two meetings for business before asking for a sense of the meeting.

Whether or not the meeting has committees, there is a need for focus on the various aspects of meeting activity. There is a need for someone or some few to give continuity to this focus, to remember across the years what has been done, what has worked, and what has not worked.

The meeting is a corporate body. One aspect of the corporate body is that the meeting is a loving, affirming community. Another aspect of the corporate body is that the responsibility for the meeting's being and actions rests with everyone. Responsibility is not delegated to a few Friends. Hence, the good order of the meeting for business and all other aspects of the meeting rest with each of us.

Friends have learned the value of contributions from serious and consistent attenders who are not members. Many meetings welcome all who care to attend at decision-making sessions. Nonmembers should show sensitive restraint when addressing meeting affairs. Because each meeting is at liberty to limit the participation of attenders, such limits should be clearly defined and communicated in advance to avoid embarrassment and hurt feelings. Prior communication is particularly important with respect to any sessions which involve confidential information or evaluations of individuals.

No one should take action on the meeting's behalf in anticipation of a minute's approval but should wait for actual approval.

The Role of the Clerk

Ideally, the clerk is both servant and leader who prayerfully and thoughtfully prepares for the meeting, maintains a worshipful spirit in the meeting, sets a helpful pace, discerns the sense of the meeting when it is present, and expresses it clearly or identifies those who can do so. Such a clerk sensitively searches for the right course of action and helps maintain the meeting's spiritual unity. All these tasks are accomplished in an active, informed, and helping spirit, facilitating but never dominating, and avoiding partisanship.

The clerk is nominated and approved by members of the meeting.

A nominated person should be given time to prayerfully test for a leading to clerk. In accepting the nomination, the clerk accepts the obligation to focus time, energies, and gifts in the fulfillment of the trust expressed by the meeting. The meeting and the clerk might benefit from an assistant to the clerk who would also be learning how to clerk.

A concern is brought to the clerk's attention usually after it has gone through a process of discernment and seasoning within the appropriate committee. If a concern is brought to the clerk by an individual before committee consideration, the matter may be sent to a committee. In the case of a need for an immediate decision, the meeting as a whole can consider the concern. The clerk prepares the agenda after consultation with others, including committee clerks. It is important that concerns and agenda items are given to the clerk before meeting for business. Impulsive agenda items can create an atmosphere of disorder, frustration, and distrust. When a clerk has a number of items to be considered at the next regular monthly meeting, prayerful reflection on them and on the order of presentation is needed. A proposed minute may be drafted before the meeting by the clerk or a committee. This can be helpful when a committee is recommending an action.

The clerk helps the meeting move through the agenda with efficient but unhurried dispatch, keeping the members' attention on the matters to be considered. The clerk listens, learns, and sifts, searching for the sense of the meeting, possibly suggesting tentative minutes or periods of silent worship to help clarify or focus Friends' deliberations. The clerk encourages those who are reluctant to speak and, in like manner, restrains those who tend to speak at undue length, too often, or with vehemence.

When the sense of the meeting becomes clear to the clerk, the clerk states the decision. Then the decision is written as a numbered minute. The minute may be formulated by the clerk, the recording clerk, or another member of the meeting. The minute may be written by any of these. It is then read back to the meeting for approval. Writing and approving the minute clarifies for everyone what the decision is. While minutes are not to be altered by a subsequent meeting for business, the decisions they reflect may be revisited, particularly in light of new information or circumstances. When the matter is revisited, probably the group of people will be slightly different, and the group may not be in the same frame of mind and spirit as at the previous meeting for business. However, another minute can always be written which supersedes the previous minute. Minutes remain in force until they are superseded.

If there is no unity, it is especially important that the clerk make clear what previous decision or custom has been established on a given issue, because lack of unity on a proposed change normally means that the previous decision will be preserved.

When the sense of the meeting seems elusive, the clerk

should be sensitive to the potential benefit of deferring the matter to a later time, to a different body, or to a different forum.

The clerk should be careful to refrain from opinionated participation in the discussion. Further, the clerk should be alert to those occasions when his or her ability to read the sense of the meeting may be blurred by deep personal convictions. In that event, the clerk stands aside and asks the meeting to recognize someone else as clerk for the moment. The clerk may then speak to the issue.

After the meeting is concluded, it is the clerk's duty to ensure that those charged by the meeting with new tasks or specific actions are informed of their responsibilities. The clerk also takes care that matters held over appear in a later agenda. Finally, letters or documents whose drafting has been entrusted to the clerk are promptly dispatched.

The Role of the Recording Clerk

The proceedings of a meeting for business should be carefully and appropriately minuted by someone designated to serve as recording clerk. Where the clerk or recording clerk has not already been appointed or is unable to serve, the meeting may ask any member to serve until a regular appointment is made. The recording clerk should state precisely the nature, extent, and timing of actions directed to be taken and the persons responsible. Ambiguity and inaccuracy are to be avoided. Minutes should be written in the knowledge that at a later date the meeting may well need a full and circumstantial account of its decision and how it was reached.

In the writing of minutes, the recording clerk is more effective when there has been detailed prior consultation with the presiding clerk so that names, dates, and proposals are already familiar. It then becomes possible for the recording clerk to prepare tentative introductory sentences for each item of business, especially those that are routine.

A recording clerk does not hesitate to ask for help in formulating minutes. In some cases the presiding clerk, rather than the recording clerk, will be in a better position to write the minute. When the action to be taken is clear but the wording of the proposed minute is not, it is sometimes useful to ask one or a few Friends to prepare a final draft for consideration later during the meeting.

The recording clerk, clerk, or another member of the meeting may at times be asked to prepare a minute on a matter of substance while the meeting waits. All others present should settle into silent and supportive prayer, holding the writers in the Light until this task is complete.

Once approved, minutes retain their authority until replaced by a subsequent minute.

The record of the meeting's proceedings consists of minutes and a brief narrative description of important aspects of the flow of the meeting. This record in its entirety is sometimes referred to as the minutes. To promote clarity and understanding, it is useful for the recording clerk to read the minutes and the narrative to have them approved from time to time during the course of the meeting. The entire record is read for approval before the closing period of worship. Since the meeting may want a record of other gatherings, the recording clerk's minutes should also state the essential purpose of each meeting, whether for decision, discussion, inspiration, or a threshing session.

An indispensable part of the corporate body is its memory. The memory of the corporate body resides in the collective memory of the members of the meeting. If the collective memory of the body no longer remembers a minute, that minute no longer has force in the discernment of the meeting.

The corporate body, just as a person, has to have aids to its memory. For clarity and ease of access, the usual practice is for action minutes and statement minutes to be numbered. Narrative minutes are not numbered. Currently Southeastern Yearly Meeting uses the following numbering system: 00EC12 or 00WIBM12 or 00YM12. The first two digits are the year; the next letters are the body; the last digits are the consecutive number of the minute, starting with the number one at the beginning of each calendar year. The minutes of the Executive Committee (EC), the fall or winter interim business meeting (FIBM or WIBM), and the yearly meeting in annual sessions (YM) are numbered independently.

It is easier for the meeting to refer to decisions already made if the recording clerk lists, in brief form, all the numbered minutes recorded during the year and puts this list as an index at the end of the minutes for the year. All minutes are to be preserved in ways that ensure their availability and permanence.

The Good Order Used Among Us

Thoughtful preparation frees the meeting to follow the leadings of the Spirit, preventing frustration arising from poor arrangements, incomplete information, or unclear procedure.

The clerks or other designated persons prepare the agenda and, if appropriate, distribute the agenda and other essential information in advance. They may need to remind persons who are to bring matters before the meeting to come prepared. They must be careful to call members' attention to issues of special moment.

Arrangements are made for the time and place of gathering, child care, meals, hospitality, and other organizational matters as needed to permit unhurried disposition of business.

Members who are prompt in arrival and disciplined in settling into worship contribute much to the depth and power of the meeting. It is vital that this time of settling and focusing not become a brief formality.

Decision making by coming to unity applies to easy issues as well as difficult ones. Matters felt to be routine but necessary are dealt with quickly in a spirit of trust. The meeting may accept without extended discussion a suggestion volunteered by the clerk or other member or may empower an individual or a committee to act on the matter.

Matters of importance are best presented by someone who is familiar with the issues. However, important concerns may come from others who may not be as widely experienced or well informed, but who nevertheless feel strongly led. The meeting is tender to the known opinions of unavoidably absent Friends.

The prompting of the Inward Teacher may come with power to any present, without respect to age or experience. Friends know that sensitive and powerful insights may come to younger and newer members and attenders. They also know the importance of those whose experience and advice, in similar matters, have been helpful in the past.

The Meeting in Conflict

Friends often find themselves most challenged when matters before them call forth strongly held but seemingly incompatible responses.

They seek for guidance through prayerful discernment. A meeting which goes forward for whatever reason without real unity in the Spirit does so at its peril. When any member present feels so strongly led as to wish to prevent the meeting from acting, it is important that the meeting take the time to test this leading in a loving spirit and examine responsibly the consequences whether or not action is taken.

The search for the course of action that will keep the meeting in unity—or the resolution of the problems caused by disunity itself—rests as much with the individual or group in opposition as it does with the other members. Often conflict is resolved through the use of listening skills. When Friends know they have been heard, movement toward unity becomes possible. Because the group listens, perspectives are enlarged, objections can be included or withdrawn, or a new resolution is found.

Moving Forward in Unity

If all efforts to include everyone in the unity of the meeting fail and one person remains outside the unity of the meeting, the rest of the meeting can still move ahead in unity after a period of discernment. Friends may use several ways of moving forward in unity.

- The meeting may move to a deeper, spiritual searching and sharing, often entering periods of silent worship. Every conviction is examined in the Light, as Friends wait together to discern whether their convictions stem from a genuine motion of the Spirit. Friends may thus be empowered to lay aside those convictions which are not so based. While seeking new Light, Friends should also remain faithful to the leadings they sense as authentic, even when these seem contrary to the weight of the meeting.

- The meeting may wait or proceed with other business while a small, temporary, representative committee withdraws, in the hope that it can bring forward to the session a proposed minute or course of action that will lead the meeting into unity.

- The meeting may reschedule the matter for another time, encouraging members in the interim to continue their search for the right action, whether in solitary prayer and meditation, or in small informal groups.

- After patient searching over a considerable period, the meeting may conclude that the sense of the meeting is clear and unity in the Spirit can be maintained if that sense is translated into action, but acknowledge that a few Friends continue to have reservations about the substance of the proposed action. In that event, those Friends may feel led to withdraw their objections, being unwilling to stand in the way of the meeting. Those Friends may say that they feel released from the burden of their concern, having laid it on the conscience of the meeting. Or they may stand aside while maintaining their objections, asking that their names and the grounds of their objections be minuted.

After a discernment process, the meeting may be led to move forward in unity despite continued objections by one or a few Friends.

Friends who stand aside are affirming their continuing spiritual unity with the meeting. That unity will require of those Friends acceptance, with good grace, of the decision's consequences for the meeting and for themselves. It will require the rest of the meeting to keep the objections firmly in mind as they proceed.

Each of these avenues expresses trust in divine guidance and a commitment to remaining in unity in the Spirit.

Queries for a Meeting in Conflict

When disagreement on an issue threatens to divide a meeting, it may be helpful for the meeting and each Friend to consider the following questions:

- Have we taken care to examine fully, in a loving and prayerful spirit, the perspective of those with whom we disagree?

- Have we truly tried to leave behind our personal desires, the better to be led by the Spirit?

- Do we seek to discern the Light in all viewpoints?

- Have we considered whether God's will for us as individuals may differ from God's will for the meeting?

- Do we in conflict regularly reaffirm, in voice and attitude, the love we feel for one another?

Queries on the Meeting for Business

Queries for Participants in the Meeting for Business

- How do I prepare myself for meeting for business? Do I approach the meeting for business as a meeting for worship, corporately seeking divine guidance? In the conduct of business, do I avoid secular practices such as debate, persuasion, coercive devices, and procedures equivalent to voting? Do I speak only once on the same issue?

- Do I accept the spiritual need to relinquish control in the meeting for business, recognizing that the meeting's corporate spiritual discernment of God's will may lead in a quite different direction from my own perception of God's will, no matter how sincere?

- Do I accept responsibility to assist the clerk by maintaining openness, sensitivity, and tenderness to others, recognizing that the true sense of the meeting can be ascertained only when all present are clerking the meeting together with the clerk, practicing spiritual discernment to the best of our abilities?

Queries for the Clerk of Meeting for Business

- Do I allow opportunity for all who wish to speak to an issue to do so? Am I mindful of those who speak seldom or with difficulty, giving them opportunity to express their discernment? In the process of seeking divine guidance, am I careful to seek the growth of all those present?

- Do I make use of periods of silent worship, when necessary? Do I avoid secular business practices and help the meeting to avoid such practices? Do I do my best to ensure a true corporate seeking after Light and the achievement of a true unity?

- When a sense of the meeting is reached, is a minute immediately written and read aloud so that all may understand and approve it or alter it until it reflects the true sense of the meeting?

- Do I carefully prepare matters for presentation to the meeting for business? Do I ask for discernment by the appropriate committee before I bring a matter to meeting for business?

"Friends, keep your meetings in the power of God, and in his wisdom (by which all things were made) and in the love of God, that by that ye may order all to his glory. And when Friends have finished their business, sit down and continue awhile quietly and wait upon the Lord to feel him. And go not beyond the Power, but keep in the Power by which God Almighty may be felt among you.

George Fox, 1658

CHAPTER 7

MEMBERSHIP IN THE RELIGIOUS SOCIETY OF FRIENDS

For as in one body we have many members, and not all the members have the same function, so we, who are many, are one body in Christ, and individually we are members one of another.

Romans 12: 4-5 NRSV

So then, putting away falsehood, let all of us speak the truth to our neighbors, for we are members one of another.

Ephesians 4:25 NRSV

The Meaning of Membership

The Religious Society of Friends is a worldwide community of faith, based on experience of a transforming power named many ways: the Inner Light, the Spirit of Christ, the Guide, the Living God, the Divine Presence. Membership includes openness to an ongoing relationship with God and willingness to live one's life according to the leadings of the Spirit as affirmed by the community of faith. The lives of Friends express their faith in accordance with their experiences with God and with the meeting community.

Membership in a monthly meeting is a commitment to a spiritual community and to responsibility for the group. Since early Friends rejected the distinction between clergy and laity, responsibility for the full range of meeting activities rests with the membership. Members are expected to participate in communal worship, to share in the work and service of the Society as they are able, and to live in harmony with its basic beliefs and practices. Membership entails readiness to live as part of the monthly and yearly meetings. Specifically, this means participation in meeting for worship, meeting for business, committee work, and giving time, skills, and financial support to the meeting. Members are encouraged to follow leadings to take part in activities such as religious education, pastoral care, and witness to the broader community. The meeting commits to providing a community where spiritual enlightenment and growth are encouraged, a community which welcomes each individual with love. We are in a spiritual community to learn from and teach each other. Noticing how the community works and how it fails to work suggests to us how to improve the community and ourselves.

Perhaps the most important understanding that may be reached in the membership process is concerning our separate and joint spiritual journeys. Everyone is growing in a relationship with God. This results in growing in our relationships with other people. Each spiritual journey is unique. The meeting aims to be a place where our spiritual journeys can thrive. We seek guidance from one another and the meeting in discerning God's will for ourselves and for the meeting. Spiritual listening is an important part of Friends' relationships and includes listening to God, listening to each other, and listening to the spirit behind the words. Since we do not ask members to subscribe to a creed or specific spiritual language, we encourage all to learn to live with and learn from the differences in spiritual perspective in our meetings.

There are regular attenders who are part of the meeting community but do not feel led to membership. We affirm their value to the community.

Initiating the Membership Process

The Meeting

All action concerning membership is taken in and by the monthly meeting. Only the monthly meeting can admit and record a member. Membership in the meeting also means association with the yearly meeting and with Quaker organizations with which the yearly meeting is associated. The meeting continually needs to be concerned with making the attenders aware of the membership process. The responsibility for encouraging membership lies with each Friend but particularly with the committee which handles membership.

As a part of the continuing care of new attenders, the meeting has a responsibility to help them learn about all aspects of the Society: the home meeting, fall or winter interim business meeting, yearly meeting, worldwide Quakers, and the other Quaker bodies with which Southeastern Yearly Meeting is affiliated. In addition, the study of Friends' literature, history, legacy, and particularly Southeastern Yearly Meeting's *Faith and Practice* will enhance attenders' understanding of our foundations.

The Attender

After a time, the attender begins to understand the unique Quaker method of shared responsibility for service to the meeting. He realizes the needs of the meeting for constant renewal of its spiritual, organizational, community, pastoral care, and physical aspects. To meet these needs, the attender participates in worship, ministry, committee work, and meeting for business. He will find that participation in the work of the meeting will help him move forward in his spiritual journey.

Before an attender applies for membership, she may find it valuable to read material on membership and discuss her spiritual goals and concerns with Friends in whose wisdom, experience, and personal sympathy she has confidence. These Friends will guide the attender in deciding whether she is ready to apply or should first become more familiar with the Religious Society of Friends.

When an attender decides to formally apply for membership, he writes a letter to the clerk of the meeting asking to become a member and giving some idea of his spiritual journey and the circumstances which led to his initiative.

Response to the Application for Membership

Appointment of a Clearness Committee

The clerk of the meeting gives the applicant's letter to the committee responsible for membership and asks the committee to appoint a clearness committee to conduct the membership process. Friends thoroughly grounded in Quaker principles and attitudes and familiar with Southeastern Yearly Meeting's *Faith and Practice,* including procedures regarding membership, are asked to be on the committee. Some of the members of the committee should know the applicant. The clerk of the clearness committee is encouraged to give the applicant and members of the committee the document, "Clearness for Membership Queries," which is found at the end of this section, or the meeting may prepare a similar document.

The Applicant and Clearness Committee Meet

The clearness committee may feel the need to meet by itself before meeting with the applicant. The committee meets with the individual as often as is beneficial. Usually the best place for meeting with the applicant is at her home. One important aspect of the membership process is that it often leads to deeper friendships among the participants and opens them to each other's gifts.

The committee is asked to discern whether the meeting should accept the applicant into membership and to help the individual discern whether he is clear that membership is right for him. Membership in the Religious Society of Friends means relinquishing membership in other religious bodies before becoming a member. It may also entail canceling membership in a secular organization that clearly promotes behavior and beliefs contrary to Friends' principles.

Throughout the membership process, the meeting affirms the diversities of religious experience in its midst. The applicant describes his expectations of membership and his beliefs. The committee shares openly the expectations the meeting has for commitment, participation, and faithfulness by its members. These expectations depend on the gifts and life situation of the individual. The applicant will have questions for the committee, which will be answered with care. Suggested questions and topics for discussion can be found under "Clearness for Membership Queries" at the end of this chapter. Loving consideration is given to the applicant's familiarity and agreement with Friends' principles and practice, but complete agreement of formal belief or practice is not expected. We urge an understanding that there is diversity in theology among Friends. This diversity is held within the framework of Friends' testimonies and Friends' willingness to move toward unity in the Spirit.

Before the close of the final meeting with the applicant, the clerk of the committee describes the remainder of the membership process for the individual.

Completion of the Membership Process

At a separate meeting without the applicant present, the clearness committee for membership writes its recommendation and forwards this to the committee responsible for membership. After prayerful consideration of this recommendation, the committee responsible for membership forwards a minute regarding the application to the monthly meeting. At this point, a member of the clearness committee shares the recommendation with the applicant.

When membership is recommended, the committee responsible for membership presents its minute of recommendation for membership to the meeting for business. The meeting receives the minute but takes no action on first reading. If any member has concerns, he shares those concerns in private with the committee responsible for membership. That committee works to resolve all concerns before bringing the minute back to the meeting for business. Final approval of membership occurs at the following business meeting. This gives time for all members to consider prayerfully the application, to converse with the applicant about this step, and to confirm that all are in unity with the new membership. After the second reading and approval of the membership minute, the business meeting welcomes the new member into the monthly meeting. The membership minute is sent to the new member. The meeting arranges a celebration of the new membership. The monthly meeting sends the minute recording a new membership to the yearly meeting membership recorder along with the following data: name, address, phone, e-mail, date of birth.

If the applicant and the clearness committee agree that membership is not appropriate at this time, this is reported to the committee responsible for membership. That committee reports their decision to the meeting for business.

If clearness for membership is not being reached, the applicant and each member of the committee need to become clear why this is so. Sometimes there is a disagreement about what the expectations are for the community and for the individual. The committee and the applicant continue to work toward resolution of the points of disagreement. If the committee and the applicant feel that progress has stopped, the committee can report to the committee responsible for membership that the committee and the applicant have not been able to reach clearness. The process will be suspended for a period of time either by the decision of the clearness committee or the applicant. If the clearness process is suspended, the committee will continue to stay in touch with and support the applicant in the meeting. The clearness process for membership can be resumed at any time. At appropriate intervals, the committee responsible for membership reports to the meeting for business.

Membership of Children in the Meeting

All children from birth to maturity need to feel themselves full participants in the fellowship of the meeting, to be nurtured in their spiritual development and their understanding of the faith and practice of Friends, and to be guided and encouraged in preparation for Quaker adulthood. The meeting should sympathetically help children prepare for the life-changing decisions they must face, such as those regarding cultural conformity and military service. As they mature, if they have received this care from their meeting, they will become increasingly conscious of the full meaning of the responsibilities of membership in the Religious Society of Friends and be ready to make their own decision regarding membership. Growing up in a meeting offers children an extended religious family. It is the meeting's joyful responsibility to provide an atmosphere of care, love, and recognition—in short, a spiritual home—for all young people in the meeting, regardless of their membership status or that of their parents.

A monthly meeting's approach to membership for children should promote the goal of a Religious Society of Friends made up of members by mature convincement. Some Friends believe the process of nurture of the young toward mature convincement is aided by a child's sense of belonging fully to a meeting, a sense that comes only with membership. Other Friends believe the process is aided by a status of "youth member" that calls for a child to make an assertion of mature convincement when ready to do so. Still others believe that any form of involuntary membership limits a child's freedom to choose. Monthly meetings are encouraged to respect parents' sense as to what is best for their children.

Thus, either on their own initiative or in response to an inquiry from the meeting, parents who are members may, at the time of their child's birth or adoption or later, (1) request membership for their child, (2) request youth membership for their child, or (3) not request any enrollment for the child. If the parents are members of different meetings, the parents decide which meeting records the child's membership. When only one parent is a member, children may be recorded upon the request of one parent and with the permission of the other or, under unusual circumstance, upon the request of one parent. Meetings are urged to recognize the diversity of family patterns and be sensitive to the concerns of all involved.

Parents requesting membership or youth membership for their child should intend to raise the child as a Friend in a meeting community. When the meeting accepts a child into membership or youth membership, it should consider whether the parents or guardians are taking seriously their responsibilities in raising their child as a Quaker and minute the discernment. The parents and the meeting should help the child to grow gradually into the responsibilities of membership and should encourage the child to take on specific responsibilities when ready. The meeting has an obligation to those recorded as members or youth members at a young age to ensure that as they reach adulthood they are aware that they should thoughtfully consider their own commitment to membership.

Youth membership is available only to children. It carries with it the full responsibilities and privileges of membership up to age twenty-five. (For yearly meeting statistical purposes, youth members will not be recorded after their twenty-fifth birthday.) Youth members, when they are led, may request adult membership. The monthly meeting should encourage youth members nearing the age of twenty-five to apply. If a youth member does not take this step by the age of twenty-five, that person's name may be dropped from membership. If a youth member is not clear by that age about applying and is dropped from membership, the meeting is encouraged to continue a caring relationship. Such a person may be encouraged to apply for membership when ready. Children whose parents requested membership for them will remain members after age twenty-five. However, they may want the experience of participating in the membership process. Under some circumstances, the meeting may want to review the young person's membership at age twenty-five.

A person may apply for adult membership in a meeting at any age, following the procedure set forth above. Meetings are urged to show a loving flexibility which recognizes the uniqueness of each person's spiritual growth. Some people are spiritually ready for membership early in their lives; others are ready only as adults. In the case of younger applicants, it may be desirable to ascertain the support of the parents or guardian.

The growth of young Friends and the health of the meeting are well served when the meeting encourages the participation of young Friends in all aspects of the meeting. Meetings need to encourage membership among their young people.

Before youth members leave home or for any reason are geographically removed from the meeting, it is important that the committee responsible for membership makes sure that youth members are clear about their relationship with the meeting and explores the question of adult membership with them.

Recording the Membership

The recorder of the monthly meeting asks the new member to fill out a membership form, which is then put in the membership file. The membership form needs to be reviewed from time to time by the member, at the request of the recorder, and kept up to date. A blank membership form is in the appendices; more can be obtained from the yearly meeting secretary. Membership information is shared with the yearly meeting as requested. The monthly meeting sends the minute reflecting any change in membership status to the yearly meeting membership recorder along with the following data: name, address, phone, e-mail, date of birth.

Transfer of Membership

Friends who live at a distance from their own monthly meeting, but near another, will do well to transfer their membership to the nearer one. Living near the meeting makes it possible to enjoy the benefits and to carry out the responsibilities of membership in a particular meeting. Inability to participate in the life of one's own meeting means a loss to both the individual and the meeting. A member of one monthly meeting who moves to the area of another is normally accepted as a member of the Religious Society of Friends and welcomed into membership. If the Friend who has moved from another meeting does not initiate a transfer of membership, the meeting he is now attending, or his home meeting begins a discussion of membership with him.

Pending transfer of membership, both meetings should

cooperate in discharging their responsibility toward the member.

When wishing to transfer membership from one meeting to another, a Friend writes a letter to the meeting where his membership is and asks for a letter of transfer to the meeting he is attending.

On occasion, Friends request a transfer of membership for reasons other than a change of residence. The transfer procedure applies in any case.

Duties of the Monthly Meeting from Which the Member is Moving

When a monthly meeting receives such an application for transfer, the committee responsible for membership prepares, in duplicate, a letter of transfer recommending the Friend to the care of the meeting to which transfer is requested. A reason for not making such a reply is if there is a strong reason to doubt the member's willingness to contribute to the life of another meeting. In such a case, communication between the meetings and with the member is advisable.

If the monthly meeting approves the application for transfer, the clerk signs the letter, the principal copy being forwarded to the receiving monthly meeting, the duplicate being retained for the records.

When the meeting issuing the transfer receives acknowledgment that the new meeting has accepted the Friend into membership, the original meeting terminates the Friend's membership, noting its action in the minutes.

Duties of the Monthly Meeting to Which the Friend Is Moving

The clerk of the monthly meeting to which a member is being transferred acknowledges receipt of the letter of transfer. Then the clerk refers it to the committee responsible for membership, which recommends action to the monthly meeting. If there is no objection, the monthly meeting accepts the transfer and records the Friend as a member. The clerk sends information to that effect to the issuing meeting, to which the Friend in the interim has continued to belong. If there is ground for serious objection to the transfer, the letter should be returned to the meeting which sent it, saying membership transfer was not accepted.

Following a transfer, the new member is welcomed into the meeting with a celebration.

Duties of the Recorder Concerning Letters of Transfer

The recorder keeps a list of all letters of transfer issued and accepted by the meeting. The accepting meeting's recorder notifies the yearly meeting of the new member. The releasing meeting's recorder notifies the yearly meeting of the transfer. Both monthly meetings send the minute reflecting the change in membership status to the yearly meeting membership recorder along with the following data: name, address, phone, e-mail, date of birth.

In the situation where a member of the meeting has moved away to a new location and has not asked for a transfer of membership within a reasonable time, the meeting should contact the member about transfer of membership.

Sojourning Members

Friends may attend a monthly meeting because they have moved temporarily into its vicinity but may not wish to give up membership in their home meeting, to which they expect to return eventually. Their desires in this regard should be set forth in a minute from their home meeting. Such Friends are listed as sojourning members of the meeting they attend and are full members of that meeting. Sojourning Friends may fulfill all functions that they are willing to undertake and that the host meeting sees fit to assign them.

The host monthly meeting sends a minute of sojourning membership to the yearly meeting membership recorder along with the following data: name, address, phone, e-mail, date of birth. However, sojourning members should not be counted in the statistical reports of the host meeting or the host yearly meeting. Their sojourning membership ends when they leave the area of the meeting where they have sojourned. Its clerk should then notify their home meeting and the host yearly meeting. If a Friend spends part of each year with the host meeting and part with the home meeting there is no need to renew the sojourning membership each year. The host meeting asks sojourning Friends who live the year round in Southeastern Yearly Meeting to examine their reasons for remaining in that status and to consider a transfer of membership.

Dual Members

Friends who hold membership in a monthly meeting belonging to another yearly meeting but regularly attend a meeting in Southeastern Yearly Meeting for all or for a regular part of the year may be recorded as dual members after informing their home monthly meeting of the proposed action and getting the approval of the monthly meeting in Southeastern Yearly Meeting. Such persons, whether sojourning or dual members, will not be counted as members of Southeastern Yearly Meeting when statistical reports are made, but in every other way will be considered as full members as long as they wish the relationship to continue. The monthly meeting sends the minute of dual membership to the yearly meeting membership recorder along with the following data: name, address, phone, e-mail, date of birth.

Laying Down Membership

Joining Other Religious Bodies

If a member wishes to leave the Religious Society of Friends and join some other religious body, that person notifies the monthly meeting. The monthly meeting may provide a letter stating the applicant's good standing in the Religious Society of Friends. When the member has been received into membership by another religious group, his membership with Friends ceases. The monthly meeting sends the minute laying down membership to the yearly meeting membership recorder along with the following data: name, address, phone, e-mail, date of birth.

Resignation by the Individual

Members may find that they are not in accord with the faith and practice of Friends or do not feel led to be involved actively in the monthly meeting. They may seek to discuss their differences with the meeting, with a member of the committee responsible for membership, or with others in the meeting whom they trust. If the member decides to leave the Society of Friends, she writes a letter of resignation to the clerk of the meeting.

When a member resigns, the meeting is not absolved from further care. A committee appointed either from the committee responsible for membership or from the meeting-at-large visits the Friend, inquiring in love and forbearance into the cause of the resignation and, if appropriate, endeavoring to bring the member back into the fellowship of Friends. A resignation may be accepted without appointing a committee when the meeting is already well acquainted with the case and is satisfied that the member's decision will not be altered by friendly efforts.

When the meeting accedes to a member's decision to resign, a minute should be made stating that this Friend is released at her own request. The individual should be informed of this action and is no longer a member of the Religious Society of Friends. Letters written in acceptance of a resignation should always show a considerate regard for the person leaving membership. The monthly meeting sends the minute of release of membership to the yearly meeting membership recorder along with the following data: name, address, phone, e-mail, date of birth.

Release by the Monthly Meeting

Long-term nominal membership is generally discouraged except when the member can not get to meeting because of poor health, disability, or location at a distance from any meeting. When a member cannot attend, the Committee for Caring communicates and connects with the member in creative ways. The member may wish to worship with Friends in her home.

When a Friend is consistently absent over a long period of time, the meeting needs to respond to the absence. If the meeting is unable to contact a member after every effort over a period of years, then, under divine guidance, membership may be laid down. Meetings try to stay in touch at least once a year with members who have moved away. Friends who have moved away may be encouraged to transfer their membership.

Either when a Friend is unresponsive to the idea of a transfer of membership or is not participating in the meeting, the meeting may wish to send a letter inquiring whether the member wishes to continue membership. If the answer is yes, the Friend should be encouraged to participate in meeting activities, such as by phone contact, e-mail, contributions, and being present when possible. If the response is negative, the meeting makes every effort to understand where the member is in his spiritual journey. Eventually, the meeting may minute that the membership is laid down, and a loving letter is sent informing the Friend of this action. The ending of membership does not mean the ending of friendship or of welcome if the person comes to meeting for a visit. The ending of membership only recognizes the choice of the individual and the meeting. The monthly meeting sends the minute laying down membership to the yearly meeting membership recorder along with the following data: name, address, phone, e-mail, date of birth.

Queries for the Meeting Laying Down Membership

- Is it really practical to keep people on the records of the meeting as members if they have not participated in the meeting for a long time?

- Is the meeting or the individual reluctant to acknowledge the reality of the situation between the meeting and the member by keeping the names of such people on the meeting's records?

The unity of Christians never did nor ever will nor can stand in uniformity of thought and opinion, but in Christian love only.

Thomas Story, 1737

Dearly Beloved Friends and brethren, in the Power, Life and Seed of God all dwell, serving one another in Love and in the Wisdom of God. . . . You must do nothing for the Lord by earthly policy ... but wait in the Power of the Lord God and be ordered by that to his glory . . .

George Fox, 1654

Clearness for Membership Queries

For meetings, these queries are suggestions or a meeting may make its own clearness for membership queries. Print out these queries or others and distribute copies to the applicant as well as the clearness committee before meeting for the first time.

For applicants, these are questions that members of your clearness committee may use to get to know you better and to guide their prayerful consideration of your request for membership in their meeting. This is not about "right or wrong" answers; rather, it is intended to ensure that you understand what you are taking on and to give you the opportunity to explore aspects of the Religious Society of Friends which may not be clear to you. Please ask any questions you may have.

YOUR SPIRITUAL JOURNEY

What has been your spiritual journey and how has it led you to seek membership in the Religious Society of Friends? We invite you to share with us ways in which you have experienced the Divine/God's presence. How can the meeting support your continued spiritual growth?

MEETINGS FOR BUSINESS

How many meetings for business have you attended (lots, a few, none)? What is your understanding of the way Friends conduct meeting for business? What has been your experience with business meeting?

MEETINGS FOR WORSHIP

How do you feel about the unprogrammed meeting for worship being based on expectant waiting? What questions do you have about the role and source of vocal ministry? What do you do with messages that you have felt as being intended for you as opposed to messages meant for the meeting as a whole?

TESTIMONIES

What do you know about the various testimonies of Friends: peace, integrity, equality, simplicity, community?

WORLD OF QUAKERISM

What do you know about the world of Quakerism: Southeastern Yearly Meeting (SEYM), Friends General Conference (FGC), Friends Committee on National Legislation (FCNL), American Friends Service Committee (AFSC), Quaker Earthcare Witness (QEW), Friends World Committee for Consultation (FWCC)?

ROOTS AND DIVERSITY OF QUAKERISM

What are your thoughts about the historical and spiritual roots of Quakerism and the diversity of Friends practice today? Have you noticed that there is within our meeting a spectrum of spiritual experience and language? How do you respond to this diversity?

QUAKER WRITINGS

Please tell us which Quaker writings, historical or contemporary, have helped you and why.

QUAKER LANGUAGE

What is your understanding of these phrases used by Friends: "discerning community," "listening to that of God within," "yielding to the Spirit," "coming to unity with Friends," "seeking inward peace," "the Inward Christ," and "way will open"?

INDIVIDUALS HELPING THE MEETING

What special gifts can you share that will enrich the life of the meeting? What other ways might you contribute to the work of the meeting, financially or otherwise? Do you realize that your presence at meeting for worship and meeting for business is a gift to the meeting as well as to yourself? Are you comfortable both with helping when you are asked and just doing a job that needs to be done?

HOW THE MEETING HELPS INDIVIDUALS

Are there forms of ministry and support that you have found helpful or that you would like to receive? How will you ask for help from the meeting? What are the various uses of the clearness process? Do you realize that you can have spiritual friends in the meeting?

RECONCILIATION

Membership in a meeting means membership in a community where people respect and love each other. Nevertheless, conflicts sometimes arise. How have you reconciled differences in the past? What have you learned from these experiences? How will it help you to resolve differences in the future?

MEETING AND YOUR CHILD

Have you requested associate membership for your child? Are there special ways the meeting can support your child's spiritual growth or your parenting?

OTHER AFFILIATIONS WITH RELIGIOUS ORGANIZATIONS

Are you currently a member of any other religious organization?

QUAKERS AREN'T PERFECT

One question you do NOT need to ask yourself is, "Am I good enough to be a Quaker?" The Religious Society of Friends is not a body of ultra-virtuous people: We all have our weaknesses as well as special gifts. In any case, who among us could judge who is "good enough"?

At the End of the Clearness for Membership Meeting

At the end of the meeting, the clerk of the clearness committee describes the remainder of the membership process to the applicant.

CHAPTER 8

MARRIAGE AND COMMITMENT

Our Life is love, and peace, and tenderness:
and bearing one with another,
And forgiving one another, and not laying
accusations one against another:
But praying one for another, and helping one
another up with a tender hand.
Isaac Penington, 1667

This is my beloved and this is my friend . . .
Song of Solomon 5:16 NRVS

Introduction

The Friends' wedding ceremony evolved from a reaction to seventeenth-century British law requiring official state clergy to assure legitimacy and inheritance. Understanding this allows the contemporary Friend insight into the wording and form of the traditional Quaker ceremony. Initially the British state did not recognize the private Friends' ceremony and considered children born to Friends' unions illegitimate. George Fox himself, to counter the attack that Friends were impulsive, recommended long engagements, public ceremonies, twelve adult witnesses, and submission of the wedding certificate to a magistrate. Friends also commenced posting public notice of their intentions to marry, as well as having all meetings open to public scrutiny. Eventually the Friends' ceremony was accepted as legal.

The spiritual journey of an individual can be enhanced and strengthened in a loving, committed relationship. Friends recognize that some couples are called into a sacred, lifelong relationship in a ministry of caring, which with divine assistance may open the door to deep and unreserved love, to forgiveness, to sharing strength, to trust, and to the nurture of each other's growth. Some call the process to recognize this relationship "marriage"; some call it "ceremony of commitment," or some may call it by another name. The couple determines the choice of the name.

> *In the true marriage [committed] relationship, the independence of the husband and wife [partners] is equal, their dependence mutual, and their obligations reciprocal.*
> **Aphorism favored by Lucretia Mott, c. 1850**
> **(adapted by North Pacific Yearly Meeting, 1993)**

When a couple, regardless of sexual orientation, feels called into such a sacred relationship, they seek clearness with their monthly meeting. When the meeting finds clearness in the couple and clearness within the meeting to take their relationship under the care of the meeting and God's guidance, a meeting for worship is specially called for public affirmation and celebration of the couple's lifetime commitment to one another. The ceremony itself takes place in a meeting for worship. In an atmosphere of quiet and reverence, the promises of the couple are made to one another without the help of a third person.

The caring friendship with a life partner is a precious thing. Selection of this person should be undertaken with prayer and great care to assure that the decision considers all aspects of compatibility. In order to explore compatibility, the partners discuss their spiritual beliefs and the Quaker testimonies. They will not agree on everything. It is essential that they respect each other and learn to live with their disagreements. Additionally, the couple considers financial arrangements and, if appropriate, considers child-rearing practices. If there are children of either partner, the couple reviews and evaluates their shared commitments to the well-being of the children. Other issues to consider are pace and style of living, sexual compatibility, and respect for each other at all levels, including intellectual understanding and the deepest spiritual outlook. The couple looks within and at each other to assure that a tender, loving, lifelong commitment is their intent. Ideally, kindness prevails in a Friends' union. Friends endeavor to support the deepening of relationships, recognizing that the quality of family life and community life are interdependent. The meeting undertakes a special responsibility for the care of the relationships in the meeting and also needs to proceed prayerfully in its decision.

> *[The joining of two people] is the work of the Lord only, and not the priests or magistrates; for it is God's ordinance and not man's, and therefore friends cannot consent that they should join them together: for we marry none; it is the Lord's work, and we are but witnesses.*
>
> **George Fox, 1669**

A Chronological List of Common Marriage and Commitment Practices

- The couple writes a letter of intention, signed by both parties, to the monthly meeting. The couple should understand that wedding plans are not to be made prior to the request and clearness process outlined here.

- The monthly meeting appoints a clearness committee for marriage/commitment.

- The couple and the clearness committee explore the rightness of the relationship for marriage or commitment. The committee makes available books and pamphlets on marriage and information on Quaker resources on marriage.

- The clearness committee reviews with the couple the promises they propose to exchange during the ceremony and makes sure the words of the certificate are consistent with them.

- The clearness committee makes sure that the welfare and rights of any children of either partner have been properly considered and legally secured.

- The clearness committee informs itself of all necessary legal requirements.

- The clearness committee reports the findings of the couple and the committee to the monthly meeting.

- When the monthly meeting approves the marriage, it appoints an arrangements committee.

- The arrangements committee is responsible for seeing that the ceremony and reception are accomplished with dignity, reverence, and simplicity.

- The couple and the arrangements committee plan the ceremony in detail. The date, time, and place of the ceremony are reported to the monthly meeting as soon as possible. Arrangements are made for the rehearsal, for the choice of persons to read the marriage certificate, and for the opening and closing of the meeting for worship.

- The couple sends out invitations and arranges for the writing of the certificate.

- The arrangements committee informs itself of all legal responsibilities. The couple informs themselves of all legal requirements and arranges for the appropriate license for use where there is no clergy. See Florida Statute 741.04 or the appropriate Georgia or South Carolina statutes.

- The couple gives the certificate and the license to the arrangements committee before the ceremony.

- The arrangements committee sees that all applicable legal requirements have been met and that the proper license has been obtained. The committee also ensures that the license is signed and dated by the couple, the clerk of the meeting, and any other legally required person and that the license is returned to the proper government office within the time required by law.

- The couple rehearses their vows. During the ceremony, they say them to each other and sign the certificate.

- The arrangements committee oversees the further signing of the certificate after the meeting for worship, seeing that it is signed by all those who were present, as witnesses. The committee also gives a copy of the text of the certificate to the recording clerk of the meeting for the records.

- The arrangements committee reports to the meeting whether the marriage has been accomplished, whether the applicable legal requirements have been satisfied, whether the certificate has been properly recorded, and whether any name changes result from the marriage, for recording in the minutes of the monthly meeting.

- At the time of the marriage, a committee for the continuing care of the marriage/commitment is appointed. This committee is led to periodically hold up in the Light the partners in this union. Often the members of the arrangements committee serve in this capacity.

The Clearness Process

When a couple, regardless of sexual orientation, feels led to affirm their lifelong commitment under the care of a monthly meeting, they must first seek clearness. When both partners are members of the same monthly meeting, they write a letter to the meeting stating their intention. This letter will be read at the meeting for worship with a concern for business. A clearness committee is appointed. Following the good order of Friends, the couple will find that they need several months or more between the sending of the request and the desired date of the celebration. If one member of the couple holds membership in another monthly meeting or is not a member of Friends, he or she requests a "letter of clearness" from his or her home meeting or other religious organization stating that organization's knowledge if any reason exists why the person should not become married at this time. This letter of clearness is sent to the hosting monthly meeting's clearness committee. If one member of a couple is unaffiliated with any religious community, the clearness committee is responsible for discerning the way forward. If neither person is a Friend, the monthly meeting must decide whether to enter into the long-term, deep and abiding process of taking the couple's relationship under the care of the meeting. Both the meeting and the couple need to recognize that this is a two-way commitment between the couple and the monthly meeting. It is important in this process that the meeting's love and care for both be affirmed.

After the request is received and a clearness committee is appointed by the monthly meeting, the couple and the clearness committee meet for thoughtful and prayerful discussions to seek God's will. The committee or the couple may present specific queries or topics to give direction to the process. Clearness may arise out of worship. Those participating in the clearness process endeavor to approach each meeting with open hearts and minds, allowing sufficient time for understanding and seasoning to occur. One of the clearness committee's responsibilities is to make sure, insofar as is possible, that there is nothing to interfere with the permanence and happiness of the proposed marriage or commitment. If either party has children, it is also appropriate for the clearness committee to ascertain that their emotional and legal rights are being considered. To help with the clearness process, the couple works with the clearness committee on the wording of the certificate, including the vows. The couple should understand that they will probably meet with their clearness committee more than one time.

When the couple and the clearness committee are clear that the ceremony should go forward, the committee reports its endorsement to the monthly meeting. They indicate that unity has been found and recommend that the monthly meeting take the relationship under the care of the meeting.

It may be that unity to move forward is not found by the couple and the committee. They may choose to continue seeking God's will in this matter, or they may choose to lay aside the request indefinitely or permanently. When the right course of action is clear, the clearness committee reports this to the monthly meeting.

The meeting for worship with a concern for business receives the clearness committee's report and, after prayerful consideration, minutes its action. Thoroughness in the clearness and guidance process is essential in seasoning the relationship and in establishing a strong basis on which to begin this lifetime journey.

Topics Suggested for Discussion During the Clearness Process

Most of these subjects will arise naturally in the course of the clearness process, and it is preferable that the prospective partners feel free to broach them themselves. It is well for the committee to have topics in mind and to see that they are covered. The aim of the clearness committee is to elicit responses so that each member of the couple hears the answers of the other. There are not specific answers necessary to the committee. The committee makes available to the couple relevant books and pamphlets on marriage or ceremonies of commitment and informs the couple of other Quaker resources.

- **Communication.** Do they understand that communication, verbal and nonverbal, is fundamental to a relationship? Have they discussed the patterns of communication they now have? Are they beginning to learn each other's style? How are uneasy feelings shared? How do they express their strongly felt concerns? How do they get what they want and cope when they do not get what they want? How do they express their love and respect for each other? How do they understand/receive the other's expressions of love, fear, passion, and other emotions? How do they know when they have been heard? How do they identify and resolve conflicts? In relating to each other, will they, in the words of John Woolman, let "love be the first motion" in their relationship?

- **Background and Acquaintance.** What brought them to decide upon this step? What benefits are they seeking? How well does the couple know each other? Do they share similar views regarding the Friends' testimonies of equality, integrity, peace, simplicity, and community? What are their basic common values? How do they adapt to differences in background, religion, temperament, and interests? Can they meet their differences with love, humor, mutual respect, patience, and generosity? Do they envision building a new family? What does this mean to them?

- **Religious Beliefs, Feelings, Aspirations.** Do they see their commitment as a spiritual relationship to be entered into with appreciation of its divine basis? How do they propose to meet their religious needs as a couple? How do they plan to make their relationship accessible to divine assistance? Do they endeavor to hold each other in the Light?

- **Growth and Fulfillment.** Do they think of themselves as trusted and equal lifelong partners, sharing responsibilities and decisions? Are they supportive of each other's goals for personal growth and fulfillment? Do they communicate their feelings and needs, their dreams and fears to each other? Are they able to discuss their sexual expectations openly? Do they have the courage and the willingness to go together for outside guidance from family, meeting, wider community, or professional?

- **Children.** Have they shared and found unity on whether they expect to raise a family? Have they discussed family planning or adoption? Do they see a child as a gift from God? If they plan to have children, do they both accept the responsibilities of raising children, including time, finances, education, and religious training? Are they aware of differences in the way each was raised and how each understands parenting? How do they expect they will resolve these differences? Have they discussed communicating with children and disciplining them? What experiences have they had in caring for children and sharing in their upbringing? Are they ready to listen to each child and to support the unfolding of the child's gifts and true nature? In relating to their children, will they, in the words of John Woolman, let "love be the first motion" in that relationship with each child? What are their feelings about the place of children in the life of the family, the meeting, and the wider community? Has the couple considered the special concerns that may arise in a family headed by a same-sex, mixed-race, or mixed-cultural-origins couple?

- **Daily Living.** Have they explored their sense of Quaker queries and advices? Have they given consideration to and found ways to resolve anger when it arises within the relationship? Have they discussed and worked through questions regarding the earning, use, and management of money? Have they considered how to resolve daily issues such as household care and personal schedules? Have they found ways to resolve lifestyle issues, such as one being a morning person and the other being an evening person? Have they explored attitudes towards holidays and gift giving?

- **Relationships with Others.** Are they aware of the need for developing a variety of other friendships that contribute both to individual growth and to their relationship? Do they share views on faithfulness? How do they view their relationships with each other's families and friends and their obligations toward society?

- **Relationship with Monthly Meeting.** What does the couple expect the monthly meeting to do to support their relationship? What do they expect their relationship to bring to the monthly meeting?

- **Outside Obligations.** Has the couple considered how existing commitments, personal or financial, may affect the union? Are they fully aware of each other's personal and financial position and obligations? Have they explored their commitments to work and discussed how they plan to balance the demands of career, family, and Quaker service?

- **Attitude of Families.** What are the views of their families toward the prospective marriage or commitment and to the new partner? What is each partner's attitude toward the other partner's family?

- **Legal Concerns.** Does the couple intend this to be a legal, as well as a religious, marriage commitment? If there is no marriage license, has the couple investigated all aspects of this situation both for themselves and their children that the ceremony will not address, especially when the ceremony is not recognized by the state? Have they discussed the legal names each will use?

- **The Vows and the Certificate.** A responsibility of the clearness committee is assisting the couple with the wording of their vows and their certificate. With the approval of the clearness committee, the wording of the vows and the certificate may be changed to conform to the wishes of the participants. Older certificates included the parents' addresses and the consent of surviving parents. At least one certificate included a children's section: "We, the children, recognizing our parents' affection for each other and for us, individually and as a family, have signed our names, knowing we shall be beloved forever."

Suggested Vows

In the presence of God and before these our Friends, I take thee, _____, to be my (wife, husband, partner), promising, with divine assistance, to be unto thee a loving and faithful (husband, wife, partner), as long as we both shall live [or words to that effect].

Or

In the presence of God and before these our Friends, I commit myself to thee, _____, promising, with divine assistance, to be unto thee loving and faithful, as long as we both shall live.

A Sample Certificate

Whereas _____ *of* _____ *and*
_____ *of* _____, *having declared
their intentions of marriage (commitment)
with each other to* _____ *Monthly
Meeting of the Religious Society of Friends
held at* _____, *their proposed union
was allowed by that meeting.*

*Now this is to certify, to whom it may con-
cern, that for the accomplishment of their
intentions, this* _____ *day of the* _____
month in the year of our Lord _____ *they,*
_____ *and* _____, *appeared in a
meeting for worship of the Religious Society
of Friends held at* _____. *And taking
each other by the hands they did declare,
each speaking in turn, that they with divine
assistance would be unto each other loving
and faithful as long as they both should live
(in agreement with their vows). And moreover they,* _____ *and* _____, *did,
as further confirmation thereof, then and
there to this certificate set their hands.*

_____

_____

*And we, having been present at the cer-
emony, have as witnesses hereunto set our
hands.*

_____   _____

_____   _____

Use enough signature lines to accommodate signing of the
certificate by everyone present.

- **The Celebration.** How do they view the meeting for worship on the occasion of marriage or celebration, which is to take place under the care of the meeting? Are they familiar with the procedure? Do they appreciate the values involved in the Quaker form of commitment? Do they understand that all arrangements, including invitations, need to wait until after the meeting has agreed to the marriage commitment under the care of the meeting?

Marriages and committed relationships pass through many phases, and through all phases the quality of the relationship is tested. The development of a relationship is a growing experience. Respect for each other and enduring, loving expression deepen the bond. With God's help, each couple finds a true path and a way of living that leads to a stronger union. Yet, whatever the style of life, all relationships need a foundation of commitment, communication, honesty, and integrity. Patience, humor, and a spirit of adventure, guided by a mutual trust in God's presence, strengthen the present and brighten the hope for the future.

North Pacific Yearly Meeting, 1993

Arrangements Committee

When the monthly meeting has minuted its approval of taking a marriage under its care, it appoints an arrangements committee after consulting with the couple. The arrangements committee and the couple come to an agreement on the time and place of the ceremony. The committee works with the couple to design their ceremony. All Quaker marriage or commitment vows take place in a meeting for worship in an atmosphere of simplicity, dignity, and reverence. Southeastern Yearly Meeting is blessed with members' experience representing a wide range of Quaker practice. In addition to the traditional exchange of vows and signing of the certificate, we experience a variety of procedures within our monthly meetings.

It is the responsibility of the couple to produce their certificate using the wording previously approved by their clearness committee. Alternatively a preprinted certificate may be ordered from the Friends General Conference Bookstore. If appropriate, the couple informs themselves of the legal requirements of the state in which the marriage is to take place and obtains the license. See Florida Statute 741.04 or the appropriate Georgia or South Carolina statutes. They rehearse their vows as approved by their clearness committee and organize their reception.

It is the responsibility of the arrangements committee to explore options with the couple and to assist in making appropriate decisions. Tradition dictates a worshipful atmosphere, with the couple saying their vows to each other without a third party officiating, the reading of the certificate, and the signing of it by all present. Some aspects of the ceremony that need to be decided include

- when the couple enters and exits and where they sit.

- general seating arrangement.

- how to let people know what to expect and how to understand a Quaker wedding. A brief printed explanation can be obtained from Philadelphia Yearly Meeting, which can be included in wedding invitations or made available at the door. A designated Friend may give an explanation after the guests and wedding party are seated.

- timing of the exchange of vows. Vows should be exchanged after the meeting has settled and early enough to allow for vocal ministry from worship afterwards.

- whether or not the couple wishes to be seated to sign the certificate or remain standing and walk to the certificate table to sign. If they wish to be seated, two people must be ready to bring the table to them.

- who reads the certificate.

- who closes meeting.

- who facilitates the signing of the certificate by those present. If desired, the number and placement of spaces to be saved for signatures of the family, the arrangements committee members, and/or members of the committee for care of the marriage may be prearranged.

- the appropriateness of any prearranged participation, such as music or readings.

The committee may also offer to help with the planning of the reception. The couple is responsible for the reception unless other arrangements are made.

The arrangements committee is responsible for ensuring that all legal documents are properly completed, signed by the clerk of the monthly meeting and any other legally required person, and filed with the county clerk or designated officer within the time required by law. The committee is responsible for recording the certificate with the monthly meeting recorder. In addition, they report to the following meeting for worship with a concern for business that the ceremony has been carried out in good order and that all legal requirements have been satisfied. The committee also reports, if appropriate, that the certificate has been properly recorded and reports the names assumed by the couple.

Traditional Friends Ceremony

The ceremony itself takes place in a meeting for worship. Guests gather in silence at the appointed time in an atmosphere of quiet and reverence. The couple and their attendants, if any, enter and usually sit facing the gathering of friends and relatives.

Following a period of worship, the couple rises, takes each other by the hand, and, each speaking in turn, makes the promises given in the certificate. The promises of the couple are made to one another without the help of a third person. Thereafter, the couple signs the certificate. It is read aloud by a designated Friend.

Worship continues, often with rich vocal ministry, and is closed in the usual manner of the meeting for worship. Afterward, everyone present signs the certificate.

Meeting's Care for the Relationship

Friends are reminded that the meeting's nurture and care of the relationship does not end with the celebration but endures throughout the whole of life. Each couple must be aware that their committed relationship has far-reaching effects on others. They need to be willing to seek divine help and meeting guidance to assist in fulfilling the vows. In taking the couple under its care, the meeting assumes the responsibility to be steadfast and direct, as well as sensitive, in fulfilling its obligation. At the time of the marriage, a committee for the continuing care of the marriage is appointed. Often, the members of the arrangements committee serve in this capacity.

Meetings have an important role in nurturing, supporting, and celebrating the couples under their care. In a loving community of persons of similar religious values and priorities, couples can be sustained and guided in their efforts to build an enduring relationship. Care of the relationships among the members of the meeting is nurtured by celebrations, workshops, and supportive discussion groups as well as by meetings for worship and meetings for business. Such nurturing may enhance the life of the meeting.

Some couples may appreciate the feeling of caring that the meeting offers when times are easy but fail to invite its guidance during difficult times. Loving concern is helpful here. As members of the meeting community deepen their friendships, one may become sensitive to the pain another is bearing. A child, another family member, or the person may communicate their pain verbally or in some nonverbal way such as behavior changes. Workshops on marriage and child rearing are particularly helpful in this context. The meeting and the individuals in the meeting assist each other through prayer and a strong belief in divine intercession in daily life. We are a community that serves God, and therefore each other. For example, one monthly meeting has had a meeting for worship for renewal of vows. Another has had a meeting for worship to recognize a divorce. Friends remain open to support members' relationships.

Marriage or Ceremonies of Commitment Outside the Care of the Meeting

If a member is married or celebrates a commitment outside the care of the meeting, the monthly meeting may arrange a committee to visit with the new couple, expressing the interest of the meeting in their new relationship. No matter how the marriage or commitment was accomplished, all couples receive the loving support and care of the meeting.

Remarriage

A new marriage or committed relationship takes much faith, strength, and courage following the loss of a partner. The processes of request, clearness, and support of the new relationship are identical to those just outlined. During the clearness process, however, special consideration will naturally be given to discussion pertinent to the changed circumstances.

Where children or other relatives are involved, it is advisable for the clearness process to include discussions with them. A new relationship often involves the creation of a blended family. The clearness committee can be helpful in resolving feelings about the new family structure by involving all parties in thorough and prayerful examination of feelings and expectations.

A common spiritual outlook, the continuing endeavor to hold others in the Light, and the awareness that love deepens and matures with time contribute to a stable relationship. The couple is encouraged in resolving and healing their respective pasts as they look to make a common future together.

Separation and Deciding to Divorce

We would counsel Friends to take timely advice in periods of difficulty. The early sharing of problems with sympathetic Friends or marriage counselors can often bring release from misunderstandings and

give positive help towards new joy together. Friends
ought to be able to do this, but much will depend on
the quality of our life together in the Society. . . .
We need to be more sensitive to each other's needs,
knowing one another in the things which are mate-
rial as in the things which are eternal.
London (Britain) Yearly Meeting, 1972

In spite of the best intentions, wisdom may dictate a separation or ultimately divorce. When dissatisfaction first arises in the
relationship, the couple is encouraged to prayerfully discuss those
differences that have arisen. Should discontent continue and it
becomes evident within the meeting community, outside counseling is recommended. Either one of the couple may request a clearness committee or seek counseling with a professional counselor
whom both people respect and trust and with whom each feels
comfortable. Through counseling, many issues can be resolved, and
the union may then remain intact. It is important to express the
meeting's love and concern to the couple and the children, if any, in
all circumstances.

If the relationship evolves into a destructive one, either
emotionally or physically, the meeting continues to reach out to
support each member of the family in seeking a solution beneficial to all. A destructive relationship may require separation and
ultimately a divorce. In the event of separation or divorce, both
persons are encouraged to consider each other beloved children of
God.

Friends often have not dealt well with the issues of separation and divorce. Ignoring a painful situation does not diminish its
impact but does isolate the people involved. When Friends com-
mence to acknowledge that differences have evolved, the couple
may be helped to come to clarity, avoiding a bitterness that can be
injurious to each other and to any children of the union as well as to
other family members.

Divorce cannot be undertaken lightly. "Laboring" is an

appropriate Quaker term for the amount of energy that must be expended within the union and within the Quaker community. Parents and the meeting need to remember and provide for the children's needs as well as the adults'. The children usually need to maintain their relationship with both parents, though circumstances may dictate otherwise.

The pain and suffering of a person going through divorce can become overwhelming for the individual and the meeting. Friends need to acknowledge their own limitations and energy commitments. Recommending professional counseling to deal with emotional issues allows the meeting to deal with the spiritual ones.

When two members face separation or divorce, one or both may feel alienated from further participation in the meeting. If the meeting has taken an active and evenhanded role in the clearness process before the separation or divorce, the sense of alienation may be lessened and separation may proceed with tenderness and charity.

Divorce

A couple that is having a troubled relationship and decides on divorce may want the meeting to witness the divorce. This may be especially true for same-sex couples that do not go through legal divorce proceedings and so do not have a formal closure of the relationship.

The meeting could provide a clearness committee for the couple and the meeting to reach clearness on the divorce.

Following much soul-searching and time required for separation, some divorcing individuals request a meeting for worship to recognize their changed status. During the meeting for worship each person, in the presence of God, releases the other from his/her vows and wishes the other well on his/her life journey. Whether privately or publicly held, this can be a healing moment for one or both parties, for any children, if any, and for their meeting.

Be kind and courteous towards one another, learning how to be quiet, how to excel in virtue and purity in everything you say and do so that your whole lives may be devoted to what is sacred and right, in a way that is fitting for saints and Christians. Let everyone, in humility, reckon others more advanced in the truth than they are, for "the one who inhabits eternity . . . lives with a humble heart" (Isaiah 57:15). And therefore, do not stifle the least prompting of God's good spirit in yourselves, or in others, but value truth and goodness, and let truth itself subdue all harshness and bitterness and abuse, so that truth can find its way through the lives of every one of you. And it will enable you to bear with one another's faults and weaknesses . . . . So be passionate and faithful in the cause of truth, but also careful and cautious, and be known for your consideration of others, your moderation and restraint. Let it be clear that it is the Lord who works through you, and let honesty and justice be evident in everything you say and in every interaction with other people. Leave no debt outstanding, but remember the debt of love you owe to others. Then each of you will be clothed in a humble and quiet spirit, which the Lord values greatly.

George Fox, 1680

We thank God then, for the pleasures, joys and triumphs of [life together]; for the cups of tea we bring each other, and the seedlings in the garden frame; for the domestic drama of meetings and partings, sickness and recovery; for the grace of occasional extravagance, flowers on birthdays and unexpected presents; for talk at evenings of the events of the day; for the ecstasy of caresses; for gay mockery at each other's follies; for the plans and projects, fun and struggle; praying that we may neither neglect nor undervalue these things, nor be tempted to think of them as self-contained and self-sufficient.

London Yearly Meeting, 1960

CHAPTER 9

Dying, Death, and Bereavement

And this is the Comfort of the Good,
That the Grave cannot hold them,
And that they live as soon as they die
For Death is no more
Than a turning of us over from time to eternity.
Death, then, being the way and condition of life,
We cannot love to live,
  if we cannot bear to die.
They that love beyond the world,
  cannot be separated by it.
Death cannot kill what never dies.
Nor can Spirits ever be divided
That love and live in the same Divine Principle,
The Root and Record of their Friendship.
Death is but crossing the world, as friends do the
seas, they live in one another still.

William Penn, 1693

For every thing there is a season, and a time to every
matter under heaven. A time to be born, and a time
to die, a time to plant, and a time to pluck up that
which is planted . . .

Ecclesiastes 3:1-2 NRSV

I have been now about 13 weeks in this violent ill-
ness, some say there is noe cure, let it be as pleases
God I am content, the sting of death hath been re-
moved from me many years agone, Glory to God
who gives Faith and victory. . . .

Robert Barrow to his wife Margaret, 1697

Quakers do have something very special to offer the
dying and the bereaved, namely that we are at home
in silence. Not only are we thoroughly used to it and
unembarrassed by it, but we know something about

sharing it, encountering others in its depths and, above all, letting ourselves be used in it . . . People so often talk of someone "getting over" a death. How could you ever fully get over a deep loss? Life has been changed profoundly and irrevocably. You don't get over sorrow; you work your way right to the centre of it.

Diana Lampen, 1979

For I am persuaded, that neither death, nor life, nor angels, nor principalities, nor powers, nor things present, nor things to come, nor height, nor depth, nor any other creature, shall be able to separate us from the love of God, which is Christ Jesus our Lord.

Romans 8:38-39 KJV

Preparing for Death

Death is part of life. It takes some experience with death to persuade us that our own death or the death of a dear one may happen any day of our lives. This realization teaches us that each day of life is precious and revises our sense of what is valuable in life. Each individual is responsible for preparing for death; members of the meeting community can aid each other in this preparation.

The following is a guide. What individuals and meetings do comes from within. The individual's preparation for diminished competency and/or death includes practical measures. These may be the making and maintenance of wills, including plans for minor children and other dependents, living wills, do-not-resuscitate directives, and durable powers of attorney for financial and medical decisions. The meeting can be of help by providing information on the current legal status and need for these documents and on how they can speak for the individual when the individual can no longer speak. Another preparation for death is writing instructions for disposal of the body and for a memorial service or funeral. These instructions go to the family and the meeting. The meeting's concept of family will be determined by relationships, not limited by legal or social attitudes.

We encourage Friends to think about what our own death means and how the death of dear ones affects us. Reading, pondering our own experiences, and sharing experiences of death help us grow to meet the challenges of death. Contemplation of death in the light of our spiritual understanding can illuminate all other aspects of dying. It is hoped that the individual and the meeting work together to learn about this view of death. The most powerful gift we can give to each other is to listen. Truly exercising our souls in this seeking will benefit ourselves and others at all times and particularly at the time of our own dying and the dying of our loved ones. Spiritual support for those who are dying is a difficult and rewarding task for each of us and for the meeting.

As Death Approaches

Each death is unique, just as each person is unique, and requires an appropriate response from the meeting. Listening is a fundamental part of this response. The focus of the meeting is on the dying person, the immediate family, and the wider family as needed. It is also a time to pay special attention to the needs of children. Sudden death or prolonged dying are extremes. Each entails its own challenges. As death approaches a member of the meeting community, the meeting gives physical, emotional, and spiritual support to the dying Friend and the family. In consultation with the family, the care and counsel committee (oversight) and the worship and ministry committee may organize a support committee with one key person designated to coordinate the meeting's loving concern. The meeting needs to continue to support the family's wishes, which may be difficult to accept. Whether the death is sudden or prolonged, it is important to offer to do specific tasks such as help with food, housework, laundry, care of children, and hospitality for people visiting from a distance. In the case of sudden death, people may not be able to cope with the routine of life because they are in shock and time is needed to integrate the loss. In the case of illness, people have many new tasks and may become overwhelmed by the usual ones.

Guided by the Spirit, the meeting can offer spiritual and emotional support to the Friend and family during the dying process, helping them to cope with pain and stress. The committees' support can include exploring spiritual disciplines, forming a spiritual friends group, finding a counselor, contacting hospice, and forming a clearness committee to help with decisions if a Friend's capacities become diminished. The meeting is sensitive to the increased need for assistance and counsels with the family about solutions such as adjusting to home care, locating suitable nursing facilities, deciding whether to prolong life, and completing legal matters. In dealing with the health care system of today, patients need advocates to look after their interests. The meeting can be helpful in providing them. All is done with sensitivity to the family's needs. Because the dying process may take a long time, the caregiver and the patient may become isolated from the community and the meeting. They need respite and help to stay in touch. The meeting can offer to gather for worship in the home. The meeting can help everyone, especially family members who are at a distance or not closely involved, by sharing practical household tasks, listening to reminiscences, and giving news of the dying person.

Dying

At the time of death, we do our best to give comfort. One way to do this is to help the dying let go. This may include reminding the person of how well he or she has taken care of affairs for their loved ones. We may need to help take care of some unfinished business or help a person with communication. Some may need permission to die, to be reassured that family and friends remaining will be all right. The simple act of being present with the dying person can give comfort. We can also encourage the family to think about whether they might want to stay in the room with the person for a while after the death, and help arrange to make this possible, especially if the setting is an institution such as a nursing home or hospital. The book *Final Gifts* by M. Callanan and P. Kelley, listed under "reference and advice to monthly meetings" at the end of this chapter, gives more examples of these needs.

Arrangements After Death

No meeting member should slip away unremembered and

unmourned. Celebrating a person's life at the end is part of our relationship with that person. The meeting may offer the bereaved family guidance with choices for care of the remains, interment, or scattering of ashes. If there is no family, the meeting is ready to do this service for the deceased Friend. A memorial meeting is the normal witness to the life of the Friend; it is usually arranged by the worship and ministry committee after visiting with the family and listening with sensitivity to their needs. There may also be a brief meeting of farewell at the time of the scattering of the ashes or interment. A memorial meeting is a meeting for worship celebrating a life that held meaning for us. As always in Quaker affairs, simplicity is a guide. Sometimes a brief biography of the deceased Friend is read and/or distributed at the memorial meeting as a keepsake. If a number of non-Friends will be present, an oral and/or written explanation of a meeting for worship should be given. It may be appropriate for refreshments to be provided after the memorial meeting so that there is an environment for informal exchanges. Comparative strangers may ask the meeting to hold a memorial meeting for a family member. It is up to each monthly meeting to make this decision. The meeting should be sensitive to the needs and wishes of parents and family in cases of loss in early infancy or through miscarriage, abortion, or stillbirth. The family may want a memorial meeting.

The death is recorded in the minutes of the monthly meeting, and the yearly meeting is notified. A memorial minute may be prepared for the records of the monthly meeting and forwarded to the yearly meeting. Quaker periodicals may be notified. The death is recorded on the membership papers of the deceased as well as the membership record of the meeting.

Adjustments After Death

The meeting offers help, listening, and clearness assistance to the bereaved in facing life anew and adapting to the new circumstances. Members of the meeting community support and acknowledge the grieving process. Counsel may be offered with regard to living arrangements and financial matters. The meeting is mindful of ways to keep the bereaved active in the meeting community and the other communities in their lives. A grieving person living alone may want a companion in the house for a short while. Answering the telephone for a grieving person or family may be an important service. The meeting may be needed to notify a prepared list of relatives and friends. Physical, emotional, and spiritual support may be needed for some time. When a difficult relationship is ended by death, there may be feelings of joy, release, and ambivalence. Let us be sensitive to the process, which will be different depending on who has died: parent, child, spouse, partner, or friend. The family is likely to be mourning for at least a year or much more. Remember that children need help with mourning. The meeting must understand that there will be periods of renewal of mourning, especially around significant dates. Each Friend should be guided by the Spirit and the needs of the grieving person.

A variety of factors may complicate and prolong grieving. There may be feelings of guilt. Survivors may not have resolved some issues of relationship with the deceased. The death may not have been anticipated, such as suicide. Some person(s) may have been responsible for the death or feel that they were.

> *"Sudden [or violent] death can bring an overwhelming shock. The survivors are left with a great sense of the precariousness of existence; the experience can be shattering, a permanent alteration of life. Some are broken by it completely, and in the desire to help, it is well to be aware of this possibility.*
>
> **Diana Lampen, 1979**

In any time of grieving, the meeting can offer remembering and understanding. We are much better able to assist others in the dying and grieving process if we have explored and been open to our own feelings about death.

> *Dear Friends, cherish each other, celebrate life, celebrate its beginning and its end.*
>
> **Diana Lampen, 1979**

Responsibilities of the Meeting

Carried Out by the Worship and Ministry Committee and the Care and Counsel Committee (Overseers):

- Providing opportunities for members to prepare for death.

- Supporting the dying person and the person's family during dying and after death.

- Arranging a memorial meeting.

- For a Friend with no family: caring for remains (disposal of body), memorial meeting, and completing arrangements of worldly affairs.

- Supporting the bereaved in their grief.

Queries for the Individual

- What influence does your attitude toward death have on your life?

- Are you able to contemplate your death and the death of those closest to you? Do you give yourself time to grieve? When others mourn, do you let your love embrace them?

- Does your final disposition of your material possessions reflect your true values?

- Are your affairs in order? Have you made and do you maintain your will? Have you included plans for minor children and other dependents? Do you have a living will, durable powers of attorney for financial and medical decisions? Have you made written instructions for disposal of your body and memorial service or funeral?

- Have you explained your preparations to those who may survive you?

- Are you ready to deal with and honor the transition process from life to death?

Queries for the Meeting and Caregivers

- Have you discussed with those close to you their preparations for dying, death, and bereavement?

- How is your meeting preparing to meet occasions of dying and bereavement?

- Are we being present in the Spirit for a dying friend, the family, and the meeting?

- Are we prepared to let go when a loved one is dying, being mindful that our need for another to resist death may come from our own needs and fears?

- In assisting a family who is facing a death or in planning for a memorial meeting, are we being tender toward the family's wishes when they do not coincide with our own?

- Are we open to thinking through the subject of life after death?

- Are you angry at God because you or a loved one is going through a terminal illness? Do you think God can handle that anger?

- Have you made arrangements for surviving pets?

- Does the meeting respect and honor each individual's way of dying?

References and Advice for Monthly Meetings

It is recommended that meetings keep on file the following references to help prepare for death or help with arrangements at the time of death:

- *Dealing Creatively with Death—Manual of Death Education and Simple Burial,* Ernest Morgan (Ed.), 1994, Zinn Communications, 35-19 215 Place, Bayside, NY 11361 (also available from most Quaker bookstores).

- *Facing Death and Finding Hope,* Christine Longaker, 1997, Doubleday.

- Pamphlet on spiritual friends, *There Is a Hunger*, by Margery Larrabee, available from Friends General Conference and Baltimore Yearly Meeting.

- *Five Wishes*, by Jim Towey, is a guide to creating a living will. Copies are free of charge and are available through the Commission on Aging with Dignity, P.O. Box 11180, Tallahassee, FL 32302-1180.

- The addresses and phone numbers of the nearest hospices, which will take care of a dying person in the home, hospital, or hospice for the last months of life and provide counseling.

- Names and addresses of memorial societies may be obtained from Continental Association of Funeral and Memorial Societies, Suite 1100, 1828 L St. N. W., Washington, D.C. 20036

- *Dear Gift of Life: A Man's Encounter with Death*, Pendle Hill Pamphlet #142, by Bradford Smith, 1965.

- Information on how to give one's body to science or become an organ donor.

- The meeting can prepare itself as a community for death by organizing worship sharing, discussions, and workshops on death as a part of life, the process of grieving, sharing on "what death has meant to my life," and spiritual aspects of death. Informational and hands-on workshops could cover wills, living wills, durable powers of attorney for financial and medical matters, and "Do Not Resuscitate" orders (at time of terminal illness) over a patient's bed and on a patient's bracelet.

- All members of the meeting are asked to fill out the request forms (see www.seym.org under the Faith and Practice icon, an open book), "Requests to the monthly meeting about death or incapacity, and related matters." It may be helpful to get Friends to fill out these forms in conjunction with a workshop or worship sharing on Dying and Death.

- "Facing Death: Helping People Grieve," Vol. III, No. 2 of *Pastoral Care Newsletter,* January 1996, Family Relations Committee of Philadelphia Yearly Meeting, 1515 Cherry St, Philadelphia, PA 19103. To obtain copies or to subscribe, contact Jill Tafoya, at 215-241-7211 or jillt@pym.org. Also check the website www.pym.org/committee/pastoral-care-newsletter.

- *Questions and Answers on Death and Dying, Living with Death and Dying, On Death and Dying, On Children and Death,* various works by Elizabeth Kubler Ross, Collier Books.

- *Final Gifts*, Maggie Callanan and Patricia Kelley, 1993, Bantam Books.

- "Committed Partners' Legal Planning: Health, Separation and Estate Planning for Florida Committed Partners." This is a flier which can be obtained from Louis D. Putney, Esquire, at <louputney@hotmail.com>, 4805 S. Himes Avenue, Tampa, FL 33611, or 813-831-3376.

- "When Someone Dies in Florida." All the legal and practical things you need to do, how to come to terms with the loss, and how to arrange your own affairs to avoid the cost of probate. By Amelia E. Pohl, Esq. Or a similar document regarding Georgia or South Carolina laws.

Information and forms for requests to the monthly meeting about death or incapacity are found on the web at www.seym.org. Click on the Faith & Practice icon (an open book) at the bottom left of the home page.

CHAPTER 10

Clearness Committees

Friends may be most familiar with clearness as the process a meeting uses to decide whether to take a marriage under its care or to accept someone into membership. More and more, however, Friends are rediscovering the power of committees for clearness to guide and support members facing a crisis in their lives, sensing a leading towards a personal witness, or considering a change in life's direction.

Philadelphia Yearly Meeting, 1997

One of the special joys of a Friends meeting is the recurring reminder that each person contributes to the spiritual strength of the loving community and that the community is a guiding and sustaining force in the life of each individual. This mutual relationship strengthens the meeting and produces a bond of love and trust among its members, helping the meeting to find unity in its spiritual life and harmony in its actions. An important evidence of such spiritual unity in a meeting is that members feel free to ask for help in clarifying personal problems and in making decisions. These may relate to such matters as family adjustments, marriage difficulties, separation, divorce, stands to be taken on public issues, a new job, a required move to a distant area, a concern for personal witness, traveling in the ministry, and other personal decisions. Meetings usually respond to such requests for help by appointing committees on clearness.

Committees on Clearness for Personal Concerns

The forming of a clearness committee may be initiated by making a request to the meeting or by asking any member of the monthly meeting committee on care and counsel (oversight). It then becomes the responsibility of that committee to see that a clearness process is held. It is the duty of the committee on care and counsel to have intentional talks with the person seeking clearness (the seeker) on the nature of the problem. Such talks may convince the committee that the seeker needs professional counseling, rather than the help of a meeting committee, and it will advise the seeker accordingly. Alternatively, it may be clear to the committee that the seeker is already clear as to the course of action to be taken but needs counsel from appropriate Friends on how to carry out the action or decision (the "how," rather than the "whether"). In such a case, the committee on care and counsel should itself counsel with the seeker.

If, however, in the judgment of the committee on care and counsel, a clearness committee is appropriate, it appoints such a committee, in consultation with the seeker, possibly designating a clerk or convener from among its members. A clearness committee should be composed of persons who, because of gifts and background, seem particularly suitable to help with the problem. It is essential that a committee on clearness include only people who are acceptable both to the committee on care and counsel and to the seeker. A committee on clearness may include people of varied ages and experience and will normally include from three to five members unless the committee on care and counsel feels that special circumstances require a different number. Members of a clearness committee are charged to remain mindful of preserving the confidentiality of the process.

A committee on clearness meets with the seeker neither as professional counselors nor as friends discussing a problem and giving advice, but rather as caring Friends who share a spiritual community, drawing on the same resources that bind us together in meeting for worship. Maintaining a spirit of openness and prayerful waiting, the committee members seek to help the individual become clear about a problem or impending decision by joining with the individual to seek divine guidance. Their purpose is not to criticize, to elder, nor to offer their collective wisdom; they are there to listen without prejudice or judgment, to help clarify alternatives, to help communication if necessary, and to provide emotional support as an individual, or a small group such as a family, seeks to find God's will. As in a meeting for business, all parties seek clearness, hoping to find "truth and the right course of action." In meetings of a committee on clearness, however, there is no need to find unity; the seeker's clearness is being served, and the committee must finally stand aside, trusting that it may have been used to help the seeker see a problem or understand a customary Friends practice more clearly or to make his or her own decision in the Light. In no case does a committee on clearness make the decision or seek to force a decision to be made.

When the problem is one in which, in the judgment of the committee on care and counsel, the meeting is too emotionally involved to be helpful, members of the committee on clearness may be selected from outside the meeting community. The committee on worship and ministry of the yearly meeting or another monthly meeting may be consulted for advice about outside members. It is worth repeating that Friends seek clearness in the Light; partisanship and emotional involvement are to be avoided, in favor of openness and a desire to be used as a channel for the Light, so that the person or persons seeking help may reach clearness.

Finally, it is important that all members of a committee on clearness feel a responsibility to help the clerk or convener establish and maintain a right spirit in all meetings of the committee. The convener has the primary responsibility, but all members should cooperate in surrounding each meeting with a waiting silence, in beginning and ending with worship, in recalling Friends to worship during a meeting, and in remembering that a meeting of a committee on clearness is not an occasion for professional or amateur counseling but a spiritual exercise. Friends hope to be channels whereby one or more seeking individuals may receive light on a problem and divine guidance for a decision which they–with God alone–must make.

Committees on Clearness for Issues Requiring Meeting Action

The term "clearness" referred originally to clearness before marriage from other entangling engagements or obligations. Today, if the problem or decision involves a possible meeting action (such as a marriage, membership, release of a member, or the like), then both the meeting and the seeker must arrive at clearness before the action may be taken. In such cases, the clearness committee must be able to offer a decision or recommendation to the individual and the meeting. A meeting needs to be careful not to offer solutions entailing aid beyond its powers. See the Chapter 7 on membership and Chapter 8 on marriage for further guidance.

Queries for Those Asked to Serve on a Committee on Clearness

- Do you feel sufficiently at ease with the seeker and with the other members of the committee to work with them? Can you labor with them truly to provide an atmosphere in which divine guidance can be sought?

- If it is a family decision, can you listen without prejudice or bias to each member who is involved?

- Can you devote sufficient time and energy to this committee, knowing that it may take several meetings and many weeks or months to clarify the problem and provide support while the decision is made and carried out?

- Can you keep the committee discussions confidential and avoid gossiping or referring to them outside the committee?

Advices for Members of a Committee on Clearness

- Remember that your task is to serve as a channel for the Light to help the seeker deal with the problem or make a decision; neither you nor the committee deals directly with the problem or makes the decision.

- Try truly to listen to the other persons present, rather than just waiting for your turn to talk. Give equal attention to each person present, whether adult or child.

- Remember that people are capable of change and growth. Do not become absorbed with historical excuses or reasons for present problems. Focus on what is happening now to perpetuate the situation or to require a decision.

- Do not take sides if it is a family problem. Each person contributes to the problem, its continuation, and its solution.

- Try to avoid all suggestion of blame. It destroys openness and makes clearness difficult or impossible to reach.

- Refrain from giving advice or presenting solutions to others. Advice can either create resistance or dependency by taking over responsibility.

- Remember that your task is to allow the Light to help the seeker deal with the problem or make a decision; neither you nor the committee deals directly with the problem or makes the decision.

- Consider creating queries and advices for those seeking clearness, to be given to the inquirer before the clearness committee meets.

CHAPTER 11

The Monthly Meeting

*I was moved to recommend the setting up of Month-
ly Meetings throughout the nation. And the Lord
opened to me what I must do . . .*

George Fox, 1667

The monthly meeting is the basic unit of the Religious Society of Friends and the body in which membership resides. The
monthly meeting consists of Friends (members and attenders) who
meet together at regular intervals to wait upon God in meeting
for worship and meeting for worship with a concern for business.
In a Quaker meeting, Friends are "joined with God and with each
other," and there is order, unity, and power. It is upon this concept
of a meeting that the good order of Friends is based.

The monthly meeting encourages members and attenders
to live their lives under the guidance of the Spirit. The monthly
meeting receives and approves the membership of individuals,
appoints committees and individuals for its needs, oversees marriage and memorial meetings, extends spiritual care and material
aid to members and attenders, and responds in a spirit of love to
members and attenders who depart from Friends' testimonies. The
monthly meeting has the authority to nurture and record spiritual
gifts; to relate to its yearly meeting, to other bodies of Friends, and
to other organizations with common concerns; and to carry out any
work or assume any function consistent with the faith of Friends.

Development of Monthly Meetings

George Fox preached the good news that "Christ has come
to teach his people himself" and that the love and power of God
are available to all people without the help of priests, ministers, or
sacraments. Early Friends testified that they were drawn together
by shared experiences of Christ, the Inward Teacher, and they knew
that Christ is present to all and in all, but that each person perceives
the Light individually and in such measure as God gives; yet, there is

but one truth. The Light operating through each individual results in a gathered fellowship, the mystical union of individuals with each other. In this welding of many persons into one corporate body, many single openings and insights are forged into a more complete and unified understanding of God's will.

In the first years of the preaching of Fox and the Valiant Sixty, those Quakers who were the first convinced by Fox and took up with him the ministry of spreading the truth to the world, organization was informal and was only as much as was necessary for communication and coordination among the Children of Light and for those traveling in the cause of truth. This ministry depended chiefly upon the personal influence and incessant work of the early leaders. As the Religious Society of Friends grew, there came to be a need for organized nurture of groups, for communication among groups, for dealing with internal problems, and for a united response to government persecution. Fox recognized that a method had to be found for Friends as a body to take up decision-making rather than for that responsibility to be assumed by a few outstanding leaders.

Perceiving hypocrisy and worldliness in the religious hierarchies and institutions of his day, Fox was led to proclaim the "true Gospel Order," an order of which Christ was clearly the head and in which all Friends participated fully according to the measure of Light they had received. Some meetings which were essentially monthly meetings were established in the north of England as early as 1653, but the systematic establishment of monthly meetings and quarterly meetings came in 1667-71 as Fox traveled extensively throughout England to set these up.

> *And the Lord opened to me what I must do, and how the men's and women's monthly and quarterly meetings should be ordered and established in this and in other nations. . . .*
>
> **George Fox, 1667**

George Fox and Margaret Fell recognized that, in the male-controlled society of that time, women could take their rightful place in the Religious Society of Friends only when they were freed from the control and interference of men. Therefore, in the beginning and for many years following, men and women met separately to conduct business. When separate business meetings became unnecessary, they were laid down two hundred years later in favor of a combined meeting.

The basic framework of the Religious Society of Friends as it exists today is essentially the system that George Fox organized, though the terminology has changed. This framework exists as a channel for the "Kingdom of God" to be lived on earth. It provides both for the care and nourishment of seekers and also for the fulfillment of God's will in the world at large. At various times in the life of the Religious Society of Friends, one or the other aspect has been foremost, but both have always been present and are necessary for healthy meetings and a healthy Society of Friends.

Organization of the Monthly Meeting

The degree of organization of a monthly meeting depends upon its circumstances. Organization does not exist for its own sake but to provide what is needed for the meeting to function in right order. Simple in its early stages, a meeting's organization evolves with its needs. Experience has shown that organizational structure which has proved useful should not be changed unless there is good reason to do so, but structure which no longer serves a vital function should be laid down. Each person in the meeting is responsible for ministry in word and action, for the good order and material needs of the meeting, visitation, and faithfulness in testimonies according to the measure of Light that each is given.

Each monthly meeting appoints whatever clerks, positions, and committees are necessary for the corporate life of the meeting. Once a position or committee is created, then the nominating committee has the responsibility to find a suitable person for the job, jointly with the candidates. While growing in strength and experience, a small meeting may be able to function with only a clerk and with the meeting acting as a committee of the whole. As soon as possible, the meeting appoints a committee on ministry and counsel (or ministry and oversight) whose clerk is someone other than the clerk of the meeting. Provision for the religious education of children who come under its care is often an early concern of the meeting. Growth in the meeting may eventually lead to separating the committee on ministry and counsel (or ministry and oversight) into two committees, such as a worship and ministry committee and a care and counsel (oversight) committee.

The meeting selects its clerks and committee members from nominations. These nominations are made out of a joint discernment of gifts by the nominating committee and the candidates. The meeting is concerned not only with appointing a qualified person to each job but also with developing and using the talents and resources of all members and attenders. In asking people to assume various responsibilities, the meeting recognizes that different individuals have different gifts that are not equally appropriate for all positions in the meeting. Members and attenders should not be asked to take on inappropriate responsibilities out of a sense of "equality" or "taking turns."

The meeting must also be able to trust its clerks and committees and spare the entire body from many small decisions. The monthly meeting provides general guidelines for committee functions. The committees are then empowered to make decisions within those guidelines. A clerk or committee should feel free to call upon persons in the meeting, other monthly meetings, and yearly meeting whenever necessary to help in carrying out a particular responsibility.

It has been the custom among Friends for the clerk, the recording clerk, the assistant clerk, the treasurer, trustees, and the members of the committees concerned with worship and ministry, care and counsel (oversight), finance matters, and nominating to be members of the meeting. In small meetings, all other organizational positions and committee clerks can be made up of members or attenders. This is necessary so that the few members are not overburdened.

Clerks and Officers of the Monthly Meeting

The meeting appoints suitable and willing members as its clerks for a definite limited term of service, as led.

The Monthly Meeting Clerk

The clerk's basic function is to facilitate the business of the meeting. The clerk performs the role well by seeing to it that all pertinent business and concerns are presented to the monthly meeting clearly and in good order. Prior to meeting for worship with a concern for business, the clerk prayerfully considers those matters that might be brought before the monthly meeting. The clerk serves at the business sessions of the meeting, is responsible for the minutes of its proceedings (in concert with the recording clerk), and carries out the instructions of the meeting on all matters pertaining to the accomplishment of its business.

The following suggestions are meant especially for the clerk of a monthly meeting, but they apply generally to the clerk of any sort of a Friends meeting and may be useful guidelines for clerks of Friends committees.

The clerk faithfully attends meeting for worship, keeps close to the work of committees, and may need to attend meetings of the worship and ministry and care and counsel (oversight) committees in order to be aware of the condition of the meeting. (In some meetings, the clerk does not attend meetings of ministry and counsel. This practice has evolved for those meetings for the following reasons: It provides greater independence for the committee, and it frees the clerk from additional duties. In these circumstances, those meetings feel that the clerk is able to be adequately informed about sensitive matters without attending the meetings.)

The clerk should be a member of the meeting who has the confidence of its membership and who, in turn, has a real respect and warm regard for its individual members and attenders. The clerk should be spiritually sensitive so that the meeting for business may be helped to discover the leadership of the Spirit. Knowledge of *Faith and Practice* is essential, and knowledge of other Quaker literature is also helpful. The clerk should be able to comprehend readily, evaluate rightly, and state clearly and concisely an item of business or a concern that comes to the meeting. In order to gather the sense of the meeting at the proper time, the clerk needs to be able to listen receptively to what is said.

The clerk serves at all meetings for worship with a concern for business; if unavoidably prevented from attending, arrangements should be made for a substitute, usually the assistant clerk or a previous clerk. The clerk prepares an agenda prior to the meeting and encourages committee clerks and others to provide ahead of time reports, concerns, and other proposals to be placed on the agenda. The clerk's judgment of the relative urgency and importance of matters and their best place on the agenda can help greatly to facilitate the meeting's business. When an action has been discerned, a minute is composed, often by the clerk, in conjunction with the assistant clerk or recording clerk. After a minute requiring action has been approved and recorded, the clerk notifies the persons involved, preferably in writing, and makes sure that they understand their responsibility in carrying out the action.

The role of the clerk, in general, is not to express his or her own views but to see that others who are present participate as fully as possible in the discernment of business and that a few do not dominate it. A clerk who feels strongly led to express an opinion on a controversial matter should ask the assistant clerk or another Friend to act as clerk and formulate the sense of the meeting before assuming the role of participant. The clerk is mindful of the Spirit to set the pace of the meeting, so that its business may be accomplished without either undue delay or undue hurry. A sense of proportion and a sense of humor are helpful.

The clerk signs all official papers, marriage certificates, and minutes unless otherwise designated by a monthly meeting minute. If there are both a clerk and an assistant clerk, it is good practice for both to sign, particularly if legal documents or action minutes are involved. The clerk prepares and endorses certificates of transfer, minutes for sojourning members, minutes of travel for religious service, and letters of introduction as well as endorsing minutes or letters of visiting Friends. The clerk sees that correspondence which comes to the meeting is properly handled.

The clerk also has the responsibility to coordinate the activities of the meeting with those of the yearly meeting and other Quaker bodies of which it is a part. This includes seeing that the meeting is represented where necessary, that reports are written and sent to the proper persons, that business and concerns are sent at the proper time to the yearly meeting, and that items received from yearly meeting go to the proper persons and committees. It is understood that the clerk will call upon the assistant clerk and other meeting members to assist in all areas whenever necessary. For a fuller discussion of the clerk's responsibilities, see "The Role of the Clerk" in the chapter "Meeting for Worship with a Concern for Business" (Chapter 6).

Assistant Clerk

An assistant clerk may be nominated by the nominating committee or may be temporarily or permanently appointed by the clerk to act as an assistant to the clerk in whatever ways are mutually agreeable. The assistant clerk may be called upon to act for the clerk when the latter is unable to serve. Generally, the assistant clerk position serves as an apprenticeship in clerking.

Recording Clerk

A recording clerk helps the clerk during meetings for business in preparing minutes and in preserving records of the minutes in an organized archival fashion. For a fuller discussion of the recording clerk's responsibilities, see "The Role of the Recording Clerk" in Chapter 6, "Meeting for Worship with a Concern for Business."

Treasurer

The treasurer receives and disburses funds as the meeting directs and keeps the account books and all financial records of the meeting. The treasurer reports regularly to the meeting for business. The accounts should be audited at regular intervals in a manner decided by the monthly meeting. For guidance, contact the SEYM treasurer.

Meeting Membership Recorder

The meeting membership recorder keeps an accurate and timely record of the membership as provided for on the form recommended by the yearly meeting. Copies of this form are available from the SEYM website (www.seym.org) and also are found herein under Appendix G and Appendix H. Such records cover vital statistics, statements of conscientious objector clearness, dying, death, and bereavement forms, and so forth pertaining to the member and the member's immediate family. It is important that changes relating to membership, such as births, deaths, transfers, releases, or marriages, be promptly recorded and shared with the SEYM membership recorder. The meeting membership recorder prepares an annual list of the members and attenders of the monthly meeting for use by the SEYM membership recorder. This list is due each year to SEYM by winter interim business meeting or Jan. 31st.

The meeting membership recorder makes sure that other important records of the meeting are being properly taken care of. Minute and record books in current use are kept by the clerk responsible for them. Committee minutes are preserved together with important correspondence and legal papers, such as deeds, conveyances, and trusts, in a permanent repository protected from fire and loss. All minutes and records should be on acid-free paper of high quality. Typewritten records are preferable to those in handwriting. Efforts should be made to convert those records to permanent digital form, such as CD or DVD format. Multiple copies should be made and a copy sent to the SEYM administrative secretary.

The Work of Committees

Committees are tools the monthly meeting may use to facilitate its business. Meetings have found that much of their work can be done more appropriately in small groups than in the body of the meeting or by individuals. Committees of the whole are used by very small meetings. Attention to the following guidelines will aid in making committees useful tools rather than burdens in carrying out the business of the meeting.

Each meeting decides which committees are necessary to carry out its business and concerns. Friends have found it useful to have three different types of committees: standing, temporary, and ad hoc. Standing committees are permanent. Temporary committees are generally the various types of clearness committees. Ad hoc committees are short-term, voluntary committees formed for a specific task. There is no obligation to create any committee, although most monthly meetings find standing committees on worship and ministry, care and counsel (oversight), and nominating committees essential. Other standing committees often found in meetings are those on religious education, finance and budget, peace and social concerns, property, and hospitality. Members of temporary committees are selected carefully for a specific purpose and length of service. Ad hoc committees are sometimes useful for a particular project or concern. When a committee is no longer needed, it is appropriate to lay it down.

Members of committees need to be selected according to their abilities and concerns. Appointments to a committee are for a definite limited term of service and often are arranged so that terms overlap, to insure continuity. Meetings customarily appoint experienced and capable members of the Religious Society of Friends to the committee on worship and ministry, the committee on care and counsel (oversight), the nominating committee, and as clerks of most other committees. The purpose of this practice is to assign those responsibilities to persons of spiritual depth who are familiar with Friends' faith and ways of organizing and conducting meeting work. Occasionally when meetings identify such persons, even though they may not be members, meetings may choose them for those responsibilities.

Friends conduct business together in faith that there is one divine Spirit that is accessible to all; when Friends wait upon and heed the Light of Truth within them, its Spirit will lead to unity. This faith is the foundation for every group decision. In practical terms, this means that all such meetings are held in a context of worship and that those present repeatedly and consciously seek divine guidance. Committees conduct business in this same manner. It is important that members of committees attend meeting for worship with a concern for business regularly in order to assure smooth coordination between the committees and the meeting.

Committees are asked to keep minutes of their meetings and report to the monthly meeting for business regularly. All proposed action of committees in the name of the meeting requires prior approval by the monthly meeting. In bringing a matter to the meeting for business, it is useful for the committee to supply a concise summary of background material and a clear statement of the kind of response wanted from the meeting. In the meeting for business, Friends need to consider carefully the recommendations of a committee and at the same time not redo the work of the committee. Mutual trust between the meeting and a committee and faith in the power of God over all will help achieve the proper balance.

It is important that all committee members feel a responsibility to help the clerk or convener establish and maintain a right spirit in all meetings of the committee. The convener has the primary responsibility, but all members should cooperate in surrounding each meeting with a waiting silence, in beginning and ending with worship, in recalling Friends to worship during a meeting, and in remembering that any meeting is a spiritual exercise, one in which Friends hope to be channels for divine guidance by focusing Light on a concern and uniting in a decision.

Special Functions of the Committees on Worship and Ministry and on Care and Counsel (Also Known as Oversight)

The closely related functions of these two committees are central to the life of the meeting. The primary focus of the committee on worship and ministry is the spiritual life of the meeting, while the committee on care and counsel (oversight) is mainly concerned with the individual members, including their relationship to the meeting. Meetings should understand the different functions of these two committees and see that these functions are faithfully carried out. These committees have a special responsibility to watch over, encourage, and develop the care of members for each other and for the life of the meeting, though all in the meeting share in the responsibility for such care. In smaller meetings the functions of both committees are often combined into one committee; some meetings may call the single committee the committee on ministry and counsel with the term "counsel" covering the functions of the term "oversight" as is currently in use in some meetings.

The Committee on Worship and Ministry

The function of the committee on worship and ministry is to foster and strengthen the spiritual life of the meeting by nurturing the meeting for worship and the spiritual growth of individuals in the meeting. Though this is a challenging assignment and one which is difficult to express in specifics, its importance to the life of the meeting cannot be overemphasized. The first responsibility of members of this committee is to deepen their own spiritual lives and their preparation for worship.

The worship and ministry committee includes members of varied ages and gifts who are faithful in worship and sensitive to the life of the Spirit. It includes both Friends inclined to speak in meeting for worship and those less inclined to do so. It also includes Friends of good judgment who have a gift for counseling with others concerning sensitivity to divine prompting.

The worship and ministry committee meets regularly to consider the meeting for worship and to keep it under constant review, prayer, and care. Their own example is an important means through which they can strengthen the meeting for worship. Their concern during the week, the promptness and reverence with which they approach the meeting for worship, and their faithfulness in responding to and staying within the guidance of the Spirit are the most effective ways through which they may deepen the quality of worship. Through self-examination, prayer, and mutual counsel they also may help one another and the meeting to grow in worship and ministry. An ever-renewed dedication to worship is almost always the best cure for what may need guidance in a meeting for worship.

> *[Committee members] thus abiding in a simple and patient submission to the will of God, and keeping down to the openings of divine life in themselves, may witness a growth in their gifts, and will also be preserved from extending their declarations further than they find the power of truth to accompany them.*
>
> **Discipline of the Yearly Meeting of Friends held in Baltimore, 1806**

The worship and ministry committee is also responsible for details in connection with meeting for worship, such as providing for the welcome of visitors (also see the responsibilities of the hospitality committee, later in this chapter), for encouraging promptness at meeting, and for signaling the rise of meeting for worship.

The worship and ministry committee should at times hold meetings for all members and attenders to share their experience and search for insight concerning the meeting for worship and the meeting for worship with a concern for business.

The worship and ministry committee should nurture the meeting for worship by giving appropriate attention to the quality of vocal ministry and the ministry of stillness that springs from a centered silence. The committee encourages all Friends to give adequate time to study, meditation, prayer, daily worship, and other ways of preparing themselves for worship. One way to encourage this is by corporate review and discussion of the queries and advices. Committee members should be mindful that there are differences in background, fluency of expression, and power of interpretation among those who may be led to speak in meeting for worship. They have responsibility to give sympathetic encouragement to those who show promising gifts and to give loving and tender guidance to those who speak unacceptably or at undue length or with too great frequency. They should endeavor to open the way for those who are timid and inexperienced in vocal ministry and should encourage all Friends in the ministry of listening as if listening to God. In trying to be helpful, they should be governed by a sense of the common seeking of human beings for right guidance rather than by an assumption of superior wisdom.

The worship and ministry committee should seek to deepen the spiritual lives of the individuals in the meeting and to encourage their varied gifts for ministry and service, whether through vocal ministry, teaching and counseling, or through aesthetic, social, and practical ways of expression. This committee should encourage private worship, prayer, meditation, and devotional reading which may promote growth in the spiritual life and prepare each individual for the corporate worship of the meeting. It may wish to obtain and circulate appropriate literature and arrange for retreats, study groups, and spiritual sharing groups.

The worship and ministry committee nurtures the religious education of all who attend the meeting. If there is a committee on adult religious education, worship and ministry should coordinate with it and develop a mutual set of priorities. Worship and ministry should be mindful of the quality of religious education being provided for the children. When concerns arise, it should consult with the religious education committee in charge of the children's First Day School to resolve these concerns.

Recognizing and Recording Gifts of Ministry

The gifts of the Spirit are diverse. Friends' ministry may include pastoral care in settings such as hospitals and prisons. Friends' work in these areas may be especially benefited by the intentional recording as ministers of those so gifted, although all Friends are considered ministers. In SEYM, meetings are continuing to undertake the recognition of the gifts of the Spirit and beginning to discern a process for recording ministers. Friends' ministry is based upon the experience that the gifts of the Holy Spirit may be bestowed upon anyone at any time.

A monthly meeting may, upon the advice of its committee on worship and ministry, record as ministers those members whom they recognize as having a clear leading to vocal ministry, to prayer, or to counseling. This recognition is not one of status or privilege and should be reviewed at least every two years. It is an affirmation based upon loving trust. The meeting trusts that the individuals so recorded will, in all humility, diligently nurture and exercise the gift of ministry in order that the meeting as a whole may be nourished. The individuals trust that the meeting will encourage and sustain them, not only to liberate them to undertake the disciplines of prayer, study and retreat that help clarify the springs of ministry but also to lovingly and faithfully counsel them. Such nurture, encouragement, and discipline are of special significance for younger members who, out of diffidence or unawareness, may discount their gifts and let them wither.

For Gainesville Monthly Meeting's process of recording the gifts of ministry, see Chapter 16, Appendix A.

The Committee on Care and Counsel (Also Known as Oversight)

The committee on care and counsel is responsible for the care of members, attenders, and the corporate life of the meeting under the guidance of the Spirit. In providing this pastoral care, the committee is concerned with the more outward aspects of building a fellowship in which all people find acceptance, loving care, and opportunity for service. Then all may grow in grace and, liberated from preoccupation with self, be helped to serve humanity creatively.

Membership on the committee on care and counsel calls for dedication, tact, and discretion and should be entered into prayerfully, with a willingness to be of service. The meeting selects members to serve on this committee who are representative of the varied make-up of the meeting and who are persons of experience, sympathy, and good judgment. Where possible, some members of the committee should have counseling skills. The committee should meet regularly, hold each person in the meeting community in the

Light, and carry on their work in a spirit of dedication and love.

Care of the Meeting Community

- The care and counsel committee should become acquainted with meeting members and regular attenders and their gifts, visit them in their homes if possible, and maintain contact with all members and attenders in a spirit of affectionate interest and loving care. To foster the knowledge of one another in things both temporal and eternal, they encourage members and attenders to visit in each other's homes and stimulate the meeting to undertake activities that will deepen the meeting fellowship.

- They also encourage Friends to attend the annual gathering of the Southeastern Yearly Meeting and similar gatherings, advising on possible financial assistance for this purpose.

- The care and counsel committee considers and recommends action upon requests for membership, transfer, and withdrawal of membership (see Chapter 7 on Membership).

- They keep in touch with inactive members, seeking ways of furthering their interest in the meeting. If non-participation and disinterest continue for a prolonged period, the Friend should be encouraged to withdraw from membership.

- At least once a year, letters should be written to nonresident members to give them news of the meeting and its activities and to let them know that the meeting is interested in their welfare.

- When appropriate, transfer of membership of nonresident Friends to a nearby meeting should be encouraged. The committee notifies other monthly meetings promptly when Friends and faithful attenders move into their area, whether or not transfer of membership is involved.

- This committee, in cooperation with the membership recorder and the treasurer, is responsible for seeing that an accurate list of meeting members and attenders is sent to SEYM every year by the date of the winter interim business meeting or as late as Jan. 31st.

- It is concerned for the nurture of the religious life of children and young people, their participation in the meeting, and their preparation for membership. When it seems right, it encourages application for membership from those who may be holding back through shyness or a sense of unworthiness.

- The care and counsel committee assists those contemplating and entering into marriage or ceremony of commitment under the care of the meeting and the laying down (divorce) of the marriage or committed relationship (see Chapter 8, Marriage and Commitment). It gives care and aid in needed arrangements at the time of death (see Chapter 9, Dying, Death, and Bereavement).

- The committee seeks to be of help in clarifying matters involving organization, practice, and procedure in the Religious Society of Friends.

- The committee seeks to be of help in clearing up misunderstandings and reconciling differences which may come about in the meeting.

- Committee members are concerned with the welfare of any who are ill, incapacitated, troubled, or in material need. The committee sees that they are visited, counseled, and assisted as may be required. The meeting needs to provide the committee with appropriate financial resources to be used at its discretion for this function.

Individual Counseling and Care

The care and counsel committee has responsibility for any needed clearness and counseling within the meeting. The committee is advised to choose counselors fitted for its needs from among themselves or other qualified persons in the meeting. Qualifications of a good counselor include approachability, warmth, empathy, spiritual insight without prejudice, the capacity to listen without judging, and ability to keep confidences. The meeting for worship can be a basic resource in counseling; through corporate worship, the strength and power of God's love may open a way that reaches to the hidden depths of personal problems, as we all strive to grow in spiritual and emotional maturity. However, the meeting for worship should remain worship centered; it should not become an occasion for dialogue on personal problems.

In dealing with particular needs, this committee keeps in mind that listening is a key part of the helping process. It needs to be sensitive to those who may not recognize their need for counseling or who hesitate to seek help. To listen helpfully and creatively involves faith in the person and in God, a desire to understand, patience, and avoidance of giving advice. The counselor or committee may suggest new ways of looking at the problem and possible solutions, but decisions are always left to the person involved in acting on their concern. Growth, independence, and standing on one's own feet are to be encouraged. Emotional support in a hard decision can be most helpful. Where a meeting ultimately determines that individual behavior precludes further involvement with the individual, then the meeting no longer allows the individual to make the decision about participation.

> *If there happen any difference among Friends, either with Friends or between Friends and the world, let it be put to reference [let it be referred to a third party], if it can not be ended between themselves: and all that are concerned to end any difference, let them have but one ear to one party, and let them reserve the other ear to hear the other party; so that they may judge impartially of matters, without affection or favour, or respect of persons.*
>
> **George Fox, 1679**

A problem may be too serious for the committee on care and counsel to handle alone; in which case a referral to professionals is appropriate. Members of the committee need to have knowledge of resources for counseling assistance in the wider community, such as clinics, family and social services, physicians, and psychiatrists. The committee may call upon the meeting to be of assistance when professional help is required. Practical assistance such as Friends offer in other times of stress, illness, or sorrow may be appropriate. Standing by, listening, and helping to plan without dictating outcomes can also be of great help in a critical time.

When an individual, family, or other group is facing a difficult situation, a committee on clearness (or a committee of concern) may be requested or suggested by members of the meeting or the clerk. The committee on care and counsel assumes responsibility for setting up the clearness committee in consultation with the individual or group concerned. Situations in which clearness is sought may include adjustments in marriage, separation, divorce, stands to be taken on public issues, a new job, a required move to a distant area, a concern for personal witness, traveling in the ministry, and other personal decisions. The committee and the individual or group meet together in worship to seek God's guidance. Valuable insights often result from the worship sharing in one or more sessions. (See "Clearness Committees," Chapter 10.)

Joint Responsibilities of Worship and Ministry and Care and Counsel

Some meetings have both a committee on worship and ministry and a committee on care and counsel. Although these committees usually meet separately, it is important that they keep in touch with each other. A joint retreat, for a day or a weekend, can be of benefit for the life of the committees and that of the meeting. They should meet together at least twice a year to review responsibilities and concerns.

These committees share two responsibilities:

• These committees are sometimes asked by a monthly meeting to share in the nurture of worship groups and preparative meetings under its care, although more often a separate committee may be appointed.

- In the fall, they begin to prepare the annual report of the spiritual state of the monthly meeting. The spiritual state of the monthly meeting report is prepared in time to be approved by the meeting for worship with a concern for business before being forwarded in early January to the SEYM administrative secretary. This report is included in the "Documents in Advance" for the annual yearly meeting sessions. The spiritual state of the monthly meeting report should be a self-examination by the meeting and its members of their spiritual strengths and weaknesses and of efforts to foster growth in the spiritual life. Reports may cover the full range of interests, concerns, and statistics but should emphasize those indicative of the spiritual health of the meeting.

To facilitate the preparation of this report, the committee on worship and ministry and the committee on care and counsel may meet together and explore the spiritual condition of the meeting. They may then formulate a series of queries for a response from the meeting as the basis of the report or may ask one or more of their members to draft a preliminary report for searching consideration by the meeting. Another approach is to use the queries from SEYM as the basis of preparation of the state of the meeting report.

The Nominating Committee

The nominating committee handles one of the most important functions of the meeting and serves throughout the year. The meeting depends upon this small group of Friends to discern the most appropriate persons to fulfill meeting responsibilities and to use to best advantage the capabilities of meeting members and attenders. The nominating committee should be representative of the meeting and its members. Committee members should serve overlapping but short terms to ensure continuity and avoid loss of experience while at the same time providing broad sharing of Friends in the nominating process. If appropriate for the meeting, the monthly meeting clerk may choose an ad hoc "naming committee." The ad hoc "naming committee" will nominate people to the nominating committee, subject to the approval of the monthly meeting, after which the ad hoc "naming committee" is laid down.

Members of the nominating committee should be familiar with the function and structure of the meeting and with the "good order of Friends." They should be aware of the interests, talents, proven experience, latent gifts, and potential leadership of meeting participants. The committee must begin its work well in advance of the date when its nominations for new clerks, positions, committees, and committee clerks are presented to the monthly meeting. As the committee meets in worship, names may rise up to serve the meeting, as the Spirit leads. Nominees are asked if they feel led to serve. After the first reading of the proposed slate of nominations, the meeting postpones action for a month, during which time any member may seek clarification or suggest changes in the nominations to the nominating committee. This committee continues to serve as a standing committee throughout the year to nominate persons to fill vacancies that may occur or to fill new positions which the meeting may establish.

Advices to the Nominating Committee

The best interests of the meeting and its participants will be served if the nominating committee keeps in mind the following suggestions:

- In approaching a person, the committee sees that details of the nominating process are understood by the potential nominee, including the fact that the meeting, not the committee, is responsible for the ultimate appointment.

- The approach to a potential nominee should not be made casually. The duties involved in any position should be fully understood by the nominating committee and relayed to the person approached for nomination, including expected length of term of service. It is strongly recommended that a written job description be prepared and given to a prospective nominee.

- Not all Friends are equally qualified for a particular responsibility, so "taking turns" and rewarding long service are to be avoided in making nominations. Friends are asked to remember that service is based on leadings and being faithful to the Light.

- The clerk of a committee may be consulted about members proposed for that committee. When two persons are to work together closely, they may both be consulted about the proposed arrangement.

- If a committee clerk cannot be identified by the nominating committee, a convener may be named to help the committee members discern, as the Spirit leads, who is best able to clerk the committee. Where appropriate, assistant clerks may be appointed to be in training to assume responsibility at the end of the term of service of the current clerks. New committee clerks are encouraged to look for a mentor for help when assuming new responsibilities. Early in his or her term of service, the committee clerk tries to identify the gifts of committee members that can be nurtured, with the intent of preparing a committee member to become the next clerk or assistant clerk.

Religious Education Committee

Religious education is a lifelong endeavor. It begins in the family, as parents take responsibility for their own religious education and that of their children. Monthly meetings have a continuing responsibility to foster understanding of the beliefs and practices of Friends to members, attenders, and children under their care, enhancing full participation in the life of the meeting. Meetings are expected to offer religious education programs for young and adult members and attenders, drawing on the many resources of the religious education committees of the yearly meeting, Friends General Conference, and others. A thriving religious education program can also include study groups, conferences, retreats, service projects, and libraries.

The worship and ministry committee and the care and counsel committee both have responsibilities linked to the religious education of the meeting, so it is important to develop a way to jointly agree on priorities while acknowledging the differences between adult and children's education.

Peace and Social Concerns Committee

Participants in the meeting may feel a responsibility to address a variety of issues in their community, state, nation, and world, for example, homelessness, health care, and migrant concerns. Ways of giving life to these leadings include the following:

- Maintaining a committee to address peace and social justice issues. This committee may recommend particular action to individuals and to the meeting itself.

- Planning and carrying out service projects as corporate activities of the meeting.

- Encouraging members and attenders to participate in the work for social change by larger Quaker groups or other bodies or to independently pursue leadings to social actions consistent with Friends' testimonies. Members and attenders who appear to be moved by a genuine prompting of the Spirit may be supported in leadings that not all share.

- Contributing services or money to help free a member to pursue a social concern as a "released Friend."

Finance Committee and Trustees

Monthly meetings solicit, maintain, and disburse operating funds for their own purposes and raise funds for the yearly meeting and other bodies they may decide to support. They may hold and maintain real property. They may hold and maintain trust funds. These tasks and responsibilities are entrusted to a treasurer and a finance committee and, if needed, trustees or other committees. The books of those holding funds are audited or reviewed at least annually. The treasurer is an ex-officio member of the finance committee.

The finance committee discerns the financial needs and resources of the monthly meeting. It prepares a budget or financial outlook for each year. It makes regular reports to the monthly meeting regarding the budget and financial outlook and, in conjunction with the treasurer, the current financial health of the meeting. From time to time the finance committee communicates with the members and attenders of the meeting regarding the financial needs of the meeting.

Trustees are entrusted with managing and disbursing long-term investments, trusts, and real property. The finance committee and trustees are charged with seeking, investing, and using the financial assets of the monthly meeting in accordance with accepted Quaker principles, approved minutes of the monthly meeting, and the expressed instructions of contributors of restricted donations, if accepted by the monthly meeting. Managing the financing of the acquisition or improvement of real property may be under the care of the finance committee, trustees, or temporary committees set up for these purposes.

Outreach Committee

By extending a welcome to people in the community and interpreting our faith to them through words and example, we practice a traditional form of Quaker ministry. Outreach is everyone's responsibility in the meeting. In larger meetings, an outreach committee can assist in the care of seekers, attenders, and new members, helping to include them in the life of the meeting and encouraging them to join in community. Another facet of outreach is to seek appropriate ways to publicize the existence and purpose of the local Friends meeting to the larger community.

Hospitality Committee

"The Quaker Practice of Hospitality" (based on an article by Nancy Fennell in the October 2005 *Friends Journal*, used by permission of the author.)

Friends want to be welcoming to all who attend our meetings, whether they are attending for the first time, are invited guests, or are regular attenders. Therefore, we don't leave this matter to chance; we make regular practices that intend to convey our sense of hospitality to all who come to our meeting.

Hospitality is a serious ministry, and it rests upon a deep base. When a guest or visitor walks through our meetinghouse door, some reflection of Spirit has arrived in our midst. One whom God loves deeply and infinitely has come to be with us; a gift has been sent. So we approach to receive our gift with open hearts and great joy; we seek to connect with that of God in our visitor.

There are four aspects of meeting hospitality we practice:
- Preparation
- Sharing
- Serving
- Follow-up.

The steps below specifically apply to hospitality for people who are new to the meeting, but they apply more broadly for all attenders.

- Preparation for hospitality includes ensuring that when folks arrive at meeting, there will be a welcoming environment. Many small steps contribute to this, including the following:

    a. Having the meetinghouse set up and ready so we can attend to visitors and not housekeeping duties.

    a. Having name tags, markers, guest books, and literature readily available.

    a. Ensuring that someone greets and quickly establishes some sense of who the newcomer is and to what extent he or she is familiar with our worship or needs more in-depth explanation. Everyone in the meeting should take on this responsibility, although some may feel too shy to comfortably meet strangers. We have found that if only one or a few meeting members are responsible to greet visitors, there are too many times that the visitor goes unwelcomed or later is left uncomfortably alone.

a. Ensuring that directions to the meeting are available so interested visitors can find us. Web sites are increasingly used by searchers, but standard information also should be available in *Friends Journal* and similar publications. Meetings that have phone numbers listed should ensure that those phones are answered and that messages are responded to.

If we are fully prepared to attend to a visitor, we make a powerful statement that "we thought about you ahead of your coming; we honor you as you are honoring us by being here."

- Sharing with a stranger who comes to our meeting for worship includes the following:

  a. In the initial introductory phase, we greet the visitor and share our name, our attention, and our interest. We share respect by listening deeply and solely to our visitor. We share companionship.

  a. Secondly, we share that which is most precious to us —our worship. Being thoughtful about this, we do not leave our visitor to worship by himself in a back row, outside the circle, or isolated by several vacant chairs on either side. Instead, we symbolically close the gap by narrowing physical space between the community and the newcomer and invite her to join close with us.

  a. Thirdly, at the rise of meeting for worship, we see that the visitor is introduced to all and introduce ourselves in return. We ask the guest to tell how he came to be with us and seek bits of information that allow us to connect and relate. When there is a time for socializing, we share the time with the visitor and ensure she is not left alone.

We must be especially sensitive to the situation when the visitor has something important to share with us; it could be a Spirit-led message, a personal problem, or an unexpected concern. Our practice should be to welcome the sharing a stranger brings, recognizing that it may call for special abilities to address concerns that come up. During our sharing, we must be alert to not use "Quakerese" or references to Friends' organizations or practices that the visitor may not know about or understand.

- Serving may simply be the offering of food and drink that often accompanies a social time following worship. Other aspects of serving may include addressing special concerns a visitor brings. Many meetings have been visited by people who need assistance with food and shelter, so providing assistance in an appropriate way is another aspect of serving. True hospitality is serving the needs of the visitor.

- Follow-up with the newcomer is simply the act of getting in touch with him at some later time (a few days at most) to ensure that the greetings and welcome we attempted to convey were successful and that the visitor understands we were grateful for his presence and interest and would welcome a return visit. This isn't understood to be an effort to convince or proselytize. We have asked guests to sign our guest book to enable us to make these follow-up contacts, so we should use the information as intended and make some contact. The meeting needs to be organized about the follow-up so it isn't forgotten or assigned to someone who wasn't present.

Once the meeting has taken an honest look at how well it is doing with hospitality, changes can be addressed and improvements made. Hospitality involves action; it is a doing and a practice.

Meeting Place, Property, or Building and Grounds Committee

This committee has care of the meeting's space and care of the property if the meeting owns any real estate. The meeting should appoint one or more Friends to have care of the meeting's material property, contractual agreements for rental space, and maintenance and cleaning of meeting-place premises whether owned or by contract if rented.

Other Committees

Additional committees may be selected by meetings as needed.

Volunteers and Paid Staff

Friends have been reluctant to deviate from the tradition of volunteerism that has marked the Society from its beginnings. Volunteers, as they work together for the meeting, often find their religious lives mutually strengthened, their sense of community deepened, and their commitment as members affirmed. These dividends of volunteerism diminish when volunteers find themselves overcommitted. Some meetings have found themselves strengthened spiritually when they have employed staff to perform a few essential functions, such as child care, general secretarial work, or maintenance of buildings and grounds.

Traveling Friends

From the beginning, Quakers have felt a special bond that has transcended geographical and cultural boundaries and has made easier the offer of hospitality to traveling Friends on the one hand and the quiet confidence of welcome on the other. Friendly intervisitation, whether formal or informal, has for more than 350 years provided an important opening for understanding and cooperation in the affairs of Friends and for mutual ministry and spiritual growth. Friends are encouraged, therefore, as they travel on business or holiday, to allow time for visits with meetings or with individual Friends and families in the regions they may pass through. Friends General Conference maintains a directory of Friends who offer hospitality to traveling Friends which is obtainable from the FGC Bookstore.

Letters of Introduction

In making such Friendly visits, many have found letters of introduction from home meetings to be helpful. Such letters, prepared by the monthly meeting clerk at the request of those members planning to travel, usually state the fact of membership, give some indication of participation and witness in the affairs of our Religious Society, and express such greetings as are deemed appropriate. Since Friends travel for a wide variety of purposes, letters of introduction do not suggest specific obligations either on the visitor or on those visited and may be issued by the clerk without formal consideration by the meeting. The letter is usually presented by the traveler to meetings or other Friends visited, who may choose to write a return greeting on the letter, which is presented to the issuing meeting upon return. When appropriate, the meeting may also grant a letter of introduction to a faithful attender.

Minutes of Travel for Religious Service

Friends may find themselves under a sense of divine leading to travel in support of an important cause or to nurture the religious life of Friends' families and meetings or of other groups. In carrying out such leadings, they find it supportive to take with them a formal minute for religious service from their monthly meeting.

A meeting should issue such a minute only after the concern has been favorably recommended to the monthly meeting by a clearness committee and approved by the monthly meeting. A minute of religious service, signed by the clerk, should state clearly the nature, scope, and duration of the proposed service. It should affirm the meeting's support of the Friend(s) involved and release the Friend(s) from meeting responsibilities until the service is at an end. The monthly meeting issuing a minute of travel for religious service should see that insofar as possible the proposed service is not hampered by a lack of funds or other support.

After adoption by a monthly meeting, a minute of religious service is usually submitted for approval, endorsement, and support by the yearly meeting committee on worship and ministry, especially if the minute will be used beyond the bounds of the yearly meeting.

Friends traveling with such minutes are welcomed by those among whom they visit and are invited to lay their concerns before appropriate gatherings. It is customary for minutes to be endorsed at the conclusion of the gatherings by the clerk of each gathering. After the completion of the service proposed, a minute for religious service should be returned promptly with a verbal or written report to those meetings who had earlier reviewed the concern and minuted their support.

A Friend who proposes to travel under religious concern may find, as have Friends in the past, that it is a source of strength and comfort to be accompanied by another Friend who is sympathetic to the concern and able to give counsel and encouragement.

Annual or Biennial Queries for Monthly Meetings

Friends have found that the regular consideration of the following queries is helpful for maintaining good order as the meeting community seeks to fulfill its responsibilities. These queries would be most helpful if addressed to meeting for worship with a concern for business on an annual basis.

State of the Meeting

- Is the meeting in a right-ordered state of spiritual and material health, its problems manageable with its own resources? If not, has it considered calling on the yearly meeting or other meetings for assistance?

Committees

- Do committees have written descriptions and a clear understanding of their responsibilities assigned by the meeting? Are they right-ordered and functioning in ways that meet the needs of the meeting, and do they report regularly to the meeting?

Economic Resources

- Are endowments and working capital invested in socially responsible ways? Is the meeting aware of the services of organizations such as the Friends Extension Corporation, the Friends Meeting House Fund, and the Friends Fiduciary Corporation? Is the income of restricted donations or endowments put to the uses specified or the concerns indicated by the donor?

- Since title to real property may be held in one of several ways, is it

    a) held by the meeting as a permanent corporate body? If held by an individual or group, what are the meeting's plans for assuming title?

    b) held by the Friends Fiduciary Corporation? If so, is the meeting aware of the potential inconveniences?

    c) held by trustees? If so, are the trustees appropriately serving the meeting?

- Are fire and liability precautions and insurance in good order, as appropriate?

- Is real property managed with care for nature's integrity? Are burial grounds, if any, simple in style and carefully maintained, with accurate records in the hands of a responsible committee?

- Are policies and practices for hiring and dismissal of employees consonant with Friends' belief? Do employees receive caring oversight and equitable compensation?

- Are patterns of spending and consumption socially and environmentally responsible?

Finance

- Does the monthly meeting have a long-term financial plan? Does it establish clear policies, including an annual budgetary process, for the raising, custody, and spending of money?

- Are the accounts of custodians of meeting funds regularly audited or competently reviewed and reports made to the monthly meeting? Does the meeting require bodies under its care to undergo regular audits or reviews and to send the reports to the meeting?

- Are the financial records in good order, up to date, and kept on archival paper?

- Have the meeting's treasurer and finance committee observed all state and federal regulations governing the incorporation of the meeting and the handling of its finances? Where there is doubt, has the yearly meeting or legal counsel been consulted?

- Is the burden for financial support appropriately carried among the members and attenders of the meeting?

- Does the meeting have a process for extending financial aid to members suffering as a result of a witness to Friends' testimonies or for other reasons?

- Does the meeting foster activities or programs such as volunteer work days, fundraising, bake sales, garage sales, and so forth that strengthen its ability to devote financial resources to good works?

Records

- Are official membership records in good order, up to date, and kept on archival paper? Are they reviewed at least annually by the committee on care and counsel (oversight)?

- Are records of members and attenders kept in good order on a formal basis with periodic backup of data? Records may be kept in a computer database or databases, from which can be drawn useful information for building the meeting community, such as newsletter mailing labels, lists of children by age groups, and telephone numbers.

- If the meeting is incorporated, are its records maintained and its corporate procedures conducted in accordance with good practice and legal requirements?

- Are minutes of the monthly meeting and of significant committees accurately and neatly kept on acid-free paper and sent from time to time to the SEYM archives committee or other suitable Quaker archives for their protection and storage in accordance with their procedures?

For those Friends wishing to understand in full the detailed responsibilities of the yearly meeting clerks, officers, standing committees, and representatives to SEYM-affiliated organizations, in addition to the *Faith and Practice*, please consult the *SEYM Operational Handbook, Procedures, and Job Descriptions* available from SEYM Publications and QuakerBooks.org.

CHAPTER 12

ESTABLISHING NEW FRIENDS MEETINGS

Ye that are turned to the light, and gathered into it, meet together and keep your meetings, that ye may feel and see the life of God among you, and know that in one another.

George Fox, 1659

Christ Jesus . . . you may see the beginning of his setting up his meetings, when he saith, "Where two or three are gathered together in my name, I am in the midst of them."

George Fox, 1667

Few at first took care for the establishing men and women's meetings, though they were generally owned when they understood them: but the everlasting God, that sent me forth by his everlasting power, first to declare his everlasting gospel; then after people had received the gospel, I was moved to go through the nation, to advise them to set up the men's meetings, and the women's, many of which were set up.

George Fox, 1681

Southeastern Yearly Meeting (SEYM) encourages all who are moved to worship God after the manner of Friends to do so by participation in a Friends worship group, a preparative meeting, or a monthly meeting.

Establishing Friends Worship Groups

In areas where no Friends meetings exist, individual Friends and those drawn to Friends' ways are encouraged to meet together for worship and to seek divine guidance. A natural experience arising out of this shared worship is a desire to participate in the wider community of Friends by becoming a recognized worship group within the yearly meeting.

A Friends worship group may also be formed when an established monthly meeting has grown so large that it becomes desirable for a group to meet separately or when some of its members live a great distance from the established Friends meeting. Such a worship group should follow a similar path as described below.

A worship group is a gathering of persons who meet regularly for public worship after the manner of Friends and desire to be identified as a Friends group. This worship group becomes part of the Quaker faith community by relating to a monthly meeting and the yearly meeting.

As a Friends worship group develops, it asks to be taken under the care of a monthly meeting. If there are no nearby monthly meetings able to undertake the care for the new Friends worship group, it may apply to be directly under the care of the yearly meeting (SEYM). The monthly meeting or SEYM will appoint a committee of care (see advices to care committees at the end of this chapter) to be available for support and guidance, but this action does not presume any particular path of development. It does, however, create a recognized relationship with the Religious Society of Friends by establishing regular contacts within the wider world of Friends and providing an avenue for membership of individuals, which comes only through a monthly meeting .

A Friends worship group names one of the group to serve as the convener and correspondent. It is beneficial if the convener/correspondent is a member of the Religious Society of Friends. Communications from the monthly meeting and SEYM (and other Friends groups and organizations) are addressed to the correspondent, who is responsible for sharing these with the entire worship group.

Each Friends worship group should organize only to the degree that is right for it at a particular time, neither over-organizing nor avoiding whatever organization is needed to nurture the interests and concerns of its participants, including children. Organization also provides an avenue for contacts with other Friends groups and with the wider body of the Religious Society of Friends, both of which can enrich the life of the worship group.

Actions that may be carried out **ONLY** with the help and clearness of the monthly meeting that has care of the worship group include the following:

- receiving requests for membership in the Religious Society of Friends,

- receiving or holding charitable contributions for tax-deduction purposes,

- holding weddings or memorial meetings,

- or otherwise acting formally as an established monthly meeting.

If a yearly meeting committee of care has the care of the worship group, it will help the worship group make appropriate application to a nearby SEYM monthly meeting and will assist in the traditional Friends clearness process. This experience will help the worship group learn about and be guided in Friends practice. Please read the **Advices for a Friends Worship Group** at the end of this chapter for more detail.

Any monthly meeting that takes on the responsibility of care for a worship group should notify SEYM and ask for a minute of recognition for this task. SEYM should then follow the development of this worship group by getting yearly reports from the monthly meeting having care of the worship group.

Establishing Friends Preparative Meetings

A preparative meeting is a meeting for worship that holds its own meeting for business and continues under the care of, and reports regularly to, a committee of care of a monthly meeting or SEYM. It looks forward to becoming a monthly meeting.

After a period of seasoning, the development of a Friends worship group often progresses in ways leading to the status of a preparative meeting. During this period, a worship group is encouraged to call upon the committee of care from the appointed monthly meeting or SEYM for encouragement, advice, or other help it needs. When a worship group feels it is ready to organize and conduct business in the manner of an established monthly meeting, it asks the committee of care of the monthly meeting or SEYM for preparative meeting status. (Or the committee of care of the monthly meeting or SEYM can also suggest to the worship group that it ask for preparative meeting status.) The committee of care of the monthly meeting or SEYM, after a clearness process, may then prepare a minute recommending change to preparative meeting status. The yearly meeting, at its annual sessions or at an interim business meeting, may approve the change in status.

A preparative meeting has the continuing care and counsel of its committee of care appointed by the monthly meeting or yearly meeting. A preparative meeting has officers and committees as needed and holds a monthly meeting for business. A preparative meeting has a budget that is a sub-budget of the budget of the monthly meeting that is caring for the preparative meeting. Each month it sends a copy of the minutes of its meeting for business to its committee of care. Both the original and copy sent to its care committee should be on acid-free paper. When the preparative meeting begins the practice of meeting for business, it should also follow the same practice of caring for minutes as a monthly meeting.

Actions that may be carried out **ONLY** with the help and clearness of the monthly meeting that has care of the preparative meeting include the following:

- receiving requests for membership

- receiving or holding charitable contributions for tax-deduction purposes,

- holding weddings or memorial meetings,

- or otherwise acting formally as an established monthly meeting.

If a yearly meeting committee of care has the care of the preparative meeting, it will help the preparative meeting make appropriate application to a nearby SEYM monthly meeting and will assist in the traditional Friends clearness process. This experience will help the preparative meeting learn about and be guided in Friends practice. Please read the **Advices for a Friends Preparative Meeting** at the end of this chapter for a more detail.

Preparative meetings can also be formed by a monthly meeting under a wide variety of circumstances, but generally such meetings will develop in order to meet the particular spiritual needs of a geographical group of Friends. Usually a group of monthly meeting members will assume responsibility for organizing the preparative meeting and for reporting frequently to the monthly meeting.

Any monthly meeting that takes on the responsibility of care for a preparative meeting should notify SEYM and ask for a minute of recognition for this task. SEYM should then follow the development of this preparative meeting by getting yearly reports from the monthly meeting having care of the preparative meeting.

Preparative meetings are encouraged to send a delegate to SEYM meetings and to prepare the annual "state of the meeting" reports to be included in the documents in advance for SEYM annual sessions. With the guidance of the monthly meeting having care for the preparative meeting, Friends will determine which group is responsible for paying the annual assessments to SEYM and for other functions typical of a monthly meeting.

Preparative meetings look forward to such growth and development as may enable them to become monthly meetings. This process depends upon a variety factors, and there may be great differences in the time required.

Establishing Friends Monthly Meetings

A monthly meeting is usually established upon the initiative of a preparative meeting, and the process follows similar paths whether it is under the care of a monthly meeting or SEYM.

When a preparative meeting under the care of the monthly meeting feels ready to become a monthly meeting and, after a clearness process, its committee of care agrees, then the preparative meeting sends a letter to the clerk of the monthly meeting requesting change in status and asking that its letter be forwarded to the yearly meeting. The letter includes a statement telling why the preparative meeting wishes to become a monthly meeting and why it feels it is ready for this step. If the monthly meeting concurs, it forwards this request and a minute of agreement to the clerk of SEYM.

If the preparative meeting has been under the care of a yearly meeting committee of care, it sends the above-mentioned letter to the clerk of that committee. If the yearly meeting committee of care, after a clearness process, agrees with the request, it will forward the letter and a minute of agreement to the clerk of SEYM.

The SEYM Visiting Committee of Care

The yearly meeting clerk will then appoint a visiting committee of care of four or five Friends to discern its readiness with the preparative meeting. This committee should include one or two members of the earlier committee of care of the monthly meeting or yearly meeting, along with suitable and experienced Friends who have not been closely associated with the preparative meeting. Because they have already established relationships with the preparative meeting, the remainder of the committee of care continues its work of nurture and support during the same period that the visiting committee is in discernment of clearness of the preparative meeting regarding becoming a monthly meeting. The committee of care is also available to consult with the visiting committee as needed. The committee of care is laid down when SEYM accepts the report of the visiting committee recommending recording of monthly meeting status.

In either of the above cases, the visiting committee of care meets as often as possible with the preparative meeting, making sure its attenders are aware of the responsibilities of a monthly meeting and giving all possible guidance. All necessary time should be taken. Great care and deliberation at this stage may prevent serious complications later. The visiting committee regularly attends meetings for worship and meetings for business and visits with attenders of the preparative meeting.

Queries for Preparative Meetings and the Visiting Committee of Care

The following guidelines and queries are suggested for consideration by the preparative meeting and the visiting committee of care:

- **Recording.** The preparative meeting compiles a complete list of names and addresses of its regular attenders, noting those who are members of the Religious Society of Friends and indicating in which monthly meeting and yearly meeting, if other than SEYM, their memberships are held.

- **Spiritual Condition.** Does the preparative meeting function under divine guidance? Is the meeting for worship the center of life of the preparative meeting? What is the vitality of the meetings for worship? Are they held in the spirit of expectant waiting and communion with God?

- **History and Experience.** How long has the preparative meeting been meeting? What relations does it have with other meetings? What geographical area does it serve? Where and when is its meeting for worship? What is the usual attendance? How many Friends, regular attenders, and children attend the meeting? Of the individuals and families taking responsibility for the meeting, how many appear well settled in the area? How do the lives of the people in this meeting speak to the outside world? Are responsibilities for the meeting's business and activities shared fairly by all? The responses to these and similar questions need to be recorded and saved to begin the history of the new monthly meeting.

- **Evidence of Good Order.** Has the preparative meeting studied the *Faith and Practice* of SEYM? Does it hold a monthly meeting for business in the manner of Friends? How are the minutes taken and approved? Are the functions of clerk and other officers understood? What committees does the meeting have? Are the functions of the committee(s) on ministry and counsel understood and carried out? Are financial matters being handled in a competent manner according to Friends' principles? How are the meeting's officers, committees, and nominating committee selected? How are children included in the life of the meeting? Are there religious education programs for children and adults?

If the visiting committee of care agrees that the preparative meeting is ready to become a monthly meeting, it prepares a written report, including evaluation of fitness in reference to the above guidelines, and presents this report at the next SEYM interim business meeting or yearly meeting, with a recommendation that the preparative meeting become a new monthly meeting in SEYM. At this session of interim business meeting or yearly meeting, the report will be reviewed. It will be accepted for submission to the yearly meeting annual session, or the visiting committee of care may be requested to obtain additional information and the application will be considered at a subsequent interim business meeting or yearly meeting annual session.

After the visiting committee report has been accepted by SEYM, a minute of recognition of monthly meeting status for the requesting preparative meeting will be prepared by the SEYM executive committee. The minute will be submitted to the next annual session of the yearly meeting.

After approval of the minute of status change by the yearly meeting, SEYM formally records monthly meeting status for the requesting meeting. The minute will be conveyed to the preparative meeting and a date set for a "meeting for organization and celebration," at which the visiting committee of care is present. Prior to the meeting for organization and celebration, the preparative meeting now may accept applications for new or transferred membership, and Friends membership procedure will be followed with the guidance of the visiting committee of care. Memberships are recorded at the organizational meeting. The visiting committee of care continues to be regularly available to the new meeting for consultation for a year or more following its recording as a monthly meeting.

Special Circumstances

SEYM has always been blessed by the presence of seasoned Friends who come into our area. At times, these seasoned Friends may make up the majority of attenders of a new worshiping group or meeting. This group, seeking together, may be led to request a different path for becoming a monthly meeting affiliated with SEYM. They will seek guidance from a wide variety of seasoned Friends in SEYM to discern whether monthly meeting structure and status is appropriate for their worshiping group. When the SEYM Friends and the worshiping group are satisfied that their knowledge and practice in Quaker principles and procedures are of a sufficient depth and duration, they may directly request that SEYM, under divine guidance, work with them to devise a procedure other than that described above for them to become a monthly meeting.

Advices for a Friends Worship Group

- Worship groups may find meeting for worship their only group activity. It is acceptable to continue in this fashion for an indefinite period of time.

- Some worship groups may have shared meals, reading groups, study groups, and discussion groups. With the guidance and support of their monthly meeting or yearly meeting committee of care they may have service projects, religious education, public witness, or worship-sharing groups.

- Worship groups need to be mindful of the dangers of attempting too many things during their initial enthusiasm or of having an individual or couple carry all of the responsibility. Remember that Quakerism is a group religious responsibility.

- It is essential that those who participate in a worship group be dedicated to the leadings of the Light and that the group be devoted to growth in the Spirit.

- Worship groups will inevitably suffer discouragements and setbacks due to the departure of participants or other difficulties that may arise. This is an opportunity for patiently working through setbacks or conflicts in a loving manner. It is important to persevere and continue to meet regularly for worship at the appointed hour even though only one or two are able to meet. In doing so, hold absent attenders in the Light and in prayer that all may come to know the comfort of an ongoing worship group.

- Worship groups are encouraged to maintain regular contact with the committee of care of the monthly meeting or yearly meeting and ask for help as needed. The purpose of a committee of care is to nurture and guide the worship group.

- It is important to keep corresponding bodies informed when a new contact/correspondent is chosen or the contact/correspondent's address changes.

- If the worship group needs to receive and distribute charitable contributions for tax-deduction purposes on behalf of its attenders, it must ask a nearby SEYM monthly meeting to act as its financial representative. Until it becomes a monthly meeting, the worship group is unable to apply for nonprofit status from the government.

We desire, dear friends, that such of you as often meet in small companies for the solem purpose of worship, may not relax in your diligence. Your situation will at times appear discouraging; but although you may be seldom assisted by the company and travail of your brethen, never forget that you are under the continued notice of the Lord; and that his tender regard extends to all those who wait upon Him in reverence and humility . . .

London Yearly Meeting, 1813

Advices for a Preparative Meeting

- It is essential that the preparative meeting be dedicated to the leadings of the Light and devoted to growth in the Spirit.

- A preparative meeting, when organizing itself, should first appoint a clerk and recording clerk and then hold meeting for worship with a concern for business monthly. The recording clerk will prepare the minutes from the meeting for business and send them to the committee of care of the monthly meeting or yearly meeting.

- A preparative meeting appoints committees and committee clerks as needed to accomplish its goals. Establishing an effective method of communication, such as a newsletter or website, is an advisable way to further contact among Friends.

- Preparative meetings should be large enough to be able to undertake, with the guidance and support of their monthly meeting or yearly meeting committee of care, such activities as service projects, religious education, public witness, or worship-sharing groups.

- Preparative meetings need to be mindful of the danger of having too many activities or having an individual or a very small group carry all of the responsibility, for this can invite exhaustion and disillusionment.

- Preparative meetings will inevitably suffer discouragements and setbacks due to the departure of participants or other difficulties that may arise. It is important to persevere and continue to meet regularly for meeting for worship and meeting for worship with a concern for business at the appointed hour.

- Preparative meetings should maintain regular contact with their committee of care. The committee's purpose is to nurture and guide the preparative meeting, and it can be of service if it is able to participate in joint corporate discernment with the preparative meeting.

- If the preparative meeting needs to receive and distribute charitable contributions for tax-deduction purposes on behalf of its attenders, it must ask a nearby SEYM monthly meeting to act as its financial representative. Until it becomes a monthly meeting, the preparative meeting is unable to apply for nonprofit status from the government.

- It is important to keep yearly meeting and other Quaker organizations informed when a new clerk or corresponding clerk is chosen or any addresses change.

The life of a religious society consists in something more than the body of principles it professes [affirms] and the outer garments of organization which it wears. These things have their own importance: they embody the society to the world, and protect it from chance and change of circumstance; but the springs of life lie deeper, and often escape recognition. They are to be found in the vital union of the members of the society with God and with one another. [This] union . . . allows the free flowing through the society of the spiritual life which is its strength. . . .

. . . Organization is a good servant but a bad master; the living fellowship within the church [meeting] must remain free to mould the organization into fresh forms [guided by the Spirit and] demanded by its own growth and the changing needs of the time.
William Charles Braithwaite, 1905

Advices for the Committee of Care of the Monthly Meeting and the Visiting Committee of Care of Southeastern Yearly Meeting

- The committee of care and the visiting committee undertake the work of forming a new Friends monthly meeting in a spirit of celebration with an eye upon how each committee can best serve and facilitate the joyous event.

- The committee of care and the visiting committee have the responsibility to nurture the growth and education of the nascent worship group or preparative meeting in Friends' practice.

- The committee of care should monitor the progress of the worship group or preparative meeting and encourage it to request the next level of formal status, e.g., move from "worship group" to "preparative meeting" when it appears suitable to do so.

- The work of the committee of care ends when SEYM accepts the favorable report of the visiting committee. After that time, the visiting committee continues to nurture and support the preparative meeting and remains available for guidance.

- It is important that the worship group or preparative meeting understand that the community is a group responsibility. The committee of care and the visiting committee are charged with helping the attenders of the worship group or preparative meeting live out their role as loving ministers to each other in the blessed community.

- The greatest gift the committee of care and the visiting committee can give to this work is their loving presence in the lives of the worship group or preparative meeting. Both committees should be prepared to have at least one member of either present as much as possible throughout the worship group's or preparative meeting's process of becoming a new Friends monthly meeting.

- After formal recording of monthly meeting status, the visiting committee should continue to nurture their relationships and be prepared to be present for guidance for the new monthly meeting at least one year or longer.

- The committee of care and the visiting committee will make regular reports to the monthly meeting having the care of the worship group or preparative meeting and to SEYM.

Love and the presence of God work together in pastoral care. Love of God, love of others, and love of oneself are all needed. We cannot grow into our whole selves, the person we were destined to be, without receiving love and learning to love. When we love and when we are loved, we are in a reciprocal relationship. This is the unseen, and often ignored, fabric of our world; God is at the center, the source of all love. Pastoral care is an activity in which all participants are learning to give and receive compassion, the fundamental skill for life.

Gay Howard, 2000

The Religious Society of Friends calls us to a God-centered way of life. We are called to shape our outward lives to reflect the inward experience of the sacred. Early Friends claimed that the second Coming is <u>now</u>. . . . [O]ur lifelong work is the ongoing conversion of manners (change in our behavior and *our very selves) as directed by the Inward Guide, submitting all relationships, habits, possessions, finances, and commitments to the Living Spirit.*

William Penn raised a high standard: "They were changed men themselves before they went about to change others" (1694). . . .

Nadine Hoover, 2000

CHAPTER 13

THE YEARLY MEETING, INTERIM BUSINESS MEETING, AND YEARLY MEETING COMMITTEES, AND REPRESENTATIVES

The thing is this: that if you had (once a year) a Yearly Meeting . . . for Friends to see one another, and know how the affairs of truth prosper, and how Friends do grow in the truth of God, to the comfort and joy of one another in it . . . all things (by the truth and power of God) may be kept in peace and love, all dwelling in the wisdom of God.

George Fox, 1681

The intent and holy design of our annual assemblies, in their first constitution, were for a great and weighty oversight and Christian care of the affairs of the churches pertaining to our holy profession and Christian communion; that good order, true love, unity and concord may be faithfully followed and maintained among all of us.

London Yearly Meeting, 1718

To follow the highest purpose always involves the setting aside of many things which in themselves are good, whether by the individuals or by the Yearly Meeting as a whole. To find the purpose of God in a gathering such as this involves bringing together of every one of our differing points of view to that place where they may be united in the power of God. If in our hearts as individuals we maintain barriers between ourselves and other Friends, we cannot be finders; and if we maintain such barriers between ourselves and our fellow men we shall not find our part in working out God's will in the world.

It has been the experience of this Yearly Meeting in the past to know that Friends have met in division and uncertainty, and that then guidance has come, and the light has been given to us, and we have become finders of God's purpose. This gives us ground for confidence. We shall not be held back by the magnitude of the questions which are to come before us, nor by a sense of our own unworthiness.

London Yearly Meeting, 1936

The Yearly Meeting

A yearly meeting is formed by monthly meetings in a region so that a larger group can undertake matters of common concern and mutual support, can communicate with each other, and can act as a unit. The yearly meeting ties all of us to the wider Quaker fellowship. In meeting for worship with a concern for business and other forums, Friends come together in annual and interim sessions for the assessment of the life of the Society of Friends, the conduct of business, spiritual refreshment and commitment, and the renewal of the ties of friendship. The yearly meeting nurtures and cares for the constituent monthly meetings, preparative meetings, and worship groups, assisting in the development of their concerns and providing inspiration and encouragement.

Members and attenders of the monthly meetings and worship groups meet together once a year at Southeastern Yearly Meeting (SEYM) Annual Gathering, which during business sessions takes up matters that have come up in the past year, new activities or problems that may arise at yearly meeting, and concerns that may require a decision at a subsequent yearly meeting. Before the next annual gathering there will be two sessions of interim business meeting that will continue to work on the business of yearly meeting, three sessions of yearly meeting committee meetings, four executive committee meetings, and a half yearly meeting for fellowship.

The SEYM Annual Gathering, traditionally held over Easter weekend, consists of meeting for business, committee meetings, workshops, groups of people getting together to talk about concerns, worship-sharing sessions, meetings for worship, the Walton Lecture, and times for Friendly fellowship. Interim business meeting is devoted to meeting for worship, committee meetings, meeting for business, and visiting time for Friends. On Sunday of the winter interim business meeting weekend, the Michener Lecture and workshops are held. Half yearly meeting, traditionally held over Thanksgiving weekend, is a time for intergenerational fellowship with an environmental focus and an opportunity for fun together.

The annual gathering may change in format or emphasis from year to year. It is an occasion for sharing information and concerns from individual members, constituent meetings, yearly meeting committees, and other Friends groups or organizations in sympathy with Friends. The gathering also receives messages in the form of epistles, letters communicating the sense of the Spirit, from other yearly meetings. It is customary to reply with an epistle approved near the close of the gathering.

The yearly meeting annual gathering is open to all participants of the constituent monthly meetings, preparative meetings, and worship groups. Members of other yearly meetings and other Friends organizations are invited to send representatives or observers to the gathering and to provide information about their organizations. Members and attenders in SEYM's constituent monthly meetings are as much a part of yearly meeting as of their own meeting and are as responsible for the well-being of the yearly meeting in addition to their home meeting.

It is helpful if all monthly meetings, preparative meetings, and worship groups send members to the annual gathering to assure a large pool of wisdom and insight at each business session, to carry the weight of the concerns and Light in their home monthly meeting to annual sessions, and to provide full and careful reports of these sessions to their home meetings. Decisions are made, under divine guidance, by all present.

Continuity of attendance is expected and is helpful for seasoned judgment and for satisfactory communication between the interim business meeting or yearly meeting and monthly meetings and their members. Information and understanding constantly flow into and out of the interim or yearly meetings so that policies and decisions may be made with broad discernment and may be widely understood and implemented.

Insight, concern, and information are received in a worshipful spirit and often evoke deeply felt responses. The yearly meeting may be led to unite in an expression of concern or in a decision for specific action. Since such expressions or actions speak for the entire membership of the yearly meeting, Friends are asked to review carefully in advance any concerns or proposals that are to come before the annual gathering meeting for business and either attend yearly meeting or ensure that their meeting's representatives understand their concerns or proposals and can share them effectively.

The meeting for business of yearly meeting may have before it many actions to consider, but each year one of the weightiest concerns is the budget. Budgetary proposals are given wide circulation well in advance of the SEYM Annual Gathering, with ample opportunity for comment from the meetings. The discussion of the budget is most useful when it explores the spiritual and testimonial implications of budgetary decisions and elicits and weighs ideas that will influence future budgets.

Friends gather in meeting for worship with concern for business at yearly meeting and interim business meetings not as instructed delegates but as individuals guided by the Spirit at that time and place. In so gathering, members may experience the tensions that may be created by discernment among the dictates of individual conscience, the sense of their home meeting, and the best interests of the whole. Implicit is Friends' understanding that we seek to discern the leadings of God throughout our sessions.

Yearly Meeting Clerks and Officers

Clerk of Yearly Meeting and Clerk of Interim Business Meeting

In its annual sessions, the yearly meeting nominates and appoints a presiding clerk for yearly meeting and a different presiding clerk for interim business meeting. Both of these clerks are present at yearly meeting business sessions and interim business meetings. The other clerks and officers serve both yearly meeting and interim business meeting. Only members of constituent monthly meetings of the yearly meeting are nominated to serve in these positions. The clerk of yearly meeting presides at yearly meeting annual business sessions, is responsible for the agenda, and is the spokesperson for SEYM. The clerk of interim business meeting presides at the fall and winter interim business meeting sessions and is responsible for those agendas.

The presiding clerk of either the yearly meeting or the interim business meeting receives information from committees, officers, staff, and individuals on suggested agenda items. Then the clerk writes the agenda. The clerk guides the meeting for worship with a concern for business, calling for worship, asking for Friends to speak, expressing the sense of the meeting when unity has been reached, guiding Friends through the process of finding the exact wording for a minute, making space for more contributions, guiding discussion to a close, directing a committee to take up the matter, and ending the meeting with worship. Finally, the clerk has to insure that the decisions of the meeting for business are carried out.

The presiding clerk of yearly meeting appoints a committee of three Friends at the beginning of yearly meeting sessions to write an epistle for the yearly meeting to be approved and sent out to other yearly meetings at the end of the gathering. The clerk also appoints, at the beginning of the annual sessions, someone to send a report of the yearly meeting sessions to be published in Friends publications.

Assistant Clerk

The assistant clerk is present at the clerks' table at yearly meeting and interim business meeting and provides assistance as needed. The assistant clerk takes over in the temporary absence, or stepping aside, of the clerk. In addition, the assistant clerk is responsible for allocating the yearly meeting's budgeted travel funds among the yearly meeting representatives to Quaker organizations and provides support to the representatives.

Recording Clerk

The recording clerk of the yearly meeting and interim business meetings writes the numbered minutes and reads them to the meeting for approval. The recording clerk also ensures that the narrative minutes contain all needed information and gives them to the administrative secretary for publication. The presiding clerk and the recording clerk are together responsible for the accuracy of the minutes, and both sign the minutes.

Treasurer

The treasurer is responsible for the integrity of the financial records of the yearly meeting and oversees all the financial transactions of yearly meeting funds that are not invested through the trustees. It is the treasurer's responsibility to see that the expenditures are in accordance with the budget or to see that changes from the budget are approved by the yearly meeting. The treasurer presents an annual report of the income and expenses in the previous fiscal year (ending May 31st) at the fall interim business meeting and an interim report at yearly meeting, winter interim business meeting, and as requested by the presiding clerks. The actual bookkeeping, writing of checks, and making of deposits are done by the administrative secretary. The treasurer answers questions and guides Friends in understanding the fiscal status of the yearly meeting.

Membership Recorder

The membership recorder keeps the membership records of the yearly meeting in a database, updating the database each year with information from the monthly meetings. From this database, the recorder produces a new Directory of SEYM annually. The membership recorder also uses the database to prepare a statistics sheet each year showing the number of members and attenders in each monthly meeting, preparative meeting and worship group and in the yearly meeting. These statistics are sent annually to Friends General Conference and, when requested, to the Friends World Committee for Consultation for inclusion in worldwide Quaker statistics.

Young Friends (Teens) Clerk(s) and Young Friends (Teens) Recording Clerk

The young Friends (teens) presiding clerk(s) and the young Friends (teens) recording clerk carry out their responsibilities in the junior yearly meeting's meeting for business during the annual sessions and make an appropriate report to the yearly meeting at the end of the annual gathering. They participate in interim business meeting and are members of the executive committee.

Young Adult Quakers Clerk(s) and Young Adult Quakers Recording Clerk

The young adult Quakers presiding clerk(s) and young adult Quakers recording clerk carry out their responsibilities in the young adult Quakers yearly meeting's meeting for business during the annual sessions and make an appropriate report to the yearly meeting at the end of the annual gathering. They participate in interim business meeting and are members of the executive committee.

In the *Southeastern Yearly Meeting Operational Handbook, Procedures, and Job Descriptions*, there are more detailed descriptions of the responsibilities of the clerks and officers as well as of committees, representatives to Quaker organizations, trustees, and the administrative secretary. The *SEYM Operational Handbook* also describes the specific procedures of yearly meeting sessions and the interim business meetings.

Yearly Meeting Responsibilities

The yearly meeting alone has authority to establish or change *Faith and Practice* or to issue statements of faith of the yearly meeting. Proposals for new sections or for revisions of existing sections of *Faith and Practice* may be initiated in any monthly meeting, in the interim business meeting, or in the yearly meeting and will be referred to the faith and practice committee. The approval of *Faith and Practice* comes from discernment and unity reached by the body of yearly meeting in plenary session after prolonged study and discernment by monthly meetings and individuals.

The yearly meeting publishes "Documents In Advance" (DIA) for the annual gathering and the fall and winter interim business meetings, which include the agenda for the meeting and other reports to be considered. The yearly meeting receives reports of the spiritual state of the meeting from monthly meetings, preparative meetings, and worship groups, publishing them in the DIA for yearly meeting annual gathering. The yearly meeting approves minutes from interim business meetings and executive committee meetings. The yearly meeting publishes *Queries and Advices*, the yearly meeting newsletter, and pamphlets from the annual Michener and Walton Lectures. In addition, the yearly meeting reports its proceedings, maintains contact with other yearly meetings and Friends organizations, and provides for due consideration of epistles and minutes of other yearly meetings.

The yearly meeting facilitates communication among its constituents and centralized record-keeping for them. The yearly meeting keeps a database with the records of the members and attenders of the monthly meetings, preparative meetings, worship groups, and other groups of Friends in the region. Membership data is regularly updated and published annually as the *Directory of Southeastern Yearly Meeting.*

The yearly meeting approves the formation of worship groups and preparative meetings and the establishment of monthly meetings. Usually, a nearby monthly meeting nurtures a worship group or preparative meeting and helps with its transition to a monthly meeting. When no monthly meeting is available, yearly meeting may take a worship group or preparative meeting under its care. The yearly meeting nurtures and cares for the constituent monthly meetings, preparative meetings, and worship groups, assisting in the development of their concerns and providing inspiration and stimulation. Much of the work of the yearly meeting is carried forward by its committees, which report to yearly meeting and to interim business meetings.

Funding the Yearly Meeting

The yearly meeting derives its operating funds from the contributions of its constituent meetings and individual members and such other monies as may be obtained from other sources such as the trustees funds and publication sales. Each meeting's share of the operating budget is determined by the number of members and attenders in the meeting as a percentage of the number of members and attenders in the whole yearly meeting. Individual members are also asked to contribute as they feel led.

Yearly Meeting Process Between Annual Sessions:

Interim Business Meeting: Functions and Responsibilities

Interim business meeting (IBM) acts for Southeastern Yearly Meeting when the yearly meeting is not in session and ensures that the work and witness of the yearly meeting are carried forward in the spirit of the preceding yearly meeting. Interim business meeting reports to yearly meeting at the annual business sessions. All the action minutes of the interim business meeting are approved or not approved at the annual sessions of yearly meeting. Both fall and winter sessions of interim business meeting are attended by SEYM clerks and officers (as listed above), SEYM committee members, monthly meeting representatives, and all other SEYM Friends and others interested in the proceedings.

The yearly meeting has delegated the following duties to interim business meeting in the time between yearly meeting sessions:

- Accepting responsibility for those concerns specifically referred by the preceding yearly meeting.

- Providing general oversight and coordination of the work of the committees of the yearly meeting and of other groups of Friends acting under leading with yearly meeting approval.

- Representing the yearly meeting and appearing on its behalf whenever required by the cause of truth, public welfare, or the interest and reputation of the Society of Friends.

- Providing for widespread consultation and discussion on matters of major import to the Society of Friends.

- Providing advice and assistance to monthly meetings, preparative meetings, and worship groups upon their request, in the administration of property and trust funds or in dealing with difficult situations.

- Providing advice and assistance for any persons or constituent group suffering because of adherence to Friends' testimonies.

- Receiving and endorsing minutes of Friends traveling in the ministry or under other circumstances related to Friends' concerns.

The IBM provides an opportunity/process for Friends to consider yearly meeting business as it develops throughout the year. In this way, Friends are made familiar with and can discuss business which will be brought for approval at the yearly business sessions. Preliminary discussion at IBM of matters to be brought before the yearly meeting can help the yearly meeting come to agreement in the annual yearly meeting business sessions. The clerk of interim business meeting may call special interim sessions as needed.

When need arises, interim business meeting may also ask the clerk of yearly meeting to call special sessions of the yearly meeting. When vacancies occur among the officers of the yearly meeting, interim business meeting makes interim appointments.

Interim business meeting may not make any changes in *Faith and Practice*, issue any statement of faith, or act upon any matters specifically reserved for the yearly meeting. It should advise the yearly meeting when a revision to the text of Faith and Practice is indicated.

Any significant change in duties or function of interim business meeting is the sole responsibility of the yearly meeting in annual sessions.

Queries for Participants of Yearly Meeting and Interim Business Meeting

- As part of Southeastern Yearly Meeting in a worshiping community, am I faithful to the responsibility of seeking God's will in carrying out the business of our yearly meeting? Do our practices provide us with spiritual refreshment? In what ways do I contribute to this spiritual refreshment?

- Am I faithful in sharing the decisions reached by yearly/interim business meeting with my monthly meeting, including all information appropriate to the understanding of those decisions? Do I share reports and information about events?

- Do I participate in a way that helps the clerk accomplish the agenda of the meeting?

- Am I careful not to speak too easily or too often, careful to discern whether my speaking is rightly ordered?

- Am I careful to listen to the Spirit as it is reflected in the contributions of others as well as within myself?

- If I am not in agreement with the discussion, do I strive to present alternatives in a way that both helps others understand my concerns and maintains the spirit of worship?

- Do I assist the clerk by remaining focused on the agenda item under discussion? Do I hold the clerk in the Light, especially when there are tensions in the decision-making process?

Committees of the Yearly Meeting

Southeastern Yearly Meeting is empowered to appoint, fund, and require regular reports from committees and working groups. The yearly meeting oversees and lays down standing committees and may name and/or lay down ad hoc committees and working groups. It also appoints or provides for the appointment of the various committees' members. Ad hoc committees may also be named at interim business meetings and at executive committee meetings as need arises.

Such bodies have as their principal purpose providing support and leadership in the following:

- The education and care of our members. This includes such functions as religious education, publications, and provision of services to the various age groups that make up our yearly meeting.

- The clarification and carrying out of our testimonies and concerns both at home and in the wider world. The particular committees and working groups that are established to implement these testimonies may change in emphasis or focus in response to the difficulties and challenges of the world we share with others. They constitute our ongoing effort to bring about a more just and peaceful world.

- The provision of services needed by our monthly meetings, preparative meetings, and worship groups, especially in communication, maintenance of current membership lists, finance, and management of property.

Generally, only members of a constituent monthly meeting are appointed to the nominating committee, the worship and ministry committee, the finance committee, and the faith and practice committee. Any change in the makeup or function of these committees is the sole responsibility of the yearly meeting annual business session.

Committee clerks and members are nominated by the nominating committee with the exception of the epistle committee, which is named by the clerk of yearly meeting at the yearly meeting sessions. Committees meet at each interim business meeting, at yearly meeting annual gathering, and otherwise as needed. Clerks and committee members serve three-year terms. Committee meetings are normally open to anyone who desires to attend.

The Executive Committee

The clerk of the executive committee is the interim business meeting clerk, who presides at the committee meetings and writes the agenda. Other members of the executive committee are the yearly meeting clerk, assistant clerk, recording clerk, treasurer, membership recorder, clerk of the archives committee, clerk of the committee for earthcare, clerk of the committee for ministry on racism, clerk of the faith and practice committee, clerk of the finance committee, the clerk of the half yearly meeting committee, clerk of the nominating committee, clerk of the peace and social concerns committee, clerk of the publications committee, clerk of the religious education committee, clerk of the worship and ministry committee, clerk of the yearly meeting gathering committee, clerk of the youth committee, clerk(s) of the young Friends (teens), clerk(s) of the young adult Quakers, and clerk of the trustees. The administrative secretary is an ex officio member of the committee. The executive committee meets four times a year, just before each interim business meeting, at the beginning of yearly meeting annual gathering, and at some time in the summer. The committee acts for the interim business meeting between sessions. The executive committee may be the place for the first discussion of concerns/ problems with which the yearly meeting has to ultimately seek discernment and minute any needed action.

Employees of SEYM are hired by the executive committee and are under the committee's direction. The committee provides guidance and loving care to the yearly meeting staff and performs duties as a personnel committee as are specified by the *Southeastern Yearly Meeting Operational Handbook, Procedures, and Job Descriptions.*

Archives Committee

The archives committee collects and preserves the records of Southeastern Yearly Meeting, which are then stored at the yearly meeting's designated repository. The committee also asks monthly meetings to store their archives with the yearly meeting archives.

Committee for Earthcare

The committee for earthcare is called to help Friends understand our roles as good stewards of the Earth today so as to ensure a healthful environment for our children's future.

Committee for Ministry on Racism

The committee for ministry on racism seeks to help Friends

as they develop their racial and ethnic awareness, increase their diversity, and strive to address the impact of the institution of racism on our society.

Faith and Practice Committee

The faith and practice committee is responsible for keeping the Southeastern Yearly Meeting *Faith and Practice* up-to-date as a document useful to the monthly meetings, preparative meetings, worship groups, and the yearly meeting. It is also responsible for reviewing the updating of the *Southeastern Yearly Meeting Operational Handbook, Procedures, and Job Descriptions* and for other responsibilities given to it by the yearly meeting. *Faith and Practice* is a record of the applied faith of the yearly meeting; it is changed to reflect the current practice of the yearly meeting and the monthly meetings.

The committee prepares drafts of proposed new sections or revises sections of *Faith and Practice* and sends them to the monthly meetings for their careful consideration and comments. The comments are returned to the faith and practice committee, and the text is revised. The revised text is threshed (a type of Friendly discussion) at the next yearly meeting annual gathering. Then the committee revises the text again and sends it to clerks, contacts, and officers in the yearly meeting. When the text seems to be acceptable to Friends, the faith and practice committee asks for approval of the section at the next year's yearly meeting business sessions. If the section is not approved, the committee continues its work in a similar manner. When a section is approved, it becomes part of SEYM's current faith and practice and is included in the *Faith and Practice* book, as well as uploaded to the seym.org website.

Finance Committee

The finance committee prepares the proposed general fund budget for the yearly meeting each year. The committee makes the proposed budget available to the monthly meetings at winter interim business meeting or in "Documents in Advance" sufficiently far in advance of the yearly meeting annual sessions to allow meetings to comment and suggest changes. The clerk of the finance committee presents the proposed budget, including any changes, to the yearly meeting annual sessions for approval. The finance fommittee may also send an appeal to individual members to help fund the budget.

Half Yearly Meeting Committee

The half yearly meeting committee secures a reservation at an appropriate site with a deposit and provides food for the half yearly meeting gathering on Thanksgiving weekend. The participants pay the cost. The clerk of the committee and the administrative secretary send out a notice about the half yearly meeting gathering. The registrar of the yearly meeting and half yearly meeting gatherings receives registration by mail or online. The clerk of the committee provides a financial report to the secretary and treasurer that becomes part of the yearly meeting's financial report.

Nominating Committee

The nominating committee is made up of Friends from every part of the yearly meeting. The nominating committee nominates Friends to serve as SEYM's clerks, officers, and trustees; as clerks and members of committees; and as representatives to other Quaker bodies. This committee distributes nominations among as many Friends and monthly meetings as possible. After these Friends have indicated their willingness to serve, their names are submitted for approval to the yearly meeting or to interim business meeting, whichever is appropriate. The clerks and officers usually serve a term of three years. A second term of three years is possible.

Peace and Social Concerns Committee

The peace and social concerns committee works on peace and justice issues in the world and brings suggested actions to the yearly meeting. This committee addresses concerns of wider scope than individual monthly meetings can accomplish. It strengthens the social consciousness of our monthly meetings, preparative meetings, worship groups, and individual Friends.

Publications Committee

The publications committee gathers news and photographs and publishes the yearly meeting newsletter periodically. The committee is responsible for the annual publication of the Michener and Walton Lectures.

Religious Education Committee

The religious education committee aids monthly meetings in developing their religious education programs.

Worship and Ministry Committee

The worship and ministry committee helps to strengthen the spiritual life of our monthly meetings, worship groups, and individual Friends. It is responsible for the worship-sharing groups at the yearly meeting gathering and developing the spiritual topic queries, which are the focus for the worship-sharing groups. It also arranges intervisitation to monthly meetings and worship groups and makes contacts with isolated Friends.

The worship and ministry committee selects the Michener Lecturer, attends to the lecturer's needs in conjunction with the lecture, and makes and oversees all physical arrangements (location, luncheon food, audio taping, and so forth). The worship and ministry committee is also responsible for the finances of the Michener Lecture and provides a financial report to the treasurer.

Yearly Meeting Gathering Committee

The yearly meeting gathering committee is responsible for planning and coordinating the annual gathering. It is this committee's responsibility to choose a theme and to bring a speaker for the Walton Lecture, who customarily conducts two or more workshops on the theme as well. The committee schedules the adult program and the youth program and organizes the workshops and interest groups.

The committee and the administrative secretary send out the program and registration information for the annual gathering. The registrar of the yearly meeting gathering receives registration by mail or online. The committee welcomes Friends to the gathering and provides them with needed information.

The clerk of the gathering committee, with the assistance of the administrative secretary, reviews proposed contracts, arranges that deposits be paid, works closely with the registrar so that reservations are submitted as required by the host site in a timely manner, and makes a budget for the annual sessions. After the gathering, the committee provides the treasurer with a financial report of the gathering that becomes part of the financial report of the yearly meeting.

Youth Committee

The youth committee plans, supervises, and facilitates youth activities throughout the year. It provides input and assistance for youth at yearly meeting functions (YM, IBMs, HYM), acts as youth coordinator at the yearly meeting gathering, and provides materials for the SEYM newsletter.

Ad Hoc Committees

Child Abuse Prevention Committee

The child abuse prevention committee reviews the Florida Department of Law Enforcement reports and makes a determination regarding an applicant's approval as a registered SEYM youth program worker. For security purposes, this ad hoc committee is appointed by and serves under the auspices of the executive committee.

Epistle Committee

The epistle committee is appointed by the yearly meeting presiding clerk early in the yearly meeting sessions. During the yearly meeting, the committee prepares the outgoing epistle, a letter communicating the sense of the spirit of the gathering, which is approved at the last business session and later sent out to other yearly meetings.

Meeting for Sufferings

The meeting for sufferings is a committee which is activated whenever there is a Friend in SEYM who, while under a leading as a witness to the world, faces the possibility of suffering or loss of civil liberties as a result of the leading. Funds in support of the Friend are collected and distributed as needed. Letter writing, visitation, and other forms of support are offered as appropriate.

Naming Committee

The naming committee is a regionally diverse group of Friends appointed by the executive committee to nominate the members of the nominating committee. The committee is appointed whenever there is a vacancy on the nominating committee and serves until it makes its report at the next yearly meeting business session after which it is laid down.

Appointees

ProNica Board

The ProNica Board serves in an advisory capacity to ProNica. ProNica grew out of a concern of St. Petersburg Monthly

Meeting and later was taken under the care of SEYM. In 2004 it became an independent organization, though retaining a five-member advisory board made up in part by three Friends nominated and approved by SEYM at yearly meeting. ProNica is a not-for-profit Friendly corporation that supplies funds, equipment, and information on community and economic development, sustainable agriculture, health, and education, creating practical opportunities to promote Quaker testimonies through friendships and partnerships that aid and empower the people of Nicaragua.

Consultants

Two groups of consultants, information technology consultants and publications consultants, have been appointed by the administrative secretary to aid in discernment. The information technology consultants provide information on new computer programs, hardware, and policy as needed. The publications consultants help with discernment on publishing submitted manuscripts and on web content.

Yearly Meeting Representatives to Wider Quaker and Religious Fellowships

Southeastern Yearly Meeting provides Friends with additional opportunities for giving expression to their faith by service to the yearly meeting in ways other than that of the clerks and committees listed above. The following are the organizations that SEYM participates in through its representatives.

SEYM has been affiliated with Friends General Conference (FGC) since 1972. FGC was originally formed in 1900 by seven yearly meetings. There are now more than fourteen yearly meetings and Friends associations, whose members predominately worship in the unprogrammed tradition of Friends. (There are a few pastoral meetings in New England and New York Yearly Meetings.) FGC serves yearly and monthly meetings, and their members and attenders, by providing resources and opportunities for spiritual growth and community building and by helping to empower Friends and their meetings to live their faith. The FGC Annual Gathering of Friends, held each summer in a different part of North America, offers an important opportunity to experience some of these services and discover additional FGC programs.

FGC's governing body consists of Friends appointed by affiliated yearly meetings and regional Friends associations, plus additional co-opted members. The work of Friends General Conference is carried out by a number of program and administrative committees, plus staff. Program committees undertake such concerns as advancement and outreach, ministry and nurture, religious education, conference planning, and a meetinghouse loan fund. FGC publishes books and pamphlets and distributes a wide variety of publications of interest to Friends through its bookstore. SEYM sends three representatives every year to the FGC Central Committee Meeting. The representatives are also asked to serve on at least one of the program committees of FGC.

The Friends World Committee for Consultation (FWCC), through visitation and periodic gatherings, offers opportunities for religious fellowship among Friends throughout the world. It sponsors the Wider Quaker Fellowship, a support group for Friends and interested others who live at a distance from a local meeting. It also sponsors, in conjunction with the American Friends Service Committee and Friends Service Council of Britain Yearly Meeting, the Quaker United Nations Office (QUNO), in two locations: New York and Geneva. SEYM sends three representatives every year to the FWCC Section of the Americas Meeting. In addition, SEYM appoints two representatives to keep the yearly meeting informed regarding UN activities and QUNO (NY office) concerns.

The American Friends Service Committee (AFSC) was founded in 1917. Its first mission was the relief of suffering during and after World War I. Since then, AFSC has developed programs in the United States and around the world intended to encourage improved understanding among different national and ethnic groups, to enable indigenous populations to improve their living conditions, and to relieve suffering caused by economic and social dislocation as well as by war. SEYM sends two representatives every year to the AFSC Corporation Meeting. In addition, SEYM sends two representatives every year to the AFSC Southeast Region Meetings (SERO) and two representatives to the AFSC/SERO Emergency and Material Assistance Program (EMAP) whenever it is activated by AFSC.

The Friends Committee on National Legislation (FCNL) was formed in 1943 to coordinate and enhance the efforts of Friends to lobby for their concerns with the executive and legislative branches of the US government. With the support of FCNL, many Quakers in SEYM participate in direct lobbying of their senators and representatives. SEYM sends five representatives every year to the FCNL annual meeting.

Quaker Earthcare Witness (QEW) began at the Friends General Conference Gathering at Oberlin College in 1987 as a response to a need among Friends there to "give forceful witness to the holiness of creation." QEW offers spiritual and material support to Friends in North America who have a growing concern for the needs of the Earth. SEYM sends two representatives each year to Quaker Earthcare Witness meetings.

SEYM sends two representatives to Friends Peace Team meetings and one representative each year to Friends for Lesbian, Gay, Bisexual, Transgender, and Queer Concerns (FLGBTQC) meetings. SEYM also appoints a representative to keep the yearly meeting informed regarding Pendle Hill programs.

Friends also participate in ecumenical bodies. SEYM is represented at the World Council of Churches through the Christian and Interfaith Relations Committee of Friends General Conference. In addition, SEYM maintains a relationship with the Florida Council of Churches with two representatives to that body.

Observers

Friends of Southeastern Yearly Meeting were once affiliated (1972-2010) with Friends United Meeting (FUM). In 2010,

SEYM withdrew its affiliation and has since appointed an observer to FUM, who attends annually a general board meeting and reports back to SEYM. FUM, founded in 1902, is a cooperative program of twenty-seven plus Friends yearly meetings in Canada, Cuba, Jamaica, Kenya, Uganda, and the United States. FUM's priorities are evangelism, leadership training, global partnership, and communication. In addition, FUM publishes books and pamphlets of interest to Friends through its bookstore. Friends United Meeting is a movement of Christian Quakers. It is their joy to share the love of God and the transforming power of the Holy Spirit with all people.

Employees

The yearly meeting currently employs one staff person, an administrative secretary who is hired by the executive committee and paid by funds from the budget. The role of administrative secretary is vital to the operations of the yearly meeting. The administrative secretary is the communication manager for the yearly meeting. He/she is responsible for the production and distribution of yearly meeting documents (pamphlets, brochures, minutes, documents in advance, and others), keeps the yearly meeting financial records including checkbook accounting (collects and deposits donations, writes checks), and provides financial records to the trustees, finance committee, and treasurer. The administrative secretary is responsible for creating and maintaining the yearly meeting website.

Trustees

The trustees of Southeastern Yearly Meeting of the Religious Society of Friends hold title to and have management rights to yearly meeting property. The trustees are endowed with the responsibility of raising and managing endowment and investment funds on behalf of SEYM.

The six trustees are members of the yearly meeting and are from diverse areas of Southeastern Yearly Meeting; two are nominated each year for three-year terms. The clerk is chosen by the current trustees and serves for three years. The yearly meeting treasurer is an *ex officio* member of the trustees. The group meets at least three times yearly: at each interim business meeting and at yearly meeting gathering. The clerk of yearly meeting or the clerk of interim business meeting may call the trustees into special session.

The trustees are responsible for investing trust and reserve funds and any additional funds as directed by the yearly meeting and are also responsible for the real property of the yearly meeting. They are entrusted with the responsibility of investing in organizations in keeping with the testimonies of Friends and the express wishes of donors.

The trustees may initiate new fund accounts and may close old accounts. The clerk of trustees makes an annual report about Southeastern Yearly Meeting's reserves and investments at the fall interim business meeting and a current status report at the winter interim business meeting and the yearly meeting business sessions. He/she explains what the reserves of the yearly meeting are, what income they are producing, and what programs they are supporting. The administrative secretary is responsible for the trustees' bookkeeping data entry and may assist in fundraising if time is available. The clerk of the trustees keeps copies of the investment records. The trustees make a recommendation to the yearly meeting about accepting the conditions specified by the donors of gifts.

CHAPTER 14

REPLACEMENT MINUTE FOR 98YM07
REVISING *FAITH AND PRACTICE*

Need for Change

The need for change in *Faith and Practice* may arise from various sources in the yearly meeting: the faith and practice committee, the executive committee, another committee in yearly meeting, a monthly meeting, or an individual. When the request for the change is communicated to the faith and practice committee, the committee may begin work on the change or may thresh out with the source of the request whether change is needed.

Process of Change

In brief, the process is as follows: The faith and practice committee writes the change or addition in draft; sends it out to the monthly meetings, preparative meetings, and worship groups; takes the replies from these meetings and groups; and writes a second draft. Then there is a threshing session on this second draft at yearly meeting annual gathering. The second draft is revised to include the information from the threshing session, making a third draft which is circulated again for comments. The revised third draft (or fourth draft if the changes are numerous) is presented at yearly meeting sessions for approval.

Here is a more detailed picture of the process: One of the members of the faith and practice committee writes the preliminary draft of the new or to-be-changed section. The author and the committee work on the section until it is ready to be sent to the monthly meetings, preparative meetings, and worship groups.

The clerk of the faith and practice committee sends draft one of each section to be considered to the clerk of each monthly meeting and preparative meeting, the contact/correspondent of each worship group, and the clerk of each unaffiliated meeting in the region. Typically, the section is sent out about September 1st with the request that the replies be returned to the clerk of the faith and practice committee by the following winter interim business meeting. The clerks and contacts/correspondents are asked to arrange for their meeting to read the section and go over it as a group. One member of the group takes notes on the comments and corrections made by the meeting. If an individual makes a comment that others do not agree with, the disagreement is noted or the comment is dropped. All the comments are discerned by the meeting before being sent back to the committee. This process allows the meetings approximately four months to read and season the first draft.

The faith and practice committee meets soon after winter interim business meeting, and, using the comments sent in by the meetings, revises the section to make a second draft.

During the next yearly meeting annual gathering, a threshing session is held to review the second draft. The clerk of the faith and practice committee presides over the threshing session, and two members of the faith and practice committee take notes. It is important that the note-takers write down the sense of the threshing session, not just everything that is said. If it seems important, the sense of the meeting (threshing session) is read back to those assembled, but often this is not necessary and can take up quite a bit of time. If it is necessary, it should be done.

The results of the threshing session are incorporated into a third draft by the faith and practice committee. The third draft is included in the "Documents in Advance" for the next yearly meeting annual gathering and circulated again to the meetings and executive committee. Sometimes, new light is found and it is necessary to prepare a fourth draft. At yearly meeting annual gathering the latest draft is brought forward in an early business session so that, if changes are called for, the changes can be worked out outside the business sessions and the revised third (or new fourth) draft brought back to a later business session of the same yearly meeting sessions asking for approval.

If at some point in the above procedure, there is considerable disagreement, the faith and practice committee can lay over the draft, repeat the above process for making a new draft, and send it out to the meetings and groups for comment. Or the committee can be creative and find a way to listen to and labor with the concerned parties before going on with or stopping the process of writing the section. All the time needed to find unity on the section in question is taken.

If agreement on a section can not be reached, the proposed addition or change is set aside for the present, to allow for all necessary seasoning.

If unity is found and the section is approved, the new section is posted on the seym.org website for immediate use by the meetings and worship groups, and included in the *Faith and Practice* at the next printing.

The committee found in practice that meetings and worship groups were were able to comfortably process two chapters or sections at a time in the revision process outlined above. Thus greatly condensing the time required for the overall revision. The process for each section/chapter takes about three years from starting draft to approval.

The process detailed above can on appearance seem endless, however, when the faith and practice committee is open to the guidance of the Spirit, the work is often blessed and uplifting. The gifts of Love and patience flow like a balm. All necessary time passes and the yearly meeting is gifted with a new *Faith and Practice*.

CHAPTER 15

A BRIEF
History of Quakers in Southeastern USA

Formally incorporated in 1964 as Southeastern Yearly Meeting, Quakers in the southeast U.S. have a long and colorful history in the area. Seventeeth-century spiritual leader George Fox almost visited the future SEYM as he traveled past Spanish-claimed Florida and the Georgia coastlines on his way from Barbados to Philadelphia.

Quakers settled in Charleston, South Carolina as early as 1657, with meeting records dating from the 1680's. Mary Fisher, one of the Valiant Sixty (the first 60 or more Quaker ministers who were convinced by Fox and spread the Quaker message worldwide) and who, c. 1660, traveled mostly by herself to the capital of the Ottoman Empire, ministering in the Light to the Grand Turk, was honored by him and allowed to return home; in later years she came to Charleston and was married and eventually buried at the Charleston meetinghouse c. 1690. The Charleston Meeting was laid down in 1837 after having been burned down twice by the slave-holding citizens in the area, thus causing most of the Quakers to migrate to more friendly environments to the north and west.

In 1696, Quaker Jonathan Dickinson, for whom the Florida state park is named, was shipwrecked near Jupiter Inlet in Florida and wrote a journal of his experiences over the year while he waited for the next ship coming by to rescue him and his party. Nearly seventy-five years later, the Quaker botanist William Bartram, inspired by Dickinson's journal, traveled extensively in the southeast, studying Florida and Georgia flora. He is perhaps the first Friend to witness the fury of a Florida hurricane, c. 1773. He also wrote that in 1793 he visited a Friends meeting near the town of Wrightsborough, (in the vicinity of modern day Augusta, Georgia), that had formed

c. 1755. By 1807, those Friends, opposed to slavery, had laid down their meeting and migrated northwest to Ohio, Indiana, or Illinois.

In the nineteenth century, the first influx of Friends in Florida arrived in Alachua County from Indiana, Nebraska and Iowa. The first Florida meetinghouse was built by Whitewater Meeting (1884-1897) near Archer, under the care of Richmond Monthly Meeting, Indiana. During the same time period, Lake Kerr Friends, having migrated from Michigan, Ohio, and London, England, started the first Friends elementary school in Florida. They sent their high school youth to Westtown Friends School near Philadelphia. The "Big Freeze" of 1892-1893 wiped out both of these Friends communities of orange grove owners. Those Friends sold their land and moved back up north.

Contemporary Quaker history commences in 1893 when the railroad transported the first Quaker farmers to Miami from the northeast. The Quaker community there waxed and waned, finally becoming firmly established in 1948 and, under the care of Friends World Committee for Consultation (FWCC), became a Monthly Meeting in 1950. Meanwhile, since about 1900, Friends had been moving to Orlando from the New Jersey and Philadelphia monthly meetings and had established a preparative meeting under the care of Moorestown Monthly Meeting in New Jersey. They became a monthly meeting in 1944 under the care of FWCC. In 1917, St. Petersburg Friends organized and have met regularly since. They, too, became a recognized monthly meeting under the care of FWCC and built Florida's first continuously used meetinghouse. Due to very poor roads and no direct transportation, there was little contact among these early Florida Friends until the late 1940s.

During World War II, a conscientious objector camp was set up near Orlando in 1942. After the war, many of the COs moved their families down to Florida which helped establish new Friends meetings.

By 1950, Friends were encouraged by American Friends Service Committee and Friends General Conference Field Secretary

J. Barnard Walton to organize further. Thus the Southeastern Conference of the Religious Society of Friends was formed. Later during the 1962 conference, it was recorded that "Seven Meetings of the Southeastern Friends Conference having indicated by official Minutes their desire to assume Yearly Meeting status, the Planning Committee recommends that these Meetings now consider themselves the Southeastern Yearly Meeting [of The Religious Society of Friends] . . ." These seven monthly meetings were Augusta, Georgia, and Florida meetings in Gainesville, Jacksonville, Miami, Orlando, Palm Beach, and St. Petersburg.

The first full sessions of Southeastern Yearly Meeting were held April 12, 1963 near Avon Park, Florida. J. Barnard Walton (Friends General Conference, 1915-1963) was instrumental in shepherding the conference from its inception in 1950 to this conclusion. In recognition of his support, the annual yearly business meeting Saturday-night lecture series was named the J. Barnard Walton Memorial Lecture.

SEYM meetings continue to grow and wane as population centers evolve. One decade into the twenty-first century, twenty-five meetings and worship groups are affiliated with or have a relationship with SEYM. In addition to the larger annual gathering/business meeting, SEYM supports two annual interim business meetings. Following the winter interim business meeting, the Dwight and Ardis Michener Memorial Lecture, begun in 1971, is held at the Orlando meetinghouse. The Walton and Michener lectures are published annually to share the experience with the wider Quaker fellowship. Also, SEYM is noted for assisting in the founding and continued support of ProNica.

CHAPTER 16

APPENDIX A

Gainesville Monthly Meeting's Practice of Recording Gifts of Ministry

Although Friends' practice of a free ministry is based upon the experience that the gifts of the Holy Spirit may be bestowed upon anyone at any time, a monthly meeting may, upon the advice of its Committee on Worship and Ministry, record as ministers those members who are recognized as having a clear leading to vocal ministry and prayer or counseling of individuals.

This recognition is not one of status or privilege and should be reviewed periodically. It is an affirmation based upon loving trust. The meeting's trust is that individuals so recorded will, in all humility, diligently nurture and exercise the gift of ministry in order that the meeting as a whole may be nourished. The individual's trust is that the meeting will on its part encourage and sustain them, and not only liberate them to undertake the disciplines of prayer and study and retreat that help clarify the springs of ministry, but also lovingly and faithfully counsel them. Such nurture and encouragement and discipline are of special significance for younger members who, out of diffidence or unawareness, may discount their gifts and let them wither.

The gifts of the Spirit are diverse, and Friends' ministry includes pastoral care in settings such as hospitals and prisons. Friends' work in these areas may be especially benefited by the recording as ministers of those so gifted.

Philadelphia Yearly Meeting *Faith and Practice*, 2002

The Process

Someone who wishes to be recorded as a minister should first write a letter to the clerk of the meeting explaining the nature of the leading and why he or she wishes to be recorded as a minister for that purpose. The clerk should read the letter aloud to those gathered in meeting for business so that everyone is aware of the request and the nature of the leading. The letter is given to worship and ministry.

Worship and ministry (or whatever committee has oversight of the meeting) appoints a clearness committee that will meet with the person making the request. After prayerful deliberation among themselves, the committee makes a recommendation to worship and ministry. Worship and ministry reports its recommendation to the meeting in meeting for business. The meeting then writes the minute to record the minister for a specific purpose to be revisited periodically, stating the time this minute will be reviewed.

A care and accountability committee is then appointed by the meeting to meet periodically with the minister to encourage and sustain him or her and to offer loving counsel. As it deems necessary this committee would report any concerns it may have to worship and ministry.

Advice

It is good to be very clear about what you are doing. Do the same as you would for any other purpose (membership, marriage) and lay over any action as long as is necessary to satisfy all concerns.

The clearness committee should not be restricted by the queries developed for this purpose. The members should consider, "Is this person leading a Quaker life? Do we want this person to represent us? What has been the quality of this person's ministry among us?" When asking about the family members (see the following queries), the committee should name specific family members that the committee may be concerned about.

The recorded minister may need a piece of paper certifying that he or she is a recorded minister of the meeting in order to satisfy legal requirements for fulfilling this ministry. The meeting should inquire exactly what is required and provide it to the extent that it is able.

The care and accountability committee needs to provide whatever support is needed and challenge the minister to remain faithful to his or her leadings.

Queries for Prospective Ministers

Leadings

What has led you to seek to be recorded as a minister in the Religious Society of Friends?

Share with us ways in which you have experienced God's presence in making this decision.

How do you understand the difference between helping to do the work of God and just doing a job that needs to be done?

What questions do you have about the role and the source of your ministry?

Quakerism

How would you apply Friends' testimonies of peace, integrity, equality, simplicity, and community to the ministry you envision?

What is your understanding of these phrases used by Friends: "listening to that of God within," "yielding to the Spirit," and "way will open"?

The Ministry

There is a wide spectrum of spiritual experiences, culture, and language among people. How will you be able to respond to this diversity (background, religion, temperament, and interests)?

Can you meet differences of opinion with those you counsel with love, humor, mutual respect, patience, and generosity?

How well do you know the work you are seeking to do?

What special gifts do you have that will help you in this ministry?

How will this ministry benefit you?

What do you expect your ministry to bring to the meeting?

Family

Have you shared your desire to undertake this ministry with your entire family, and have you found unity in this undertaking?

What are the views of your family members towards this ministry?

Have you discussed with your family plans to follow in case there is adverse reaction to your ministry from the wider community?

What are your feelings about the possibility of placing your family in any jeopardy because of your ministry?

Will this ministry have any effect on your ability to earn money, and if so have you made provisions to support your family?

Meeting Support and Accountability

How can the meeting support your continued attempts/ effort to walk in the Light, to let God lead you in this work?

Is there a form of oversight and support that you have found helpful and would like to receive from the meeting?

If you have uneasy feelings about your ministry, how would you share these with a support committee?

Do you have the courage to go to a support group for guidance, not only for spiritual renewal but also for burdens this ministry may place upon your family, the meeting, or your professional life?

What do you expect the monthly meeting to do to support your ministry?

Queries for Reflection on the Well-being of the Recorded Minister

1. What kind of experiences have you had?

2. Do you still feel led to do this work?

3. How have you been able to minister to these people (callers)?

4. Have you felt the ministry of this work beyond counseling?

5. Do you have any uneasy feelings about your ministry?

6. Have your expectations changed?

7. Do you feel the support of the meeting?

8. How can the meeting support your continued attempts to let God lead you in this work?

APPENDIX B

Gainesville Monthly Meeting's Testimony of Stewardship Stewardship of Economic Resources

All that we have, in our selves and our possessions, are gifts from God, entrusted to us for our responsible use. Jesus reminds us that we must not lay up earthly treasures for ourselves, for where our treasures are, there will our hearts be also. We cannot serve both God and Mammon.

Stewardship is a coming together of our major testimonies. To be good stewards in God's world calls on us to examine and consider the ways in which our testimonies for peace, equality, and simplicity interact to guide our relationships with all life.

> *O that we who declare against wars, and acknowledge our trust to be in God only, may walk in the light, and thereby examine our foundation and motives in holding great estates! May we look upon our treasures, the furniture of our houses, and our garments, and try whether the seeds of war have nourishment in these our possessions.*
>
> **John Woolman, c. 1770**

In a world of economic interactions far more complex than John Woolman could have imagined, Friends need to examine their decisions about obtaining, holding, and using money and other assets, to see whether they find in them the seeds, not only of wars, but also of self-indulgence, injustice, and ecological disaster. Good stewardship of economic resources consists both in avoidance of those evils and in actions that advance peace, simple living, justice, and a healthy ecosystem. Good stewardship also requires attention to the economic needs of Quaker and other organizations that advance Friends' testimonies.

Right Sharing

*Friends worldwide have accepted the idea that the
testimony of equality in the economic realm implies
a commitment to the right sharing of the world's resources. Friends in comfortable circumstances need
to find practical expression of the testimony of simplicity in their earning and spending. They must
consider the meaning for their own lives of economic
equality and simplicity, and what level of income is
consonant with their conclusions. They should consider likewise what portion of that income should be
shared beyond the immediate family. That decision
entails balancing the social value of self-sufficiency
against the social value of greater help for those
more needy. It also requires judgments about what
expenditures are essential and what are discretionary, and about the values that will underlie discretionary expenditures.*

Excerpted from Philadelphia Yearly Meeting
Faith and Practice, **2002, pp. 80-81.**

Walk Gently on the Earth

*And out of the ground the Lord God made to grow
every tree that is pleasant to the sight and good for
food. . . . The Lord God took the man and put him
in the garden of Eden To till it and keep it. And the
Lord God commanded the man, saying, "You may
freely eat of every tree of the garden . . ." Then the
Lord God said, "It is not good that the man should
be alone; I will make him a helper fit for him." So
out of the ground the Lord God formed every beast
of the field and every bird of the air, and brought
them to the man to see what he would call them;*

Genesis 2: 9; 15-16; 18-19 (RSV)

For the Lord showed me that . . . I might not eat and drink to make myself wanton but for health, using the creatures in their service, as servants in their places, to the glory of him that hath created them; they being in their covenant, and I being brought up into the covenant, as sanctified by the Word which was in the beginning, by which all things are up-held; wherein is unity with the creation. But people being strangers to the covenant of life with God, they eat and drink to make themselves wanton with the creatures, devouring them upon their own lusts, and living in all filthiness, loving foul ways and de-vouring the creation; and all this in the world, in the pollutions thereof, without God; and therefore I was to shun all such.

George Fox, The Journal of George Fox, John L. Nickalls, ed., 1997, p. 2

We recognize that the well-being of the earth is a funda-mental spiritual concern. From the beginning, it was through the wonders of nature that people saw God. How we treat the earth and its creatures is a basic part of our relationship with God. Our planet as a whole, not just the small parts of it in our immediate custody, requires our responsible attention.

As Friends become aware of the interconnectedness of all life on this planet and the devastation caused by neglect of any part of it, we have become more willing to extend our sense of community to encompass all living things. We must now consider whether we should lay aside the belief that we humans are acting stewards of the natural world and instead view human actions as the major threat to the ecosystem.

Friends are indeed called to walk gently on the earth. Wasteful and extravagant consumption is a major cause of destruction of the environment. The right sharing of the world's remaining resources requires that people in underdeveloped nations can have more and that the earth's life-sustaining systems can be restored. The world cannot tolerate indefinitely the present rate of consumption by technologically developed nations.

Friends are called to become models and patterns of simple living and concern for the earth. Some may find it difficult to change their accustomed lifestyle; others recognize the need and have begun to adopt ways of life which put the least strain on the world's resources of clean air, water, soil, and energy.

A serious threat to the planet is the population explosion and consequent famine, war, and devastation. Called on to make decisions to simplify our lives, we may find that the most difficult to accept will be limiting the number of children we have.

> *Voluntary simplicity in living and restraint in pro-creation hold the promise of ecological redemption and spiritual renewal.*
> **Excerpted from Philadelphia Yearly Meeting**
> ***Faith and Practice*, 2002, p. 81**

Submitted by Gainesville Monthly Meeting

APPENDIX C
NOMINATIONS TO SERVICE WITHIN SEYM

Clerks and Officers
1. Yearly Meeting Clerk
2. Interim Business Meeting Clerk (serves also as Executive Committee Clerk)
3. Assistant Clerk (serves both YM and IBM Clerks)
4. Recording Clerk (serves both YM and IBM Clerks)
5. Treasurer
6. Membership Recorder
7. Young Friends (Teen) co-Clerks (they select their own clerks)
8. Young Adult Quakers co-Clerks (they select their own clerks)
9. Clerk of Trustees (Trustees select their own clerk)
10. Trustee
11. Trustee
12. Trustee
13. Trustee
14. Trustee

Standing Committee Clerks
15. Archives
16. Committee for Earthcare
17. Committee for Ministry on Racism
18. Faith and Practice
19. Finance
20. Half Yearly Meeting
21. Meeting for Sufferings – currently inactive
22. Nominating
23. Peace and Social Concerns
24. Publications – currently inactive
25. Religious Education – currently inactive
26. Worship and Ministry
27. Yearly Meeting Gathering
28. Youth
29. Website

All Clerks, Officers, and Standing Committee Clerks are members of the Executive Committee. All serve for three-year terms.

APPENDIX D
Nominations to the Wider Quaker World

Representatives to Organizations
1. American Friends Service Committee Corporation (AFSC, Philadelphia) – 2 representatives
2. American Friends Service Committee, Southeast Region Office (AFSC/SERO) – 2 representatives
3. Friends Committee on National Legislation/William Penn House (FCNL/William Penn) – up to 5 representatives
4. Friends General Conference (FGC) Central Committee – 3 representatives
5. Friends for Lesbian, Gay, Bisexual, Transgendered, and Queer Concerns (FLGBTQC) – 1 representative
6. Friends Peace Teams – 2 representatives
7. Friends World Committee for Consultation, Section of the Americas (FWCC) – up to 4 representatives
8. Florida Council of Churches – 1 representative
9. Florida IMPACT – 1 representative
10. Palmetto Friends Gathering – up to 3 representatives
11. Quaker Earthcare Witness – 2 representatives
12. Quaker United Nations Office (QUNO) – 2 correspondents

Observer to Organizations
13. Friends United Meeting (FUM) General Board Observer – 1 observer

Appointees to Organizations
14. ProNica Board – 3 appointees

Ad Hoc Committees
15. As requested by the Yearly Meeting Clerk or the Interim Business Meeting Clerk

All serve for three-year terms.

APPENDIX E
SUGGESTED FORM LETTER FOR
REQUESTING DUAL MEMBERSHIP

Date

TO [YOUR HOME MEETING] Monthly Meeting of [YOUR HOME YEARLY MEETING] Yearly Meeting:

Because of the special situation in many of our monthly meetings for those Friends who hold primary membership in some other monthly meeting and wish to retain that membership, but who also reside in the South all or part of the year and take an active interest in the life and work of one of our meetings, Southeastern Yearly Meeting recognizes dual membership.

Such Friends are not counted as members in any statistical report, but in every other way are considered as full members as long as they wish the relationship to continue. We welcome them, not only for the added strength they bring to our meetings, but also for the closer ties of fellowship which this association brings with their home meetings.

Southeastern Yearly Meeting welcomes into sojourning membership those Friends who are temporarily within our area and who bring sojourning minutes from their home meetings. However, where the association is on a more regular or permanent basis it seems appropriate to record Friends as dual members under the conditions described above.

[YOUR NAME/S] (have/has) requested membership with us on this basis. Before enrolling (them/his/her), we would like to notify your Meeting of this intended action, and if it meets with your approval, we would appreciate receiving from you a Minute of acknowledgment and approval.

Signed _____
Clerk of (SEYM Meeting Name) Monthly Meeting

Signature(s) of Friend(s) requesting Dual Membership

APPENDIX F
SUGGESTED FORM LETTER FOR
CERTIFICATE OF TRANSFER

A member residing in the area of another monthly meeting is encouraged to transfer his or her membership to that monthly meeting. This certificate of transfer is to be used for that purpose.

After the committee of the meeting from which the certificate is to be sent have satisfied themselves as to the condition of the individual(s) to be transferred, they should prepare this certificate of transfer in duplicate and present it to their monthly meeting, one copy to be retained by the clerk. Husband and wife and minor children may be included on one form, but separate certificates must be provided in other cases.

TO [NEW MONTHLY MEETING] Monthly Meeting of the Religious Society of Friends:

Dear Friends,

Our certificate of transfer has been requested on behalf of [TRANSFERRING FRIEND] [TRANSFERRING FAMILY MEMBERS],
member(s) of this monthly meeting who now reside(s) within your area. The usual inquiry has been made, and no obstruction appearing we recommend
[TRANSFERRING FRIEND] [TRANSFERRING FAMILY MEMBERS]
to your care and remain with love your Friends.

Signed on behalf of [MONTHLY MEETING NAME] Monthly Meeting of the Religious Society of Friends, held the [NUMBER OF THE DAY] of the [NUMBER OF THE MONTH], 20XX

Signed _____
Clerk

APPENDIX G

The following form is available in 8.5 x 11 inch downloadable pdf from the seym.org website. It is provided here for your perusal.

MONTHLY MEETING MEMBERSHIP RECORD

Monthly Meeting: _____

    Membership No.: _____

Member's full name: _____

    Birth Name: _____

    Birth Date: _____

    Place of Birth: _____

    Mother's birth name: _____

    Father's birth name: _____

Membership

    By birth: _____

    By application: _____

    By certificate of transfer from: _____ Meeting

    Dual membership (2 YMs) with _____ Meeting

    and _____ Meeting

Member's current address: _____

Member's former addressees: _____

If Applicable

Spouse or Partner's name: _____

    Optional: birth date, place of birth, parent's names

_____

_____

Ceremony date: _____

If separated and/or divorced, date: _____

Deceased: _____

Member's former spouse(s) or partner(s) name(s):

_____

Children (list each child and provide following information.
Name(s), Birth date:(s), Places of birth:

_____

_____

_____ :

Membership(s) held in _____Meeting

Optional information for contact purposes:

Termination date:

By certificate of transfer to: _____Monthly Meeting

By resignation: _____

By release: _____

By death_____; location of ashes or burial _____

Information supplied by: _____

<u>PLEASE RETURN THIS DOCUMENT PROMPTLY TO</u>
<u>MONTHLY MEETING RECORDER</u>

APPENDIX H

The following forms are available in 8.5 x 11 inch downloadable pdf from the seym.org website, which is a more useable size. The text and layout of the forms are provided here for your perusal.

Requests to the Monthly Meeting About Incapacity or Death

INTRODUCTION TO DYING, DEATH, AND BEREAVEMENT FORMS

The meeting can offer assistance around the process of death. The individual may ask the meeting for any level of assistance or none at all. It is very difficult for us to face the prospect of our own death so there may be reluctance to fill out these forms even if we would like the meeting to be involved. It is suggested that the meeting periodically bring Friends together to discuss end-of-life issues and to give Friends a chance to ask questions about the forms and to fill out the parts they find useful. The completed forms are retained by the meeting recorder, until such time as they are needed. It may happen that a Friend may not get around to filling out the forms until death is imminent. If a member of the meeting community is dying, it would be appropriate for someone from the meeting to make clear to the dying person what assistance the meeting can provide. The meeting recorder is responsible for having blank copies of these forms available to anyone in the meeting. Forms may also be available for downloading from the Southeastern Yearly Meeting website <www.seym.org>.

It is recommended that Friends prepare a Will, a Living Will, Designation of Health Care Surrogate, a Durable Power of Attorney, and a Living Trust. Such legal documents, of course, are drawn up with regard to the laws of the state the individual lives in. Instructions and sample forms are available at your local Hospice office and at Aging with Dignity, P.O. Box 1661, Tallahassee, Florida 32302-1661, 1-888-594-7437, <www.agingwithdignity.org>. The

Advanced Directives from Aging with Dignity are called Five Wishes.

It would be well for meetings to note that the laws and customs in the end-of-life area are constantly changing. These forms are as good as we can make them now, but changes are bound to occur. Individuals are encouraged to file a Living Will with their primary care doctor and their hospital and verify that the doctor and hospital will follow it.

Legal resources within SEYM are available for those Gay, Lesbian, Bi-sexual, Transgender and Queer persons who face special problems in preparing for their death.

REQUESTS REGARDING
MY POSSIBLE INCAPACITY

Name: _____ Date: _____

Address: _____

_____

Phone:_____

E-mail: _____

I request _____ Monthly Meeting to do the
following things for me if I become incapacitated:

1. To notify these persons of my incapacity.
   Yes _____   No _____
   If yes, **Attach a List** including: name, address, phone number, e-mail, and relationship.
2. To notify my health care surrogate and the person who has a durable power of attorney for my financial affairs.
   Yes _____   No _____
   If yes, **Attach a List** including: name, address, phone number, e-mail, function and relationship.
3. I have a Living Will?   Yes _____   No _____
   If yes, what is the location of the document?
   Attach Instructions.

Signature of person
making request:_____

Date _____ Dates reviewed _____   _____   _____

Received for _____ Monthly Meeting.   Date: _____

Clerk or Recorder's
Signature:_____ Date: _____

REQUESTS REGARDING MY DEATH

Name: _____ Date: _____

Address: _____

_____

Phone:_____

E-mail: _____

I request _____ Monthly Meeting to do the
following things for me if I become incapacitated:

1. To notify these persons at the time of my death. Yes _____
   No _____
   If yes, **Attach a List** including: name, address, phone number, e-mail, and relationship. You may include the executor
   of your will if you wish.
2. If I have minor children or other dependents and there is
   no surviving parent or guardian, I ask the meeting to notify
   those responsible for their care. Yes _____ No _____
   If yes, **Attach a List** with the necessary information.
3. To oversee the disposal of my body in the manner I request.
   Yes _____ No _____
   If yes, complete, sign and attach the corresponding form
   provided in this packet, including your financial arrangements to carry this out.
4. To plan and carry out a memorial meeting for me. Yes _____
   No _____
   If yes, complete, sign and attach the corresponding form
   provided in this packet.
5. To provide information, if necessary, for the completion of
   the Death Certificate. Yes _____ No _____
   If yes, complete, sign and attach the corresponding form
   provided in this packet.
6. I have a Will and a Living Will? Yes _____ No _____
   If yes, what is the location of these documents?

Attach Instructions

Signature of person
making request:_____

Date _____ Dates reviewed _____   _____   _____

Received for _____ Monthly Meeting.   Date: _____
Clerk or Recorder's
Signature:_____ Date: _____

❖   ❖   ❖   ❖   ❖

REQUESTS REGARDING DISPOSAL OF MY BODY

Name:_____ Date: _____

Address: _____

_____

Phone:_____

E-mail: _____

I request _____ Monthly Meeting to notify my
next of kin/significant other of my wishes for disposal of my body as
follows at the time of my death. In the event of no surviving next of
kin/significant other, I authorize _____ Monthly
Meeting to carry out my wishes and have made financial arrangements to do so. **Attach Instructions.**

1.   __ Burial   __ Cremation   __ Medical Research   __
Organ Donations   ___ Eye Bank
If you have decided to donate your body to Medical
Research, Organ Donations or Eye Bank, please designate
a second choice of Burial or Cremation in the event your
wishes are unable to be carried out.

2. Do you own a plot for your interment?

    Cemetery: _____

    City: _____

    State: _____

    Plot : _____

    Location of deed to cemetery plot: _____

3. If your body is to be cremated, what do you wish done with your ashes? Please provide enough detail so that the meeting can carry out your wishes. **Attach Instructions.**

4. If your body is to be given for medical use, who needs to be contacted? **Attach Instructions.**

5. Member of a Memorial Society: Yes _____ No _____

    Name: _____

    Address: _____

    _____

    Phone: _____

6. Undertaker preferred: _____

    Phone: _____

7. Burial insurance company: _____

    Policy number: _____

    Location of Policy: _____
    If no insurance, expenses are to be met as follows:
    Attach Instructions.

8. Special instructions if death is distant from home:
    Attach Instructions.

Signature of person
making request: _____

Date _____ Dates reviewed _____   _____   _____

Received for _____ Monthly Meeting.   Date: _____
Clerk or Recorder's
Signature: _____ Date: _____

❖   ❖   ❖   ❖   ❖

REQUESTS REGARDING
MY MEMORIAL MEETING

Name: _____   Date: _____

Address: _____

_____

Phone: _____

E-mail: _____

Unless otherwise specified the usual practice would be a memorial meeting for worship as described in the *Faith and Practice* in the Dying, Death, and Bereavement Section. Please indicate any specific requests.

Special requests: _____

_____

_____

Flowers accepted? Yes _____   No _____

   Where? _____

In lieu of flowers, contributions may be made to: _____

_____

_____

Do you wish the meeting to put an
obituary in the paper?   Yes _____ No _____

(Funeral homes will provide a simple notice without extra cost and
might submit your obituary for you at the newspaper's rate.)

Do you have an obituary you wish
the meeting to use?   Yes _____ No _____

Please attach the obituary or information about your life.

Signature of person
making request:_____

Date _____ Dates reviewed _____   _____   _____

Received for _____ Monthly Meeting.   Date: _____

Clerk or Recorder's
Signature:_____ Date: _____

❖   ❖   ❖   ❖   ❖

INFORMATION FORM
FOR DEATH CERTIFICATE

Name:_____ Date: _____

Address: _____

_____

Phone:_____

E-mail: _____

ONLY FILL THIS FORM OUT **IF** YOU ARE ASKING THE MEETING TO FILE YOUR DEATH CERTIFICATE
Information must agree with legal records and policies

Full legal name: _____

Other names on legal documents : _____

Address :_____

County you live in: _____

Social Security Number: _____ _

Date of Birth: _____

Birthplace: _____

Citizenship: _____

Present Employer:_____

Occupation: _____

Kind of business or industry: _____

Marital Status: _____

Surviving Spouse (Partner): _____

Address of surviving
spouse (partner): _____

Education:

_____ 10 – 12, _____ college 1 – 4, _____ college 5 + _____

Race: _____

Father's full name:: _____

Mother's full name
including maiden name: _____

Surviving children: _____

_____

_____

Addresses of surviving children:

Signature of person
making request: _____

Date _____ Dates reviewed _____   _____   _____

Received for _____ Monthly Meeting.   Date: _____

Clerk or Recorder's
Signature: _____ Date: _____

❖   ❖   ❖   ❖   ❖

FORMS FOR MY LIVING WILL

Name: _____   Date: _____

Address: _____

_____

Phone: _____

E-mail: _____

Included are sample forms for a Living Will and a Designation of Health Care Surrogate, circa 2003. Friends are urged to find current forms applicable to your situation.

Definitions useful in understanding Living Will and Designation of Health Care Surrogate forms.

"Health care decision" means:
- Informed consent, refusal of consent, or withdrawal of consent to any and all health care, including life-prolonging procedures.

- The decision to apply for private, public, government, or veterans' benefits to defray the cost of health care.

- The right of access to all records of the principal that are reasonably necessary for a health care surrogate to make decisions involving health care and to apply for benefits.

- The decision to make an anatomical gift pursuant to Part X of Chapter 732, Florida Statutes, or the corresponding statutes in other states.

"Incapacity" or "incompetent" means the patient is physically or mentally unable to communicate a willful and knowing health care decision. For the purposes of making an anatomical gift, the term also includes a patient who is deceased.

"Life-prolonging procedure" means any medical procedure, treatment, antibiotics or intervention, including artificially provided sustenance and hydration, or other which sustains, restores, or supplants a spontaneous vital function. The term does not include the administration of medication or performance of a medical procedure, when such medication or procedure is deemed necessary to provide comfort care or to alleviate pain.

"Terminal condition" means a condition caused by injury, disease, or illness from which there is no reasonable medical probability of recovery and which, without treatment, can be expected to cause death.

"End-stage condition" means a condition caused by injury, disease, or illness which has resulted in severe and permanent deterioration, indicated by incapacity and complete physical dependency, and for which, to a reasonable degree of medical certainty, treatment of the irreversible condition would be medically ineffective.

"Persistent vegetative state" means a permanent and irreversible condition of unconsciousness in which there is:

A. the absence of voluntary action or cognitive behavior or any kind; or

B. an inability to communicate or interact purposefully with the environment.

Legal resources within SEYM are available for those Gay, Lesbian, Bi-sexual, Transgender and Queer persons who face special problems in preparing for their death.

SAMPLE: LIVING WILL

Declaration made this _____ day of _____, 20__,

I, _____, willfully and voluntarily make known my desire that my dying not be artificially prolonged under the circumstances set forth below, and I do hereby declare that, if at any time I am incapacitated

And (initial one or more of the following three conditions)

_____ (initial) I have a terminal condition

or _____ (initial) I have an end-stage condition

or _____ (initial) I am in a persistent vegetative state

And if my attending or treating physician and another consulting physician have determined that there is no reasonable medical probability of my recovery from such condition, I direct that life-prolonging procedures be withheld or withdrawn when the application of such procedures would serve only to prolong artificially the process of dying, and that I be permitted to die naturally with only the administration of medication or the performance of any medical procedure deemed necessary to provide me with comfort care or to alleviate pain.

It is my intention that this declaration be honored by my family and physician as the final expression of my legal right to refuse medical or surgical treatment and to accept the consequences for such refusal.

In the event that I have been determined to be unable to provide express and informed consent regarding the withholding, withdrawal, or continuation of life-prolonging procedures, I wish to designate, as my surrogate to carry out the provisions of this declaration:

Name: _____

Address: _____

Phone: _____

I understand the full import of this declaration, and I am emotionally and mentally competent to make this declaration.

Additional Instructions (optional):

Signed: _____

Date: _____

Witnesses' signature, address, and phone number:

1. _____

_____

2. _____

_____

Sample: Designation of Health Care Surrogate

Name: (Last)_____(First)_____(I.)__

In the event that I have been determined to be incapacitated to provide informed consent for medical treatment and surgical and diagnostic procedures, I wish to designate as my surrogate for health care decisions:

Name::   _____

Address: _____

Phone: _____

If my surrogate is unwilling or unable to perform his or her duties, I wish to designate as my alternate surrogate:

Name: _____

Address: _____

Phone: _____

I fully understand that this designation will permit my designee to make health care decisions, except for anatomical gifts, unless I have executed an anatomical gift declaration pursuant to law, and to provide, withhold, or withdraw consent on my behalf; to apply for public benefits to defray the cost of health care; and to authorize my admission to or transfer from a health care facility.

Additional Instructions (optional):

I further affirm that this designation is not being made as a condition of treatment or admission to a health care facility. I will notify and send a copy of this document to the following persons other than my surrogate, so they may know who my surrogate is.

Name: _____

Name: _____

Name: _____

Signed: _____

Date: _____

Witnesses' signature, address, and phone number:

    1. _____

       _____

    2. _____

       _____

RECOMMENDED READING REFERENCE LIST

All Titles used as references in this list have been rated by Five or more professional Quaker librarians as to their suitability for each level of Quaker experience.

A Friendly Reading List, 2nd Edition

TOP PICKS

Compiled by Phoebe Andersen and Sally Rickerman
Published by Troll Press, 2011
Used with permission of the authors

PUBLICATIONS OF INTEREST TO FIRST-TIME AND NEW ATTENDERS

BIOGRAPHY

Bacon, Margaret Hope. *Valiant Friend: The Life of Lucretia Mott.*
Rose, June. *Elizabeth Fry: A Biography.*

CONCERNS AND PRACTICE

Cox, Fabianson, Farley & Swennerfelt. *Earthcare for Friends: A Study Guide for Individuals and Faith Communities.* Quaker Earth Witness, 2004, 254 PP. Spiral Bound.

Dandelion, Ben Pink. *An Introduction To Quakerism.* Cambridge, 2007, 296 PP. Paper.

Gee, David. *Faithful Deeds: A Rough Guide to the Quaker Peace Testimony.*

Kreidler, William J. *Conflict Resolution in the Middle School.*

Manousos, Anthony, ed. *Western Quaker Reader: Writings by and about Independent Quakers in the Western United States, 1929-1999.*

FAITH AND PRACTICE

Faith & Practice Publications. Books of *Faith & Practice* from 12 different Yearly Meetings.

Jones, Rufus M. *The Faith and Practice of the Quakers.*

FAITH, MINISTRY AND SPIRITUALITY

Allen, Richard. *Silence and Speech: For Those New to Meeting for Worship.* Britain Yearly Meeting, 2004, 14 PP. Paper.

Allen, Richard. *Yours in Friendship: An Open Letter to Enquirers.*

Ambler, Rex. *Light to Live by: An Exploration in Quaker Spirituality.* Britain YM, 2002, 60 PP. Paper.

Beasley-Topliffe, Keith. *The Sanctuary of the Soul: Selected Writings of Thomas Kelly.*

Beasley-Topliffe, Keith. *Walking Humbly with God: Selected Writings of John Woolman.*

Bill, J. Brent. *Holy Silence: The Gift of Quaker Spirituality.* Paraclete Press, 2005, 165 PP. Paper.

Bill, J. Brent, ed. *Imagination & Spirit: A Contemporary Quaker Reader.* Friends United Press, 2002, 240 PP. Paper.

Black, Klos, Reddy, Smith & Stacy, eds. *Whispers of Faith: Young Friends Share their Experience of Quakerism.* Quaker Press of FGC, 2005, 168 PP. Paper.

Gates, Tom. *Opening the Scriptures: Bible Lessons from the 2005 Annual Gathering of Friends.* Quaker Press of FGC, 2005, 64 PP. Paper.

Gillman, Harvey. *A Light That Is Shining: An Introduction to the Quakers.*

Gorman, George H. *The Amazing Fact of Quaker Worship.* (1973).

Gulley, Phillip & James Mulholland. *If Grace is True: Why God Will Save Every Person.* HarperCollins, 2004, 225 PP. Paper.

Gulley, Phillip & James Mulholland. *If God is Love: Rediscovering Grace in an Ungracious World.* HarperSF, 2005, 288 PP. Paper.

Joliff, William. *The Poetry of John Greenleaf Whittier: A Readers Edition.*

Kelly, Thomas. *Reality of the Spiritual World & Gathered Meeting.*

Kelly, Thomas. *Testament of Devotion.*

Kelly, Thomas. *The Eternal Promise.*

Macy, Howard. *Laughing Pilgrims: Humor and the Spiritual*

Journey. Paternoster Press, 2006, 137 PP. Paper.

Mullen, Tom. *A Very Good Marriage.*

Outreach Committee of Philadelphia YM. *William Penn.* (Video).

Outreach Committee of Philadelphia YM. *The Quakers: That of God in Every One.* (Videotape).

Palmer, Parker. *A Hidden Wholeness: The Journey Toward an Undivided Life.* Jossey-Bass, 2004, 192 PP. Cloth.

Palmer, Parker. *Courage To Teach – 10th Anniversary Edition.* Jossey-Bass, 2007, 272 PP. Cloth & CD.

Palmer, Parker J. *The Active Life: A Spirituality of Work, Creativity and Caring.*

Punshon, John. *Encounter with Silence: Reflections from the Quaker Tradition.*

Pym, Jim. *Listening to the Light: How to Bring Quaker Simplicity and Integrity into Our Lives.*

Smith, Robert Lawrence. *Quaker Book of Wisdom: Life Lessons in Simplicity, Service and Common Sense.* HarperCollins, 1999, 144 PP. Paper.

Steere, Douglas V. *Dimensions of Prayer: Cultivating a Relationship with God.*

Steere, Douglas V. *Introduction from Quaker Spirituality.*

Watson, Elizabeth. *Wisdom's Daughters: Stories of Women Around Jesus.*

Watson, Elizabeth. *Guests in My Life.* (reprinted 1984).

West, Jessamyn. *The Quaker Reader.*

Whitmire, Catherine. *Plain Living: A Quaker Path to Simplicity.*

Whittier, John Greenleaf. *Selections From The Religious Poems.* Tract Association, 2000, 84 PP. Paper.

FICTION

Allen, Irene. *Quaker Indictment: An Elizabeth Elliot Mystery.*

Allen, Irene. *Quaker Witness: An Elizabeth Elliot Mystery.*

Allen, Irene. *Quaker Testimony: An Elizabeth Elliot Mystery.*

Bacon, Margaret Hope. *Year of Grace: A Novel.*

Gulley, Philip. *A Change of Heart: A Harmony Novel.* Harper San Francisco, 2005, 247 pp. paper.

Gulley, Philip. *Almost Friends: A Harmony Novel.* HarperSan Francisco, 2006, 224 PP. Cloth or paper.

Gulley, Philip. *Home to Harmony: A Harmony Novel.* HarperSF, 2004, 240 PP Paper.

Gulley, Philip. *Just Shy of Harmony: A Harmony Novel.* HarperSanFrancisco, 2004, 256 PP Paper.

Gulley, Philip. *Life Goes on: A Harmony Novel.* HarperSan Francisco, 2004, 245 pp. cloth or paper.

Gulley, Philip. *Porch Talk: Stories of Decency, Common Sense, and Other Endangered Species.* HarperOne, 2007, 176 PP. Paper.

Gulley, Philip. *Signs & Wonders: A Harmony Novel.* HarperSF, 2006, 226 PP Paper.

Gulley, Philip. *The Christmas Scrapbook.* Harper San Francisco, 2005, 96 PP. Cloth.

Newman, Daisy. *Autumn's Brightness.*

Newman, Daisy. *I Take Thee, Serenity.* (1975).

West, Jessamyn. *Friendly Persuasion.* (1945).

HISTORY

Bacon, Margaret Hope. *Mothers of Feminism: The Story of Quaker Women in America.*

Bacon, Margaret Hope. *The Quiet Rebels: The Story of Quakers in America.*

Brinton, Howard H. *Friends for 350 Years: The History & Beliefs of the Society of Friends Since George Fox Started the Quaker Movement,* updated by Margaret Hope Bacon.

Newman, Daisy. *A Procession of Friends: Quakers in America.*

Punshon, John. *Portrait in Grey: A Short History of the Quakers.*

LECTURES

Saunders, Deborah. *Equality, 2nd Ed. 36th Annual J. Barnard Walton Lecture 1999.* Southeastern Yearly Meeting, 2006, 36 PP. Paper.

Steere, Douglas V. *Quaker Meeting for Business – 1973 Michener Lecture.*

MAGAZINES

Friends Journal. *Friends Journal.*

Quaker Life. *Quaker Life.*

PAMPHLETS

Brinton, Howard H. *Guide to Quaker Practice.* PHP 20.

Morrison, Mary. *Approaching the Gospels Together.* PHP 219.

Peck, George T. *What is Quakerism? A Primer.* PHP 277.

Taber, William. *Four Doors to Meeting for Worship.* PHP 306.

TRACTS

Bill, J. Brent. *Holy Silence.* Western Quarterly Meeting, 2006, Leaflet, Tract.

Brown, Thomas. *When Friends Attend to Business.*

Cronk, Sandra. *Peace Be With You: A Study of the Spiritual Basis of the Friends Peace Testimony.*

Griswold, Robert. *Quaker Peace Testimony in Times of Terrorism.* Friends Bulletin, 2003, 18 PP. Paper.

Hutchinson, Dorothy. *Friends and Service.*

Kelly, Thomas. *The Gathered Meeting.*

Outreach Committee of Philadelphia YM. *Welcome Poster and/or Postcards.*

Philadelphia Yearly Meeting. *Friends and Wedding.*

Rickerman, Sally. *ABCs of Quakerism.*

Steere, Douglas V. *Friends and Worship.*

Steere, Douglas V. *A Quaker Meeting for Worship.*

Western QM Membership Brochure Working Group. *A Quaker Path: A Spiritual Journey from Visitor to Attender to Member.*

YOUTH ORIENTED

Bacon, Margaret Hope. *The Back Bench: A Novel.* Quaker Press of FGC, 2007, 127 PP. Paper.

Clarke, Marnie, ed. *Lives that Speak: Stories of 20th Century Quakers.* Quaker Press of FGC, 2004, 168 PP Paper.

FGC Religious Education Committee. *Lighting Candles in the Dark: Stories of Courage and Love in Action.*

Quaker Tapestry at Kendal. *Quaker Tapestry Coloring Book: Costumes.*

Yolen, Jane. *Friend: The Story of George Fox.* Quaker Press of FGC, 2005, 192 PP. Paper.

PUBLICATIONS OF INTEREST TO LONG-TIME ATTENDERS AND MEMBERS

BIOGRAPHY

Anderson, Jervis. *Bayard Rustin: Troubles I've Seen.*

Bacon, Margaret Hope. *Valiant Friend: The Life of Lucretia Mott.*

Fager, Chuck, ed. *Tom Fox Was My Friend Yours, Too.* Kimo Press, 2006, 102 PP. Paper.

Massey, Vera. *The Clouded Quaker Star: James Naylor, 1618-1660.*

Miller, Larry. *Witness for Humanity: A Biography of Clarence E. Pickett.*

Richmond, Ben. *Reminiscences of Levi Coffin.* Friends United Press, 2001, 430 PP.

Rose, June. *Elizabeth Fry: A Biography.*

Ross, Isabel. *Margaret Fell: Mother of Quakerism.* Sessions of York, 1996, 421 PP. Paper.

Slaughter, Thomas P. *The Natures of John & William Bartram: Two Pioneering Naturalists, Father and Son, in the Wilderness of 18th Century America.*

Wriggins, Howard. *Picking up the Pieces from Portugal to Palestine: Quaker Refugee Work in WW II – A Memoir.* University Press of America, 2004, 258 PP. Paper.

CONCERNS AND PRACTICE

AFSC American Friends Service Committee. *Coming Home, Criminal Justice Program Prisoners Resource Center.* AFSC, 2003, 58 PP Paper.

AFSC International Working Party. *When the Rain Returns: Towards Justice & Reconciliation in Palestine & Israel.* AFSC, 2004, 326 PP. Paper.

Dandelion, Ben Pink, ed. *The Creation of Quaker Theory: Insider Perspectives.* Ashgate, 2004, 208 PP. Cloth.

Fager, Chuck. *A Quaker Declaration of War.* Kimo Press 2003 72 PP. Paper, DVD or VHS.

Greene, Jan & Marty Walton. *Fostering Vital Friends Meetings: A Handbook for Working with Quaker Meetings.*

Greenleaf, Robert K. *Power of Servant Leadership.*

Heller, Mike, ed. *The Tendering Presence: Essays on John Woolman.* Pendle Hill, 2003, 360 PP. Paper.

Heron, Alaistair. *Caring, Conviction, Commitment: Dilemmas of Quaker Membership Today.*

Hickey, Damon. *Unforseen Joy: Serving a Friends Meeting as Recording Clerk.* North Carolina Yearly Meeting (F), 1987, 35 PP. Paper.

Intrator, Sam M. *Living the Questions: Essays Inspired by the Work and the Life of Parker Palmer.* Jossey-Bass, 2005, 416 PP. Cloth.

Intrator, Sam M. *Stories of the Courage To Teach: Honoring The Teacher's Heart.* Jossey-Bass, 2007, 337 PP. Paper.

Kelley, Martin. *Quaker Ranter Reader: A Slapped Together Collection of Essays.* Martin Kelley, 2005, 87 PP. Paper.

Lacey, Paul A. *Growing into Goodness: Essays on Quaker Education.*

Manousos, Anthony, ed. *Western Quaker Reader: Writings by and about Independent Quakers in the Western United States, 1929-1999.*

New England Yearly Meeting. *Addressing Sexual Abuse in Friends Meetings.*

Palmer, Parker. *Courage To Teach Guide For Reflection and Renewal.* Jossey-Bass, 2007, 176 PP. Paper & DVD.

Palmer, Parker J. *Courage to Teach: Exploring the Inner Landscape of a Teacher's Life.*

Quakers & Business Group, The. *Good Business: Ethics at Work – Advice and Queries on Personal Standards of Conduct at Work.*

Richmond, Ben. *A Guide for Friends on Conscientious Objection to War.*

Seeley, Robert. *Choosing Peace: A Handbook on War, Peace and Your Conscience.* Central Committee for Conscientious Objectors, 1994, 245 PP. Paper.

Sheeran, Michael J. *Beyond Majority Rule.*

Walton, Marty. *The Meeting Experience: Practicing Quakerism in Community.*

Watson, Will. *Before Business Begins: Notes for Recording Clerks.* New England Yearly Meeting, 1996, 64 PP. Paper.

Wilson, Robert Cowan. *Authority, Leadership And Concern: A Study In Motive and Administration In Quaker Relief Work.* Britain Yearly Meeting, 2007, 92 PP. Paper.

FAITH AND PRACTICE

Christian Faith and Practice in the Experience of the Society of Friends. London Yearly Meeting, 1960.

Church Government. London Yearly Meeting, 1968.

Faith & Practice. Baltimore Yearly Meeting, 2011 Draft.

Faith & Practice. New England Yearly Meeting, 1985.

Faith & Practice. New York Yearly Meeting, 1995.

Faith & Practice. North Pacific Yearly Meeting, 1993.

Faith & Practice. Pacific Yearly Meeting, 1985.

Faith & Practice. Philadelphia Yearly Meeting, 1997

Faith & Practice. From six other Yearly Meetings.

Jones, Rufus M. *The Faith and Practice of the Quakers.*

Kaiser, Geoffrey & Bruce Grimes. *The Religious Society of Friends in North America Chart.* Quaker Press of FGC, 2005, Poster.

The Old Discipline: Nineteenth-Century Friends' Disciplines in America. Friends Heritage Press, 1999.

FAITH, MINISTRY AND SPIRITUALITY

Abbott, Margery Post & Peggy Senger Parsons, Eds. *A Walk Worthy of Your Calling: Quakers and the Traveling Ministry.* Friends United Press, 2004, 302 PP. Paper.

Abbott, Marjorie Post. *A Certain Kind of Perfection: An Anthology of Evangelical and Liberal Quaker Writers.*

Ambler, Rex, ed. *Truth Of The Heart An Anthology Of George Fox.* Britain Yearly Meeting, 2007, 202 PP. Paper.

Angell, Stephen W. & Paul Buckley, eds. *The Quaker Bible Reader.* Earlham School of Religion, 2006, 310 PP. Paper.

Barbour, Hugh & Arthur Roberts, ed. *Early Quaker Writings.*

Barclay, Robert, Dean Freiday, ed. *Barclay's Apology in Modern English.*

Bauman, Richard. *Let Your Words Be Few: Symbolism of Speaking and Silence Among Seventeeth-Century Quakers.*

Benson, Lewis. *Catholic Quakerism: A Vision for All Men* (1966).

Bill, J. Brent, ed. *Imagination & Spirit: A Contemporary Quaker Reader.* Friends United Press, 2002, 240 PP. Paper.

Birkel, Michael. *A Near Sympathy: The Timeless Quaker Wisdom of John Woolman.* Friends United Press, 2003, 140 PP. Paper.

Birkel, Michael. *Silence and Witness: The Quaker Tradition.* Orbis

Books, 2004, 164 PP.   Paper.

Birkel, Michael.   *Engaging Scripture: Reading the Bible with Early Friends.*   Friends United Press, 2005, 152 PP.   Paper.

Boulding, Elise.   *One Small Plot of Heaven: Reflections on Family Life by a Quaker Sociologist.*   (1989).

Bownas, Samuel.   *A Description of the Qualifications Necessary to a Gospel Minister: Advice to Ministers and Elders Among the People Called Quakers.*   (1750).

Brinton, Howard H.   *Quaker Journals: Varieties of Religious Experience Among Friends.*

Buckley, Paul.   *Twenty-First Century Penn.*   Earlham School of Religion 2003 415 PP.   Paper

Cadbury, Henry J.   *George Fox's 'Book of Miracles'.*

Cooper, Wilmer A.   *Growing Up Plain: A Journal of a Public Friend.*

Cronk, Sandra.   *Dark Night Journey: Inward Re-Patterning Toward a Life Centered in God.*

Dandelion, Ben Pink.   *God the Trickster: Eleven Essays.*

Drayton, Brian.   *On Living with a Concern for Gospel Ministry.*   Quaker Press of FGC, 2005, 196 PP.   Paper.

Drayton, Brian.   *Selections From the Writings of James Naylor.*

Foster, Richard J.   *Freedom of Simplicity.*

Foster, Richard J.   *Streams of Living Water: Celebrating the Great Traditions of Christian Faith.*

Foster, Richard J.   *Celebration of Discipline: The Path to Spiritual Growth, Revised Edition.*

Foster, Richard J. & Emilie Griffin, eds.   *Spiritual Classics: Selected Readings for Individuals and Groups on the Twelve Spiritual Disciplines.*

Fox, George. John L. Nickalls, ed. *The Journal of George Fox* (1694).

Freiday, Dean & Arthur O. Roberts, ed. *Barclay's Catechism and Confession of Faith: A New Edition.*

Gates, Tom.   *Opening the Scriptures: Bible Lessons from the 2005 Annual Gathering of Friends.*   Quaker Press of FGC, 2005, 64 PP.   Paper.

Gorman, George H.   *The Amazing Fact of Quaker Worship* (1973).

Grundy, Martha P.   *Resistance and Obedience to God: Memoirs of David Ferris, 1707-1779.*

Gulley, Phillip & James Mulholland.   *If Grace is True: Why God Will*

Save Every Person. HarperCollins, 2004, 225 PP. Paper.

Gulley, Phillip & James Mulholland. *If God is Love: Rediscovering Grace in an Ungracious World.* HarperSF, 2005, 288 PP. Paper.

Gulley, Phillip. *If the Church Were Christian: Rediscovering the Values of Jesus.* Harper One, 2010. 197 PP., Cloth.

Gwyn, Douglas. *Apocalypse of the Word: The Life and Message of George Fox.*

Gwyn, Douglas. *Unmasking Idols: A Journey Among Friends.*

Gwyn, Douglas. *Seekers Found: Atonement In Early Quaker Experience.* Pendle Hill, 2000, 410 PP. Paper.

Joliff, William. *The Poetry of John Greenleaf Whittier: A Readers Edition.*

Jones, Rufus Mather. *Studies in Mystical Religion.* Wipf & Stock, 1909, 2004, 518 PP Paper.

Jones, T. Canby. *The Power of the Lord is Over All: Pastoral Letters of George Fox.*

Judson, Sylvia Shaw. *The Quiet Eye.*

Keiser, Melvin & Rosemary Moore, eds. *Knowing the Mystery of Life Within: Selected Writings of Isaac Penington in their Historical and Theological Context.* Britain Yearly Meeting, 2005, 322 PP.

Kelly, Thomas. *Testament of Devotion.*

Kelly, Thomas *The Eternal Promise.*

Kuenning, Licia, ed. *The Works of James Naylor: Volume 1.* Quaker Heritage Press, 2004, 604 PP. Cloth.

Kuenning, Licia, ed. *The Works of James Naylor: Volume 2.* Quaker Heritage Press, 2004, 604 PP. Cloth.

Kuenning, Licia, ed. *The Works of James Naylor: Volume 3.* Quaker Heritage Press, 2007, 762 PP. Cloth.

Lacey, Paul A. *Nourishing the Spiritual Life.*

Loring, Patricia. *Listening Spirituality, Vol I: Personal Spiritual Practices Among Friends.*

Loring, Patricia. *Listening Spirituality, Vol II: Corporate Spiritual Practice Among Friends.*

Maloy, Kate. *A Stone Bridge North: Reflections in a New Life.*

McBee, Patricia, ed. *Grounded in God: Care and Nurture in Friends.* Quaker Press of FGC, 2002, 288 PP. Paper.

Morrison, Mary. *Let Evening Come: Reflections on Aging.*

Moulton, Phillips, ed. *Journal and Major Essays of John Woolman.*

Nayler, James, Evamaria Hawkins, ed. *Milk for Babes and Meat for Strong Men: A Feast of Fat Things; Wine Well Refined on the Lees.* Hawkins, 2004, 30 PP. Paper.

Nickalls, John L., ed. *The Journal of George Fox.*

Nickalls, John, ed. *Early Prophetic Openings of George Fox.*

Niyonzima, David & Lon Fendall. *Unlocking Horns.* Barclay Press 2001 129 PP. Paper.

O'Reilley, Mary Rose. *The Barn at the End of the World: The Apprenticeship of a Quaker Buddhist Shepherd.*

Palmer, Parker. *A Hidden Wholeness: The Journey Toward an Undivided Life.* Jossey-Bass, 2004, 192 PP. Cloth.

Palmer, Parker J. *Let Your Life Speak: Listening for the Voice of Vocation.*

Penington, Isaac. *The Works of Isaac Penington. Volume 1 – 4.* Quaker Heritage Press Vol. 1, 1995, 538 pp. cloth; Vol. 2, 1994, 508 pp. cloth; Vol. 3, 1996, 538 pp. cloth; Vol. 4, 1997, 474 pp. cloth.

Penington, Isaac. *The Light Within and Selected Writings.*

Penn, William. *No Cross, No Crown.* Sessions of York edition.

Penn, William, Edwin Bronner, ed. *The Peace of Europe, the Fruits of Solitude and Other Writings.*

Punshon, John. *Reasons for Hope: The Faith and Future of the Friends Church.*

Punshon, John. *Encounter with Silence: Reflections from the Quaker Tradition.*

Punshon, John. *Testimony and Tradition: Some Aspects of Quaker Spirituality.*

Pym, Jim. *Listening to the Light: How to Bring Quaker Simplicity and Integrity into Our Lives.*

Ratliff, Bill. *Out of Silence: Quaker Perspectives on Pastoral Care and Counseling.*

Rickerman, Sally, ed. *Universal Religious Truths as Found in World Religions.* Troll Press, 2006, 67 PP. Looseleaf.

Roberts, Arthur O. *The Sacred Ordinary: Sermons and Addresses.* Barclay Press, 2006, 313 PP. Paper.

Scott, Janet. *What Canst Thou Say? Towards a Quaker Theology.* Britain Yearly Meeting, 2007, 100 PP. Paper.

Searl, Sanford. *Voices From the Silence.* Authorhouse, 2005, 216 PP. Paper.

Southeastern Yearly Meeting. *Marriage and Commitment.* Southeastern Yearly Meeting, 2006, 28 PP. Paper.

Steere, Douglas V. ed. *Quaker Spirituality: Selected Writing.*

Stephen, Caroline. *Quaker Strongholds.* 1898.

Trueblood, D. Elton. *The People Called Quakers.*

Vining, Elizabeth Gray. *Facing One's Own Death.*

Walters, Kerry, ed. *Rufus Jones: Essential Writings.*

Watson, Elizabeth. *Wisdom's Daughters: Stories of Women Around Jesus.*

Watson, Elizabeth. *Guests in My Life.* (reprinted 1984).

West, Jessamyn. *The Quaker Reader.*

Whitmire, Catherine. *Plain Living: A Quaker Path to Simplicity.*

Whittier, John Greenleaf. *Selections From The Religious Poems.* Tract Association, 2000, 84 PP. Paper.

Wilson, Lloyd Lee. *Essays on the Quaker Vision of Gospel Order.* Pendle Hill Publications, 1993, 200 PP. Paper

Woolman, John. *The Journal and Major Essays of John Woolman.* (1776) (Phillips P. Moulton, ed.).

HISTORY

Abbott, Chijioke, Dandelion & Oliver. *The A to Z of the Friends (Quakers).* Scarecrow Press 2006 376 PP. Paper.

Bacon, Margaret Hope. *Mothers of Feminism: The Story of Quaker Women in America.*

Bacon, Margaret Hope. *Wilt Thou Go On My Errand? Three 18th Century Journals Of Quaker Women Ministers.* Pendle Hill, 1994, 400 PP. Paper.

Bacon, Margaret Hope & Emma Lapansky, eds. *Back To Africa, Benjamin Coates And The Colonization Movement In America, 1848-1880.* Penn State Press, 2005, 385 PP. Cloth.

Barbour, Hugh & J. William Frost. *The Quakers.*

Braithwaite, William. *Beginnings of Quakerism to 1660, 2nd Edition* (1955).

Braithwaite, William. *Second Period of Quakerism.* (1979).

Brinton, Howard H. *Friends for 350 Years: The History & Beliefs of the Society of Friends Since George Fox Started the Quaker Movement,* updated by Margaret Hope Bacon. Pendle Hill Publications, 2002, 320 PP. Paper.

Brock, Peter. *The Quaker Peace Testimony, 1660-1914.* (1990).

Brown, Elizabeth Potts & Susan Mosher Stuard. *Witnesses For Change: Quaker Women Over Three Centuries.* (1989).

Cherry, Charles, Caroline Cherry & William Frost, eds. *George Fox's Legacy: Friends for 350 Years - Essays.* Friends Historical Association, 2006, 149 PP. Paper.

Cooper, Wilmer A. *A Living Faith: An Historical Study of Quaker Beliefs.* (1990).

Cope-Robinson, Lyn. *The Little Quaker Sociology Book: with Glossary.* Canmore Press, 1995, 220 PP. Paper.

Dorland, Arthur G. *Quakers in Canada.* (1968).

Fell, Margaret. *A Sincere and Constant Love: An Introduction to the Work of Margaret Fell.* Terry Wallace, ed.

Foulds, Elfrida Vipont. *George Fox and the Valiant Sixty.*

Foulds, Elfrida Vipont. *The Story of Quakerism, 1652-1952.*

Garman, Benefiel, Applegate & Meredith. *Hidden In Plain Sight: Quaker Women's Writings 1650-1700.* Pendle Hill, 1995, 512 PP. Paper.

Glines, Elsa, ed. *Undaunted Zeal: The Letters of Margaret Fell.* Friends United Press, 2003, 509 PP. Paper.

Gwyn, Douglas. *The Covenant Crucified Quakerism And The Rise Of Capitalism.* Britain Yearly Meeting, 2006, 404 PP. Paper.

Hamm, Thomas D. *The Quakers.*

Hamm, Thomas D. *Transformation of American Quakerism.*

Hill, Christopher. *The World Turned Upside Down: Radical Ideas During the English Revolution.*

Holton, Sandra Stanley. *Quaker Women: Personal Life, Memory, and Radicalism in the Lives of Women Friends, 1800-1920.* Routledge, 2007, 304 PP. Paper.

Ingle, Larry. *First Among Friends: George Fox & the Creation of Quakerism.*

Ingle, Larry. *Quakers in Conflict: The Hicksite Reformation.* (1986).

Kuenning, Licia. *Historical Writings of Quakers Against War.*

Leach, Robert & Peter Gow. *Quaker Nantucket: The Religious Community Behind the Whaling Empire.*

McDowell, Nancy Parker. *Notes from Ramallah, 1939.* Friends United Press, 2002, 133 PP. Paper.

McFadden, David & Claire Gorfinkel. *Constructive Spirit: Quakers in Revolutionary Russia.* Intentional Productions, 2004, 232 PP. Paper.

Moore, Rosemary Anne. *Light in Their Consciences: Faith, Practices, and Personalities in Early British Quakerism, 1646-1666.*

Murphy, Andrew R., ed. *The Political Writings of William Penn.* Liberty Fund, 2002, 439 PP. Paper.

Newman, Daisy. *A Procession of Friends: Quakers in America.*

Palmer, Beverly Wilson, ed. *The Selected Letters of Lucretia Coffin Mott.* University of Illinois, 2002, 580 PP. Cloth.

Penn, William. *The Journal of William Penn: While Visiting Holland and Germany in 1677.* Penn State University Press, 2006, 189 PP. Paper.

Punshon, John. *Portrait in Grey: A Short History of the Quakers.*

Schmitt, Hans. *Quakers & Nazis: Inner Light in Outer Darkness.*

Sharman, Cecil W. *George Fox and the Quakers.*

Skidmore, Gil, ed. *Strength in Weakness: Writings of 18th Century Quaker Women.* AltaMira Publishers, 2003, 200 PP. Paper.

Sox, David. *John Woolman: Quintessential Quaker.*

Trevett, Christine. *Women and Quakerism in the 17th Century.*

Vipont, Elfrida. *George Fox & The Valiant Sixty.* Quaker Press of FGC, 1997, 160 PP. Paper.

Wellman, Judith. *The Road to Seneca Falls: Elizabeth Cady Stanton and the 1st Women's Rights Convention.* University of Illinois Press, 2004, 297 PP. Paper.

Worrall, Jr., Jay. *The Friendly Virginians: America's First Quakers.*

LECTURES

Birkel, Michael. *Mysticism and Activism – 2002 Michener Lecture.* Southeastern Yearly Meeting, 2002, 21 PP. Paper.

Brown, Charles. *Pray and Pay Attention: Or How to Enjoy Meeting for Business – 1991 Michener Lecture.*

Calvi, John. *The Dance Between Hope and Fear – 1992 Walton Lecture.*

Chidsey, Linda. *Intimations of Renewal in New York Yearly Meeting: 42nd Annual Walton Lecture 2005.* Southeastern Yearly Meeting, 2005, 30 PP Paper.

Corbett, Jim. *Leadings – 1994 Walton Lecture.*

Fisch, Deborah. *Being Faithful as Friends, Individually and*

Corporately – 2006 Weed Lecture. Beacon Hill Friends House, 2006, 32 PP. Paper.

Gould, Lois Lofland. *Be Ye Perfect: A Quaker Call to Wholeness – 2002 Walton Lecture.* Southeastern Yearly Meeting, 2002, 37 PP. Paper.

Lakey, George. *New Theory, Old Practice: Nonviolence and Quakers – 2004 Michener Lecture.* Southeastern Yearly Meeting, 2004, 30 PP Paper.

Larrabee, Arthur. *Leadership & Authority In the Religious Society of Friends – 2007 Walton Lecture.* Southeastern Yearly Meeting, 2007, 24 PP. Paper.

Lord, Mary. *A Vision of Peace – 2004 Walton Lecture.* Southeastern Yearly Meeting, 2005. 30 PP Paper.

Seeger, Dan. *Finding our Sacred Ground: Quakerism's Place in a Globalized Future – 2001 Michener Lecture.*

Shaw, Deborah. *Being Fully Present to God – 2005 Michener Lecture.* Southeastern Yearly Meeting, 2005, 45 PP Paper.

Steere, Douglas V. *Quaker Meeting for Business – 1973 Michener Lecture.*

Taber, William & Frances. *Building the Life of the Meeting – 1994 Michener Lecture.*

Trueblood, D. Elton. *The Trustworthiness of Religious Experience – 1939 Swarthmore Lecture.*

Wajda, Michael & Alison Levie. *Shaped by the Light: The Quaker Experience of Worship, Community and Transformation – 2001 Walton Lecture.* SEYM, 2001, 23 PP. Paper.

Walton, Marty. *Blessed Community – 1993 Walton Lecture.* Southeastern Yearly Meeting, 1994, 21 PP. Paper.

MAGAZINES

Friends Journal. *Friends Journal.*
Quaker Life. *Quaker Life.*
Quaker Religious Thought. *Quaker Religious Thought.*

PAMPHLETS

Anderson, Paul. *Navigating the Living Waters of John: On Wading with Children & Swimming with Elephants.* PHP 352. Pendle Hill Pamphlet, 2001, 32 PP. Paper.

Boulding, Kenneth. *There is a Spirit: The Nayler Sonnets.* PHP 337.

Boulding, Kenneth. *Mending The World: Quaker Insights on the Social Order.* PHP 266.

Brown, Thomas. *When Friends Attend to Business.*

Cadbury, Henry J. *A Quaker Approach to the Bible.*

Clement, Daphne. *Group Spiritual Nurture: The Wisdom of Spiritual Learning.* PHP 373. Pendle Hill Pamphlet, 2004, 32 PP. Paper.

Cooper, Wilmer A. *The Testimony of Integrity.* PHP 296.

Cronk, Sandra. *Gospel Order: A Quaker Understanding of Faithful Church Community.* PHP 297.

Cronk, Sandra. *Peace Be With You: A Study of the Spiritual Basis of the Friends Peace Testimony.*

Drayton, Brian. *Getting Rooted: Living in the Cross, a Path to Joy and Liberation.* PHP 391. Pendle Hill Pamphlet, 2007, 35 PP. Paper.

FGC Ministry & Nurture Committee. *Dealing with Difficult People in Meeting for Worship: Meeting the Needs of the Many While Responding to the Needs of the Few.*

Fox, George. *To the Parliament of the Commonwealth of England: 59 Particulars.* Quaker Universalist Fellowship, 2002, 21 PP. Paper.

Gates, Thomas. *Members One of Another: The Dynamics of Membership in Quaker Meeting.* PHP 371. Pendle Hill Pamphlet, 2004, 40 PP. Paper.

Gillman, Harvey. *Spiritual Hospitality: A Quaker's Understanding of Outreach.*

Griswold, Robert. *Creeds and Quakers: What's Belief Got to Do With It?* PHP 377. Pendle Hill Pamphlet, 2005, 35 PP. Paper.

Griswold, Robert. *Quaker Peace Testimony in Times of Terrorism.* Friends Bulletin, 2003, 18 PP. Paper.

Grundy, Martha P. *Tall Poppies: Supporting Gifts of Ministry and Eldering in the Monthly Meeting.* PHP 347.

Heath, Harriet. *Answering That of God in Our Children.* PHP 315. Pendle Hill Pamphlet, 1994, 39 PP. Paper.

Hoffman, Jan. *Clearness Committees and Their Use in Personal Discernment.*

Kelly, Thomas. *The Gathered Meeting.*

Lacey, Paul. *The Authority of Our Meetings is the Power of God.* PHP 365. Pendle Hill Pamphlet, 2003, 40 PP. Paper.

Lacey, Paul A. *On Leading and Being Led.* PHP 264.

Loring, Patricia. *Spiritual Discernment: The Context and Goal of Clearness Committees.* PHP 305.

Loring, Patricia. *Spiritual Responsibility in the Meeting for Business.*

Maddock, Keith. *Living Truth A Spiritual Portrait Of Pierre Ceresole.* PHP 379. Pendle Hill Pamphlet 2005 35 PP. Paper

Martin, Marcelle. *Invitation to a Deeper Communion.* PHP 366. Pendle Hill Pamphlet, 2003, 39 PP. Paper.

Mather, Eleanor Price. *Edward Hicks: His Peaceable Kingdoms and Other Paintings.* PHP 17.

McIver, Lucy Screechfield. *A Song of Death, Our Spiritual Birth: A Quaker Way of Dying.* PHP 340.

Morley, Barry. *Beyond Consensus: Salvaging Sense of the Meeting.* PHP 307.

Murer, Esther. *Reflections on Quaker Worship* (formerly From Worship and Ministry). Central Philadelphia Monthly Meeting, 2003, 30 PP. Paper.

Muench, Elizabeth. *Friendly Audits.*

Ostrom, Warren. *In God We Die.* PHP 385. Pendle Hill Pamphlet, 2006, 36 PP. Paper.

Palmer, Parker. *Meeting For Learning: Education In A Quaker Context.* Friends Council on Education, 2007, 13 PP. Paper.

Rehard, Mary Kay. *Bringing God Home: Family Spirituality.* PHP 362. Pendle Hill Pamphlet, 2002, 39 PP. Paper.

Rickerman, Sally *Trust: My Experience of Quakerism's Greatest Gift.* Troll Press, 2008, 23 PP. Looseleaf.

Schenck, Patience. *Answering the Call to Heal the World.* PHP 383. Pendle Hill Pamphlet, 2006, 34 PP. Paper.

Seeger, Dan. *I Have Called You Friends: One Quaker's Reflections Concerning Jesus.*

Smith, Steve. *A Quaker in Zendo.* PHP 370. Pendle Hill Pamphlet, 2004, 38 PP Paper.

Stanfield, David. *Handbook for The Presiding Clerk.* North Carolina Yearly Meeting (F) 1989 20 PP. Paper.

Steere, Douglas V. *On Speaking Out of Silence.* PHP 182.

Steere, Douglas V. *A Quaker Meeting for Worship.*

Taber, William. *Four Doors to Meeting for Worship.* PHP 306.

Taylor, Phyllis. *A Quaker Look at Living with Death & Dying.*

Vining, Elizabeth Gray. *The World in Tune.* PHP 66.

Welsh, Anne Morrison. *Fire of the Heart: Norman Morrison's Legacy in Viet Nam and at Home.* PHP 381. Pendle Hill Pamphlet, 2006, 39 PP. Paper.

Watson, Elizabeth. *Marriage in the Light: Reflections on Commitment and the Clearness Process.*

Woolman, John. *A Plea for the Poor.* PHP 357.

GLOSSARY OF TERMS

Note: Some of the terms that follow are in common usage but Friends have given them a particular meaning. Others are essentially limited to Quaker usage.

Advices: Ideals stated as a continuing reminder of the basic faith and principles held to be essential to the life and witness of Friends. They arose from extracts from the minutes and epistles of early Friends and were intended to supply guidance, caution. and counsel to monthly meetings and their members on various aspects of daily life. The word Advices is also sometimes used to encompass the whole of a Friends book of discipline (*Faith and Practice*).

Affirm: A legal declaration provided for Friends and others who conscientiously refuse to take (or swear) judicial oaths. Following Jesus' directive "Swear not at all," Matthew 5:34, Quakers try to be truthful at all times. Swearing an oath implies having a double standard in regard to speaking the truth. Sometimes also used in meetings to recognize items of business not requiring a formal minute, i.e., "affirming" a committee report rather than "accepting" or "approving" it.

Anchor Committee: An anchor committee, or anchoring committee, is a support committee that guides and nurtures a Friend who is pursuing a ministry that leads him or her to travel away from meeting frequently. This term is heard most frequently in reference to traveling ministries supported by Friends General Conference (FGC).

Attender: Someone who attends with some frequency and participates in meeting for worship and other meeting functions but who has not yet sought and been accepted into membership in the meeting.

Birthright Friend: In early practice, an individual whose parents were both members of a Friends meeting and who as a consequence was automatically recorded at birth as a member of that meeting. Most meetings no longer have this category of membership and instead use associate membership for children in the meeting.

Book of Discipline: A document describing a yearly meeting's spiritual practice and procedures, including advices, queries, and often quotations or extracts from the experience of Friends. *Faith and Practice* is a book of discipline. The word *discipline* comes from the root word *disciple.*

Breaking Meeting: Term used to indicate the ending or closing of meeting for worship when a designated member shakes hands with Friends nearby. Friends then greet their neighbors in the same fashion. See also Rise of Meeting.

Called Meeting: A meeting of the monthly or yearly meeting specially called by its clerk to address a particular concern or item of business. In a called meeting for business, decisions are recorded as in a regular meeting for business.

Centered: Condition of an individual or group in touch with the divine presence.

Centering/Centering Down: The initial stage of worship when Friends endeavor to quiet our restless thoughts and open our hearts, in order that we may hear the divine presence speak directly to us.

Christ Within: That of God in everyone especially as illustrated in the teachings of Jesus. Also called the Truth, the Spirit of Guidance, the Inward Light, the Inner Teacher, the Seed, or the Holy Spirit.

Clearness: Confidence that after prayer and reflection an action or next step is consistent with the divine will.

Clearness Committee: Originally, a term for those appointed by a monthly meeting to oversee a request for membership or a marriage under the care of the meeting and conscientiously satisfy the meeting that there is nothing to interfere with the accomplishment of the membership or marriage. Other kinds of clearness committees have been used to help persons be clear about their leading to take a particular action, such as tax resistance or to witness publicly or to travel for Friends ministry. More recently, clearness committees have been requested to help individuals come to clearness regarding divorce issues, employment issues, gay marriage issues, and so forth.

Clerk: The person responsible for the administration of a Friends body and for being particularly sensitive to the guidance of the Spirit in the conduct of the business of that body, which also includes preparation, servant-leadership, and follow-up of meetings for business.

Concern: A concern, whether of an individual or a meeting, is a quickening sense of spiritual leading that motivates Friends to take action about a situation or issue in response to what is felt to be a direct intimation of God's will.

Conscientious Objection: A principled refusal to participate in certain social or political practices; commonly applied to the refusal to undertake military service or pay war taxes.

Consensus: A secular method, involving rational process and producing general agreement. The authority is in the group, with individual readiness to accept a decision reached by cooperative search. Not to be confused with "Sense of the Meeting."

Conservative Friends: Three unaffiliated yearly meetings in the USA—Iowa, North Carolina, and Ohio—call themselves Conservative. Historically, they share John Wilbur's objections to the pastoral system; at the same time they are more explicitly Christ-centered than most meetings in Friends General Conference. It is a descriptive term, not an organization.

Continuing Revelation: A central Quaker belief that the revelation of God's will is an ongoing process. George Fox and the other early seekers believed that the same Spirit that rendered the original Biblical words was available to those who waited prayerfully and quietly upon the Lord for the truth. Howard Brinton in *Friends for 350 Years* says that Friends in unprogrammed meetings believe that "the Spirit of God which gave forth the Scriptures [is] still at work ... in the human heart. It [is] more important to hear what He [is] saying directly ... than what He once said centuries ago."

Convener: Member of a committee, usually the first person listed by the nominating committee, who is asked to convene the first meeting of the group before a committee clerk is named. Also, it is the correspondent or contact person of a worship group.

Convinced Friend: A person who, after deciding that the Religious Society of Friends provides the most promising home for spiritual enlightenment and growth, becomes a member of a monthly meeting. Traditionally distinguished from a birthright Friend.

Corporate Worship: The action of a group's seeking together the will of God for their individual and community life. The meeting for worship is corporate worship. The activity of the group decision process – quiet waiting and group discussion – is intended to reflect the group's corporate search for truth.

Covered Meeting: A meeting for worship or business in which the participants feel the power and inspiration of God so strongly that they all are united in that Spirit and understanding which is the reward of waiting upon God. See also Gathered Meeting.

Discernment: The process of arriving at the right course of action through spiritual perception and clear rational thought. Seeks to incorporate God's will to rise above mere "deciding." It is wisdom to see clearly and to differentiate the truth from other impressions.

Discipline: Following a particular path. Also see *Faith and Practice.*

Disownment: The practice of dismissing an individual from membership in the Society of Friends. Historically, a person could be put out of meeting ("read out" or "disowned") by a monthly meeting for violating prohibitions or practices of the Society regarding worldly dress, amusements, marrying a non-Quaker, and so forth. This practice is no longer used among Friends.

Elder: Elders (regardless of their age) are spiritually sensitive persons appointed by the monthly meeting to foster the ministry of the meeting for worship both vocal and silent and the spiritual condition of the members. Historically, he or she was often appointed as a traveling companion to a minister traveling beyond the monthly meeting.

Eldering: The act of encouraging and/or questioning an individual's behavior and/or expression. Eldering is to be done with courtesy and loving concern for the spiritual well-being of the individual, even when offered as a correction.

Embraced Friend: A Friend whose leading for ministry has been affirmed by the yearly meeting and is supported at the yearly meeting level.

Epistle: A public letter of greeting and ministry. Such letters are sent from a Friends meeting or organization to other Friends groups to supply information, spiritual insight, and encouragement.

Evangelical Friends: Evangelical Friends emphasize Christian doctrine based on the authority of the Bible. They point to Jesus Christ as the unique revelation of God. Through their deep concern for mission, they have parented groups of Friends in Latin America, Africa, and India. Their worship is programmed, and their theology is evangelical, with a strong scriptural base. Like other Friends, they hold testimonies of peace, simplicity, and equality.

Experiential Religion: A religion in which personal spiritual experience is the foundation for belief and practice. The word *experimental* was used by early Friends with this meaning.

Facing Benches: In older Friends meetinghouses, rising tiers of benches facing the meeting, traditionally occupied by recognized ministers and elders. Metaphorically, the group of leaders occupying those benches. Meeting houses without benches most often have seats arranged circularly or squarely around the room to emphasize equality.

Faith and Practice: An official edited book of Friends' testimonies, beliefs, experiences, and practices compiled by a yearly meeting body of Friends. The book is meant to provide guidance (queries and advices) for individuals and organizational groupings of the religious body. The structure and membership of the group, the procedures of well-ordered business, the formalities of marriage and other events (death, divorce), and stewardship of group property are explained. These are sources of tradition and not dogma. They are periodically updated to respond to current needs. Sometimes called "A Book of Discipline."

First Day: The first day of the week, Sunday. Historically, the Society of Friends numbered the days and months rather than using the names which came from non-Biblical often pagan sources. This custom is still in common usage for official documents and optional usage among the meetings.

First Day School: Friends' designation for the Sunday religious education program provided by a monthly meeting for children and adults.

Friends: Members of the Religious Society of Friends; also called Quakers. The term "Friends," or "Friends of the Truth," was used as early as 1652. The name "Friends" is inspired by John 15:12-14.

Friends Education: See Quaker education.

Gathered Meeting: A phrase used to describe those special occasions when in the meeting for worship or for business those present feel a particularly deep meditative quality and a sense of the Divine Presence touching each worshipper, uniting all in the shared experience of holy fellowship. See also Covered Meeting.

Good Order: Those procedures for the conduct of Friends' business and witness that encourage a meeting to carry out its corporate activities under divine leading. The term "rightly ordered" is also used in this sense.

Gospel Order: A term used by George Fox and others to describe the new covenant order of the church under the headship of Christ. It concerns how we live faithfully in relationship with God and with each other.

Half-Yearly Meeting: The name of a regional gathering of Friends who meet socially, or for business, between yearly meetings.

Hold in the Light: To ask that divine guidance and healing will illumine a person, situation, or problem, whether in concern or thanksgiving; also, to give prayerful consideration to an idea.

Inner Light/Inward Light/The Light Within: Terms which represent for Friends the presence of God in our hearts and lives. Some other equivalent terms often found in Quaker writings are the

Spirit, Spirit of Truth, the Divine Principle, the Seed, the Guide, the Christ Within, the Inward Teacher, that of God in every person, and the Holy Spirit.

Integrity: One of the basic practical principles or testimonies of Friends. It involves both a wholeness and harmony of the various aspects of one's life and truthfulness in whatever one says and does.

Interim Business Meeting (IBM): In Southeastern Yearly Meeting, a broadly representative body open to all, meeting twice annually [fall (FIBM) or winter (WIBM)] to conduct the business of the yearly meeting between its annual sessions.

Lay Down: A decision to discontinue a committee or concern when its work is complete; occasionally, a decision to discontinue a meeting or other Friends organization when it is no longer viable.

Lay Over: In Quaker business process, to postpone or continue the discernment on an issue or the presentation of a report from one meeting for business to another, which allows time for further reflection, discussion, and discernment.

Leading: A sense of being called by God to undertake a specific course of action. A leading often arises from a concern. A Friend may submit a leading to the meeting for testing by corporate wisdom.

Letter of Introduction: A Friend who is traveling socially or otherwise may request a "Letter of Introduction" from her or his monthly meeting to affirm association with Friends.

Liberal Friends: Liberal Friends hold that belief must be verified by religious experience. Religious experience derives from the direct revelation of God through the Light of Christ within. For Liberals, Jesus' life, teachings, and death are a supreme example of love.

Historically, Liberal Friends have reconciled science and religion, incorporating freedom of thought, tolerance and humanitarian service in their expression of religious faith and practice, maintaining a balance between individual liberty and community. It is a descriptive term, not an organization.

Lift Up: To emphasize or make explicit a particular point or concern.

Marriage After the Manner of Friends: See Chapter 8 – "Marriage and Commitment" of this *Faith and Practice*.

Marrying Out: Marrying someone who is not a member of the Society of Friends. Until 1859, many were disowned for marrying those who were not Quakers.

Meeting for Worship: A gathering of individuals in quiet expectant waiting for the enlightening and empowering presence of God, which may inspire any one of the group to offer a message or prayer; the central focus of the corporate life of the Religious Society of Friends.

Meeting for Worship with a Concern for (Attention to) Business: A meeting for worship during which the corporate business of the meeting is conducted. All business meetings, held in the spirit of worship, deal corporately with both spiritual and practical aspects of Friends' community and/or action. There is never a vote but instead a careful search to find unity with the divine will, or more commonly known as "the sense of the meeting."

Meetinghouse: The building in which Friends meet. The name is used in place of "church."

Message: A spoken message of ministry by an individual inspired by divine leading in a meeting for worship. A message may come to an individual that is personal or not for the group, and it is a matter of discernment whether or not to stand and deliver the message to a gathering.

Mind the Light: An admonition to attend to the Light Within for guidance in one's life. It means both active obedience to divine leadings and careful nurturing of one's openness to the Light.
Ministry: Sharing or acting upon one's gifts, whether in service to individuals, to the meeting, or to the larger community.

Minute: The record of a corporate decision reached during a meeting for worship with a concern for business formalizing the sense of the meeting. More broadly, the account of a single transaction in the written record of a meeting for business or other body. In the plural it is a compilation of transactions at a single session.

Minute of Exercise: An expression of insights and concerns on a specific unresolved topic at the close of a meeting for business. Historically, a closing summary of vocal ministry and spiritual concerns expressed during yearly meeting sessions.

Monthly Meeting: 1] A recognized congregation of Friends who meet regularly for worship and to conduct corporate business. 2) A monthly gathering of such a body for worship and business.

Moved: Led or prompted by the Spirit.

Opening: A moment of unexpected enlightenment or inspiration from God.

Overseers: A committee of those members who are appointed by the meeting to give pastoral care and nurture to all members and attenders.

Pacifist: A person who renounces war and any use of violence and seeks to resolve conflicts peacefully.

Pastor: The preferred term in programmed Friends churches for minister.

Pastoral Meeting: A meeting or church relying on a minister or a Friend (with spiritual gifts) to provide direction for a programmed worship service of sermon and song. See Programmed Meeting.

Peace Testimony: The corporate commitment of Friends to pacifism, nonviolence, and peace-making.

Pendle Hill: 1) The hill in northern England where George Fox, in May 1652, envisioned "a great people to be gathered." 2) In 1930, a Quaker study and retreat center near Philadelphia, PA was founded and named Pendle Hill.

Plain Dress/Plain Speech: The witness of early Friends to the testimonies of equality and integrity by dressing and speaking simply. These served into the twentieth century as outward symbols and reminders of our distinctive beliefs.

Plain Friend: A plain Friend is a Friend who adhered to simple dress and plain language to protest ornamentation and use of the formal second-person pronouns (you) to individuals as indicative of class.

Plain Language: Friends' language using the familiar second- person singular "thee" and "thou" for all persons including judges and royalty, who in the seventeeth century were accustomed to the formal second-person "you" as a statement of respect for their social class. Early Friends based their choice on the principle of all persons having equal status. Friends generally have not used honorific titles, such as Rev., Mrs., Dr., and Your Honor, as a further testimony to their belief in the equality of all persons.

Popcorn Meeting: As implied, numerous speakers "pop up" to "minister" to the meeting for worship, often elaborating upon each other's messages and leaving very little "silence" for reflection between speakers. A contemporary term.

Preparative Meeting: 1] In Southeastern Yearly Meeting, an organized group of attenders and members of other monthly meetings and/or yearly meetings who meet together usually under the care of a nearby monthly meeting to prepare to become a monthly meeting. 2] An organized group of members of an established monthly meeting which ordinarily gathers for worship at another place.

Presiding Clerk: The person who presides at a meeting for business. See Clerk.

Proceed As Way Opens: To undertake a service or course of action without prior clarity about all the details but with confidence that divine guidance will make these apparent and assure an appropriate outcome.

Programmed Meeting: A Friends meeting under the leadership of a pastor, with an arranged order of worship that usually includes a short period of silent worship. See also Unprogrammed Meeting.

Quaker: Originally, a derogatory term applied to Friends because their excitement of spirit when led to speak in a meeting for worship was sometimes expressed in a shaking or quaking motion. Now this term is simply an alternative designation for a member of the Religious Society of Friends.

Quaker Education: A style of education that seeks to provide an integrated curriculum appropriate to the needs of the whole individual, emphasizing the personal value of each student. Both in Britain and in the Americas, Quakers emphasized education and were among the first to provide coeducational schools for their children and among the first to teach the sciences.

Quakerism: Quakerism is a way of life in which Quakers try to live their religious convictions. Distinctions may include actions for peace, striving for a consistently simple lifestyle, a respect for all people and conditions, and a reliance on God's leadings from the Spirit.

Quarterly Meeting: A regional gathering of members of constituent monthly meetings, traditionally on four occasions each year. Some quarterly meetings also oversee the operations of institutions. This practice is usually used in large yearly meetings and not by Southeastern Yearly Meeting.

Queries: A set of questions, based on Friends' practices and testimonies, which are considered by meetings and individuals as a way of both guiding and examining individual and corporate lives and actions. As such, they are a means of self-examination. Queries to be considered regularly are included in *Faith and Practice*; others may be formulated by a committee or meeting that seeks to clarify for itself an issue it needs to address.

Recorder: The person appointed by a meeting to maintain statistics and contact information of the members and attenders of that meeting.

Recording Clerk: The person appointed to take minutes at regular and called meetings for business of a monthly meeting or other Friends body.

Released Friend: A Friend whose leading to carry out a particular course of action has met with approval from a monthly meeting which then promises to provide such spiritual and material support as would enable the Friend to follow that leading.

Religious Society of Friends: Official name of the denomination (movement) commonly called Quakers. Many variations of this name are in use. The name Friends is inspired by John 15:12-14.

Rise of Meeting: A term used to indicate the end of a meeting for worship or business. Meetings for worship "break" (are sensed complete) when the clerk or other designated person initiates "shaking of hands" to signify meeting is over. Also called "close of meeting."

Seasoned Friend: See Weighty Friend.

Seasoning: Taking the time to seek the Light rather than moving into a matter hastily.

Sense of the Meeting: An expression of the unity of a meeting for worship with a concern for business on some issue or concern; the general recognition, articulated by the clerk or some other person, that a given decision is in accordance with the divine will.   It is not the same as consensus or unanimity.

Settled: All together under the leading of the Spirit. A well-established monthly meeting.

Silence: Solemn waiting, meditation, and quiet time in meetings. The holding of hands in a circle, involving the children in being "silently thankful" before meals, is another way Friends practice silence in the meeting community.

Silent Meeting: See Unprogrammed Meeting.

Simplicity: A Quaker testimony that is closely associated with integrity, equality, and stewardship. Essentially, to limit the material circumstances of one's life in a way that allows/enables one to follow divine leadings. Quaker simplicity is living without extravagance in order that a person may give time and money to the most meaningful things as the person is led by Spirit.

Sojourning Friend: A member of a monthly meeting who may temporarily reside at some distance from that meeting but close to another monthly meeting and who upon formal request is accepted by the latter as an active member in Southeastern Yearly Meeting, with the financial obligations of an attender.

Speaking to My/One's Condition: The conviction that a message, whether directly from God or through the words or actions of another, meets one's own deepest needs and purposes.

Spirit: Spirit of God, Christ, Truth, Holy Spirit, Holy Ghost, Inner Light, Inner Spirit, and Teacher Within are terms which Friends use to refer to the Divine Presence.

Standing Aside: An action taken by an individual who has genuine reservations about a particular decision but who also recognizes that the decision is clearly supported by the weight of the meeting. The action of standing aside allows the meeting to reach unity. A person may ask to be recorded as standing aside.

Standing in the Way: A seasoned Friend who feels a spirit-led objection to a decision or proposed action of the meeting may stand in the way, thus preventing further action at that time until the objection is heard and resolved.

State of the Meeting (Society): A self-evaluation of the meeting done at intervals by members. This report usually includes spiritual matters, the way members have involved themselves in ministries, statistics of membership, and so forth. In Southeastern Yearly Meeting, meetings are asked to prepare a written report annually that is due to the administrative secretary by winter interim business meeting and printed in the "Documents In Advance" of the yearly meeting annual gathering. See Advices; Queries.

Stewardship: For Friends, stewardship is an element of integrity. Good stewardship directs Friends' investment of time and money in sustainable and renewable resources and in work that supports Quaker values and beliefs.

Stop/Stop in the Mind: A clear uneasiness in the face of a proposed decision or action and an unwillingness to follow it.

Testimonies: Friends testimonies (religious and social) are an outward expression of inward spiritual leadings and discernments of truth and the will of God. Testimonies are the application of Friends' beliefs to situations and problems of individuals and society: i.e., equality, integrity, peace, simplicity, and community. They constitute the moral and ethical fruit of the inward life of the Spirit. Testimonies are our outward witness to the world.

"That of God in everyone": A Quaker belief that all humans have a divine spirit enabling them to hear, be aware of, and respond to the movement of the spirit of God in the heart.

Threshing Session: A meeting to consider in depth a controversial issue, but in a way that is spirit-centered and free from the necessity of reaching a decision.

Traveling Minister: A Friend traveling with a concern who received approval by the monthly meeting releasing him or her to speak to specific groups or persons. Traveling ministers have been called "visiting Friends" by their hosts.

Travel Minute: The endorsement a meeting gives to one of its members who is traveling under the weight of a concern.

Truth: The revealed will of God, as experienced in communion with the Inner Light or Inward Christ. Early Quakers called themselves the Religious Society of Friends of the Truth.

Under the Care Of: Describes an activity, program, or event for which a meeting takes responsibility and to which it gives oversight: thus, a marriage, a preparative meeting, a traveling minister, or a school might all be said to be under the care of a monthly meeting.

Under the Weight Of: Giving high priority to an issue arising from a deep feeling of concern. Said of an individual or meeting that is struggling to reach an appropriate decision about such an item of business.

Unity: A recognition of the truth emerging from a group's corporate search and yielding to the Holy Spirit in its decision-making.

Universalism: The belief that there is a universal spiritual truth to be found at the base of all religious traditions.

Unprogrammed Meeting: A meeting for worship with the emphasis being on members and attenders centering down in silence to seek spiritual unity and guidance, minus the need for a pastor or prearranged program. Any worshiper may feel led to speak briefly during the meeting for worship. Meetings for worship in which the whole time is spent in silence can also be occasions of great inspiration.

Valiant Sixty: A group of fifty-four men and twelve women who were first convinced by George Fox. As early as 1654, they traveled extensively preaching the Quaker message.

Visiting Friends: See Traveling Ministry.

Vocal Ministry: The sharing of a Spirit-inspired message or prayer during a meeting for worship.

"Wear it as long as thou canst": Words (perhaps legendary) of George Fox to William Penn's question about his sword. The expression is used to indicate that each person must seek to know and decide on which issues he or she will stand.

Waiting upon God: Actively seeking and attending to God's will in expectant worship.

Weighty Friend: A Friend who is respected for spiritual depth, wisdom, and long service to the Religious Society of Friends. Also called a seasoned Friend.

Witness: To let one's life speak. To stand up for a truth or deeply held belief.

Worship Group: A group of worshipers who meet regularly but who may or may not have established a formal affiliation with an established monthly meeting or yearly meeting and therefore is unable to "keep" official membership records or to certify marriages.

Worship Sharing: A modern group practice in which participants share personal and spiritual experiences, thoughts, and feelings, often in response to a prearranged theme or questions and in a manner that acknowledges the presence of God and respect for all participants.

Yearly Meeting Friends: Quakers known for their involvement at the yearly meeting level.

Yearly Meeting: Those Friends from a geographically extended area who gather in annual session to worship and conduct business together. Yearly meeting has an advisory and supportive role to the monthly meetings.

Youth Member: One of several membership designations in the Religious Society of Friends used by many monthly meetings. A youth member is a minor child recorded as a member at the request of parents, one or both of whom are members of the monthly meeting. Youth members may be transferred to full membership at their own request, in writing, after they have reached an age of decision and when they are familiar with Friends' principles or at age twenty-five when youth membership expires.

Index

A

B

D

E

F

204, 266, 268, 269, 271

Family, Love Binds the 71

Fell, Margaret 42, 49, 51, 59, 185

Fifth Monarchy 55

Finance Committee and Trustees 205

Finance Committee, SEYM 247

Fisher, Mary 261

Fox, George 13, 16, 17, 18, 40, 41, 43, 45, 50, 51, 54, 55, 65, 76, 79,
81, 82, 84, 88, 91, 97, 110, 111, 113, 128, 143, 147, 149, 165, 183,
184, 185, 200, 217, 233, 261, 272, 282, 285, 289, 295

Fox, Margaret Fell 59

Franklin, Ursula 15

Friends and Military Activity 57

Friends Committee on National Legislation 253

Friends Declaration to King Charles II 55

Friends for Lesbian, Gay, Bisexual, Transgender, and
    Queer Concerns 254

Friends General Conference 252

Friends Peace Team 254

Friends United Meeting 254

Friends World Committee for Consultation 253, 262

Friends World Conference 72

G

Gambling 63, 105

Gathered Meeting 22, 23

God 13-24, 26-38, 40-50, 52-56, 58, 61, 64-67, 69-73, 75-77, 79,
80, 81, 83, 84, 87, 88, 90-94, 97-100, 102-111, 113-117, 127-130,
143-145, 148, 149, 152, 154, 156, 158, 161, 163, 165-168, 174, 178,
179, 183-185, 192, 194, 195, 199, 200, 207, 217, 223, 233, 234, 236,

L

M

N

V

Volunteers and Paid Staff 210

W

Walking Gently on the Earth 61
Walton, J. Barnard 262
Walton, Marty 77, 78, 84, 87
Watson, Elizabeth 52
Wilson, Lloyd Lee 81
Wilson, Roger 38
Woolman, John 24, 42, 43, 53, 56, 59, 65, 79, 82, 153, 154, 270
World Order 58
Worship 13, 18, 19, 20, 21, 25
Worship and Ministry Committee, SEYM 249

Y

Yamanouchi, Tayeko 16
Yearly Meeting Clerks and Officers 237
Yearly Meeting, Funding the 241
Yearly Meeting Gathering Committee 249
Yearly Meeting Representatives 252
Yearly Meeting Responsibilities 240
Young Adult Quakers Clerk(s) 239
Young Friends (Teens) Clerk(s) 239
Young, Mildred Binns 61
Youth Committee 250
Youth Membership 136

CPSIA information can be obtained
at www.ICGtesting.com
Printed in the USA
FFHW020346231019
55659456-61516FF